CORPUS
FONTIUM
MANICHAEORUM

SERIES IRANICA

I

CORPUS FONTIUM MANICHAEORUM

Edited by
AN INTERNATIONAL COMMITTEE

Samuel N. C. Lieu
Robinson College
Cambridge
Editor in Chief

Johannes van Oort
University of Utrecht/
Nijmegen/Pretoria
Editor in Chief

Nils Arne Pedersen
Aarhus University
Editor in Chief

Aloïs van Tongerloo †
University of Göttingen
Founding Editor in Chief

SERIES IRANICA
Enrico Morano, Turin
Director of the Series Iranica

with the support of

THE BRITISH ACADEMY

UNITED NATIONS EDUCATIONAL, SCIENTIFIC
AND CULTURAL ORGANIZATION

INTERNATIONAL UNION OF ACADEMIES
(Union Académique Internationale)

THE LEVERHULME TRUST (U. K.)

THE SEVEN PILLARS OF WISDOM TRUST (U. K.)

THE CHIANG CHING-KUO FOUNDATION
FOR INTERNATIONAL SCHOLARLY EXCHANGE

THE AUSTRALIAN ACADEMY
OF THE HUMANITIES

THE AUSTRALIAN RESEARCH COUNCIL

THE ARTS AND HUMANITIES RESEARCH COUNCIL (U. K.)

THE NATIONAL RESEARCH COUNCIL (S. A.)

THE ANCIENT INDIA AND IRAN TRUST (Cambridge, U. K.)

CORPUS FONTIUM MANICHAEORUM

Series Iranica I

A MANICHAEAN

PRAYER AND CONFESSION BOOK (BBB)

Edited and translated by

Nicholas Sims-Williams

Introduction by

John S. Sheldon

Codicology by

Zsuzsanna Gulácsi

BREPOLS

D/2022/0095/203
ISBN 978-2-503-59790-4

Printed in the EU on acid-free paper.

CONTENTS

Introduction (John S. Sheldon) vii

Editor's note xx

Bibliography & bibliographical abbreviations xxi

Part 1. A Middle Persian and Parthian Bema liturgy 1

Part 2. A Sogdian Confessional 61

Part 3. The manuscript M801a (III 53) as bound in antiquity 97

Part 4. Codicology (Zsuzsanna Gulácsi) 111

Codicology of an Iranian Manichaean Bema Service Book from Uygur Kocho 113

Bibliography to Part 4 160

Appendix: Additional texts a–f 163

INTRODUCTION

John S. Sheldon[1]

Among the Iranian Manichaean texts brought back to Berlin from Central Asia by the German expeditions in the first decade of the twentieth century, M801a is unique. It is the only bound book, although at some stage it had been pulled apart and roughly rebound.[2] A number of pages are missing. Since at first sight it seemed to provide a more continuous text than most of the fragments in the first batch of texts to reach Berlin, it was early to claim the attention of F. W. K. Müller, who published a small section of it in 1904 to illustrate the fact that, although much of the text is in Middle Persian, another unknown Iranian language was also found.[3] This language, which Müller referred to as a 'Pahlavi dialect', is what we now call Sogdian.[4]

The first German expedition to the Turfan oasis was undertaken in 1902–1903 by Albert Grünwedel with two companions. It was almost certainly at Qočo, the ancient capital of an Uighur Turkish kingdom, that this book was discovered among many other fragmentary manuscript remains, before being brought back in one of the 46 crates which reached Berlin on 6 July 1903. The element of uncertainty about its exact provenance comes from the fact that, although the fragments had been put into envelopes on site and each envelope given a signature indicating the place of discovery, the envelopes were discarded when they were opened in Berlin and a new signature with M (for Manichaean script) and a number was given to each manuscript written in this handwriting. Thus the original signature of the small codex subsequently known as M801a, as MIK III 53 (referring to the Museum für Indische Kunst, now the Museum für Asiatische Kunst, which became the home of the codex), as III 53,[5] or as BBB (the initials of the German

[1] This introduction was written by John Sheldon in 2012 and has been edited and updated where necessary by Nicholas Sims-Williams.

[2] For the reconstruction of the original sequence of folios see Henning 1937, 3–7, and Zsuzsanna Gulácsi's study on pp. 111–62 below.

[3] Müller 1904, 99–100, cites the headline to p. 42 and lines 650–664 of BBB.

[4] In the addenda to his work Müller (1904, 111) refers in passing to the language as 'Sogdian'. By this time he knew of Andreas' identification of the language, on which see below.

[5] The prefix 'MIK' was dropped in about 2010, after the incorporation of the Museum für Indische Kunst into the Museum für Asiatische Kunst.

title 'Bet- und Beichtbuch' given to it by W. B. Henning), was unfortunately not preserved.[6]

Müller was at that time head of the Eastern Asiatic Department of the Ethnological Museum in Berlin, and a well-equipped scholar in many eastern languages and cultures. It was his knowledge of Semitic scripts and languages that enabled him to decipher the Manichaean script, which he compared with the estrangelo alphabet used for writing Syriac. He may be justly considered the founder of all future scholarship in the field of Middle Iranian Manichaean texts. A huge field had opened up, but competent labourers were, and have remained, few. Among these a special place must be accorded to F. C. Andreas, who is best known to the world at large as the husband of Lou Salomé,[7] less well known as having identified Müller's 'Pahlavi dialect' as Sogdian.[8] Although Andreas published very little during his lifetime, his brilliant insights into the new Middle Iranian material not only greatly advanced knowledge in this field, but also inspired a number of his pupils, notably Wolfgang Lentz and W. B. Henning. When Andreas died in 1930 he left a large collection of papers including ground-breaking work on the Manichaean manuscripts, such as a series of important Middle Persian and Parthian texts which were published by Henning from Andreas' Nachlass under the title 'Mitteliranische Manichaica'.[9] Lentz and his colleague Ernst Waldschmidt published two hymns from M801a,[10] but this unique book remained otherwise untouched until Henning undertook the task of editing and translating it in its entirety in the mid 1930s. M801a provided him with a great challenge. His work hitherto had chiefly involved Manichaean Middle Persian and Parthian. The codex included a liturgy in these languages, but its second part was a confessional text in the vernacular of the worshippers, a form of Sogdian hardly studied before. Buddhist and Christian material was known in this language and had been interpreted with a considerable degree of success, but M801a offered a wealth of new vocabulary, morphology and syntax for which the previously studied Sogdian texts provided only a starting point. Henning's finished work, published in 1937,[11] was a masterpiece; so much so that to this day no further edition has been deemed necesssary. BBB, as it is generally known, has been continuously quoted, especially in work on the Sogdian language such as the *Grammar of Manichean Sogdian* written under Henning's supervision by his pupil Ilya Gershevitch. Henning's presentation is directed to a specialist scholarly readership; to read and

[6] See Sundermann 1991, 426–38. It is also possible that BBB was purchased from local people who had been removing items from the Qočo site for sale to interested Europeans. Grünwedel mentions such purchases but does not systematically distinguish them from the archaeological finds.

[7] He appears as such in the opera *Lou Salomé* by Giuseppe Sinopoli, first performed in 1981.

[8] For details see Sims-Williams 2020.

[9] Andreas–Henning 1932; 1933; 1934.

[10] Waldschmidt–Lentz 1926, 120–21 (= BBB 164–99). Albert von Le Coq had previously described the external appearance of the book with an illustration of it as well as a transcription of two pages with a partial translation by Müller (Le Coq 1923, 40).

[11] Henning 1937 (often cited below merely as 'Henning'). Most of the text of Part 1 is reproduced as Text 'cu' in Boyce 1975, 153–9, with some useful notes but without any substantial changes. Klimkeit 1993, 133–44, provides an English translation of both parts of BBB with some notes.

to understand it requires a knowledge of German and much more. The current undertaking is intended to make this text and Henning's brilliant work on it more accessible to a wider audience and to bring it up to date.

The text of BBB

Most of the manuscript fragments of the Berlin Turfan collection are now housed in the Berlin-Brandenburg Academy of Sciences and Humanities where they were re-united in 1992 after years of disruption and dispersal, and where the Turfan Research project, led for many years by Werner Sundermann, the leading Manichaean scholar of his generation,[12] has now almost completed the work of conserving, publishing and digitizing the Iranian material. M801a, however, was one of the manuscripts selected for display at the Berlin Ethnological Museum, from which it passed to its successor institutions, the Museum of Indian Art, later the Museum of Asian Art. The beautiful miniature book is sealed under glass so that only one double-page spread is visible to the beholder and the sheets have only rarely been removed, one such occasion being when the book was photographed for publication by Dieter Weber in 2000 in a volume entitled *Iranian Manichaean Turfan texts in publications since 1934: Photo edition* (Corpus Inscriptionum Iranicarum, Supplementary Series 4). Weber's photographs, which are somewhat enlarged, are of good quality and provide almost all that is needed for someone working on this material. However, the double-page spreads are inevitably presented in the order in which they are bound, which was not the correct order established by Henning, although Weber does provide a concordance showing the recontructed original sequence of pages.[13] It is unfortunate that the photos are in black and white, not only because this detracts from the aesthetic appeal of the manuscript, but also because the different inks used in the headings of each page have significance in determining the correct order of the sheets, as Henning demonstrated. The colour photographs published here, with the kind permission of the Museum für Asiatische Kunst, make it possible for the first time for readers to appreciate the artistic quality of the manuscript's calligraphy and decoration as well as to see the pages in their original order.

Henning published the manuscript under the title *Ein Manichäisches Bet- und Beichtbuch* 'A Manichaean Prayer and Confession Book'. It has always been abbreviated as BBB and this designation will replace its signature M801a in what follows. There are three languages in the manuscript, which is in two parts. The first part, a liturgy containing substantial fragments of hymns and songs of praise, is principally in Middle Persian (henceforth MP), the traditional church language of the Manichaean community in Central Asia, sanctified through its use by Mani himself in at least one of his writings, the *Šābuhragān*. As in other Manichaean collections of sacred songs, the closely related Parthian (= Pa.) language is also

[12] The sad news of his death on 12 October 2012 after a long and courageous struggle with illness was conveyed to me by Professor Lieu while I was writing this introduction.

[13] Weber 2000, 27–8. In a few places (which will be referred to in the footnotes to the edition) Weber's photos show letters which have now broken off or cannot be seen on the new photos for some reason.

strongly represented. The second part is a confessional formula for the Manichaean elect, largely an examination of conscience, which seems to have been part of the same liturgy. Apart from occasional citations in MP, this part is written in Sogdian (= Sogd.). That this was the vernacular of the users of the book there can be little doubt; there is in fact a Sogdian rubric early in the first part. Like the MP and Pa. texts of Part 1, the Sogdian text is written in the Manichaean script which is clearer and less ambiguous than the native Sogdian script. Though the tradition that the Manichaean script was the creation of Mani himself is no longer accepted,[14] the founder of the religion was no doubt rightly remembered as a fine artist and illustrator of his own work. Correctness and painstaking care in the writing tasks of the elect are stressed and any carelessness or delinquency in these tasks is regarded as a sin against the second commandment, as we discover in BBB 524–32. The presentation of the text bears this out. Apart from the clarity and evenness of his writing, the scribe has adorned the heading of each page with more elaborately written words and decorative rosettes in four colours. As the book in its original condition would clearly have been something of a work of art, it is sad to see that it must have fallen to pieces or been pulled apart and the surviving folios roughly rebound in an arbitrary order with coarse string. Henning was of the opinion that this act of vandalism belonged to a time when Manichaean book-craft had fallen into abeyance and a rough and ready repair job would have to suffice.

The Bema liturgy in BBB

The surviving part of BBB, as reconstructed by Henning, begins with an extract from the 'Seal Letter', the last letter which Mani wrote before his death in prison.[15] There follow 14 short hymns or invocations described in MP as *mahr ī gāh* 'Bema hymns', a designation which already serves to identify the whole as part of the liturgy of the annual Bema festival, when the founder of the religion was believed to be present on a throne or raised dais (Greek βῆμα, MP *gāh*). The next group of hymns are 'blessings' or 'songs of praise' (MP *āfurišn*) addressed to a series of deities (with some lacunae between them): Narisah-yazad, the 'Third Messenger'; Srōšahrāy, the 'Column of Glory'; Yišōʿ Zīndakkar, 'Jesus the Life-giver'. There follow two 'songs of praise' addressed to the *frēstagān*, the 'messengers' or 'apostles', the first in MP, the second a Parthian reworking of the same text. The next group of three songs are described in the rubrics at the beginning and end as *āfurišn gāhīg* 'hymns of praise to the Bema' or *āfurišn ī*

---

[14] Durkin-Meisterernst 2000.

[15] As Mani's last words, the Seal Letter would have had a special resonance for his followers. One may compare the homily of Jesus at the last supper, occupying five chapters in the Gospel of St John, which is especially treasured by Christians as the last message of the Saviour to his apostles and hence to all his flock. Unfortunately very little of the Seal Letter survives (see Reck 2009) and the significance of its title is unclear. Seals are part of testamentary procedure in general and the title may simply be meant to indicate that this is Mani's last will and testament to his followers; on the other hand, the title may be capable of a metaphorical interpretation in view of the special significance of the word 'seal' in Manichaean ethics, where the 'three seals' of mouth, hand and heart encapsulate the whole disciplinary code of behaviour.

gāhrōšn 'hymns of praise to the light Bema' but in the page headings as *āfurišn frē[stagīg]* or *āfurišn ī [frēstag]* 'hymns of praise to the Apostle'. Like the fourteen 'Bema hymns' earlier in the liturgy, these are addressed to Mani, the Apostle, who is imagined to be spiritually, possibly physically, present at the rite. The surviving portion of Part 1 is completed by seven short hymns described as *mahr ī šādčanān* 'hymns of the joyful' or *mahrān ī šādīhān* 'hymns of joy', which are addressed to Mani and rejoice at his coming. As occurs from time to time in other such hymns, the melody to which they are to be sung is named at the beginning of five of these.

It is no accident that the second part of the text, the confessional or examination of conscience for the elect, is found in a book whose first part contains the liturgy of the Bema festival, as confession of sins was an essential part of the rite. The logical juxtaposition of the two parts has been highlighted recently by a series of publications by Christiane Reck. In her edition of MP and Pa. Bema hymns, she discussed M5779, published in Henning's BBB as Text c, and confirmed the suspicion of some earlier scholars that the two sides of this text should be read in the opposite order to that adopted by Henning. Like BBB itself, 'Text c' can be identified as a Bema liturgy (in this case rather briefly summarized), in which the singing of hymns is interspersed with other liturgical elements, including (near the beginning) the reading of the 'Seal Letter' and (at a much later point) the confession of sins (*xwāstwānīft*).[16] In two subsequent articles, Reck edits fragments of a manuscript which contains both a Sogdian translation of Mani's Seal Letter (including the same passage as is found in BBB) and transcriptions into Sogdian script of MP and Pa. Bema hymns, two of which correspond to those found in BBB 74–85.[17]

The confessional part of BBB no doubt began with the first commandment, *ršty'k* 'Truth', but this is missing from our text.[18] The surviving portion begins at a point where the examination of conscience has reached a review of the second commandment *pw 'zrmy'* 'Non-injury'. The rubrics indicate a twofold division of the matter for confession under this heading, which is in fact a feature of all five commandments.[19] The first section of the third commandment *dyncyhryft* 'Behaviour according to the religion', i.e. 'Purity', is substantially preserved, but the second part is lost in a lacuna; its likely content may be suggested by 'Text a', in which the passage dealing with this second part begins with a reference to 'male (and) female bodies'.[20] What follows in the text of BBB may possibly be a short fragment reviewing the fourth commandment *qwcyzprty'* 'Purity of mouth',[21] but of the fifth commandment *frnxwndc δšt'wc* 'Blessed poverty' there is no trace. It

16 Reck 2004, 30–31. For 'Text c' see now below, pp. 178–81.

17 Reck 2008, 318–28; 2009.

18 The Sogdian names of the five commandments for the elect are known from M14, V21–2 (Waldschmidt–Lentz 1933, 548). Sims-Williams 1985a collects references to these commandments in Chinese, Turkish, MP and Sogdian. On the fifth commandment see Colditz 2005, 285–7.

19 See Henning 1937, 15. Cf. also the reference to 'five commandments in ten parts' in Sundermann 1981, 44 with n. 15.

20 For 'Text a' see now below, pp. 164–5.

21 Cf. esp. BBB 589–93: 'If ... mixed food (or) intoxicating drinks have entered my mouth'.

is difficult to interpret the next section (lines 594–618) owing to the disrupted text, but some words could be seen as a formula for personal confession following the above examination of conscience.[22] This 'personal confession' is preserved clearly from the point that sins against the 'five gifts' are mentioned (lines 619 ff.).[23] In similar vein we next have passages concerning 'the closing of the five gates (i.e. senses)', neglect of prayer and other religious observances, lack of zeal, specific neglect of the Monday observances,[24] and improper attitude to the reception of the daily gifts from the divine table. Here our text breaks off.

It seems clear that our tiny book was specifically designed for use at the Bema festival or that it was a miniature copy of the liturgy lovingly made by an elect who treasured the text and believed in the merit gained by such copying. Our detailed knowledge of the festival is put together from scattered references and does not allow us to assume that what we have in BBB is a canonical text in use at all annual celebrations. It can be said, however, that the contents of BBB are appropriate for use at the festival and that there is no discrepancy between them and what we can gather from elsewhere. Apart from evidence for the celebration gleaned from BBB itself and from some related fragments, we need to look at other Bema hymns preserved in MP and Parthian as well as those found in the Coptic Psalm-book.[25] There is also a clearly identifiable illustration of the festival scene in one of the manuscripts from Turfan.[26] It is perhaps paradoxical that possibly the most detailed information comes to us in the anti-Manichaean writings of Augustine.[27]

The Bema festival was the major event of the Manichaean ecclesiastical year and came at its conclusion, at the end of February or early in March. It may have lasted four days and was preceded by a month of fasting.[28] The whole community, hearers and elect, gathered for a general confession and absolution, as well as a meal at the 'table of the gods' of which only the elect partook. These quasi-sacramental celebrations were surrounded by hymn singing, scripture readings and spiritual instruction including homilies and parables. The Bema throne or dais took centre stage and it was either left empty or more likely provided with an image of Mani who, in any case, was believed to be present and who gave the absolution. This celebration recalled Mani's death and his last testament, the 'Seal Letter', was read at it. It is no wonder that Augustine saw here an imitation of the Christian Easter rites which also occurred in spring and which involved commemoration of the Saviour's death, readings from His scriptures, confession and communion. We learn from a Coptic Bema psalm that the throne was also thought to

22 e.g. *wynd'yd pywhyd*, lines 597–8, cf. Asmussen 1965, 128 n. 81.

23 The 'five gifts (of the Light Nous)' are the five cardinal virtues: love, faith, perfection, patience and wisdom (see Asmussen 1965, 244, with many references; Sundermann 1992, 109).

24 Monday was a special holy day of the week for the elect, as was Sunday for the hearers. See Reck 2004, 10, citing the clear statement of An-Nadīm's *Fihrist*.

25 See Wurst 1995.

26 See Gulácsi 2001, 71 (fig. 32.1), 74–5.

27 *Contra Epistulam Fundamenti* 8. The most relevant passage is translated in Gardner–Lieu 2004, 237.

28 See Reck 2004, 28–30 (summarizing the work of Henning, Sundermann and others).

represent the throne of Christ on the day of judgement at the end of time. This psalm, no. 222 in the Medinet Madi Psalm-book,[29] is, in my opinion, one of the most beautiful things in the entire range of Manichaean literature. There is a passionate fervour in these Egyptian followers of Mani, many no doubt recent converts, which finds full expression in the poetry here. The psalmist is praying before the Bema throne which he sees as a visible symbol of the remission of his sins: 'Lo, there has come for you, the grace of the day of joy, do, for your part reveal without fear all your sins today'. The five steps upon which the Bema is raised according to Augustine's description become here a ladder to the paradise of forgiveness which the psalmist will ascend:

> May the Bema become for you a landing-place of your days,
> a place of cleansing of your life, a chest filled with teaching,
> a ladder to the heights, a counting-balance of your deeds;
> and as you see the likeness of these things in the Bema, bless it.

This is the season of spring when all is renewed. In words prophetic of Wagner's evocation of nature weeping at the Saviour's death on Good Friday, then smiling at the thought of his coming Resurrection, all in empathy with the work of man's salvation,[30] we read:

> Every tree today has become new again,
> Lo, the roses have spread their beauty abroad,
> for the bond has been severed that does harm to the leaves;
> do you also sever the chain and the bond of our sins.
> All the air is luminous, the sphere glitters today,
> even the earth puts forth blossom, the waves of the sea are still:
> for the gloomy winter has passed that is full of trouble;
> let us too escape from the iniquity of evil.

This psalm radiates sincere contrition, but even more does it express the deep feeling of joy brought by the grace of this holy day and its rite.

Confession in Manichaeism[31]

Consciousness of guilt or sin is a common element in many though not all religions. Forgiveness of sin is therefore required and, in the religions which are potentially relevant to Central Asian Manichaeism, this is achieved by confession.

---

[29] Allberry 1938, 7–9; Wurst 1996, 32–7; Gardner–Lieu 2004, 238–40.

[30] 'Karfreitagszauber', *Parsifal* Act III.

[31] [*Editor's note*. The argument presented by John Sheldon in this section largely follows the fundamental work of Jes P. Asmussen (1965). It is worth noting, however, that Jan Nattier argued that Buddhist confessional texts from Central Asia are dependent on the Manichaean, rather than vice versa. Building on this, Jason BeDuhn has drawn attention to striking Ancient Near Eastern parallels to the Central Asian Manichaean confessional formularies and postulated that 'formal, publicly performed confession texts were an original part of early Manichaean religious practice in West Asia' (BeDuhn 2004, 162; see further BeDuhn 2013).]

The formalization and ritualization of confession is a different matter. There is no evidence for such a practice in the early Judaeo-Christian communities, so that, while we may be sure that Mani was aware of the importance of confession, he would not have been accustomed to the use of a confessional formulary such as we have in BBB. It is also highly improbable that Zoroastrian practice in this matter was an influence. The Pahlavi *patīt*, a formulary of confession of the same general type as is found in BBB, is known only from late Sasanian or Islamic times. Owing to the gap in Zoroastrian literary sources it may well be that this type of formulary existed in Mani's time, but there is nothing to substantiate any contact between the two religions in this matter.

When a formalized practice of confession was adopted in Manichaeism we do not know, but in all probability it is to Buddhist practice that we must turn to find a source for Manichaean confessional ritual. In the Turfan region where BBB was discovered there was a strong and ever increasing Buddhist presence which made its mark on the way the followers of Mani conducted their lives. For example, the robing of the elect and the existence of two sets of commandments for elect and hearers—Buddhists had different commandments for monks and laity—all bear strong marks of Buddhist influence. It is not unreasonable to assume that, while confession of sin must always have been a requirement for Manichaeans, its ritualization, in particular the use of confession formulae, was something that they most likely learned from neighbouring Buddhists. We know that in China, at the likely period of BBB's composition, confessional rituals evolved for both laity and monks, which consisted of readings from the *sūtras* and prayers addressed to statues of Buddha and Bodhisattvas, and BBB shares many resonances with the Buddhist genre of *deśanā* 'confession' texts.

The strong emphasis on guilt and sinfulness which pervades the second part of BBB and other Manichaean confessional texts has its origin in Mani's explanation for the existence of both good and evil in the world, a seemingly insoluble problem which must be faced by all religions. According to Mani, all mankind is a mixture of light and dark elements. The sinfulness inherent in man's nature through the dark elements within it can be reduced, if not totally eliminated, by good actions, of which confession is a major part. Opponents of Manichaeism such as Augustine, who after his conversion from Mani's teachings to Christianity could invoke the doctrine of the fall of Adam and original sin, pointed to an inherent contradiction here. If the soul is by its very nature sinful or at least is clothed in a totally sinful body, how can it be purified by confession or any other means? This was no doubt an academic question to Mani's educated followers, who would claim that we must do the very best we can to redeem our light elements and that good living and confession among other things were steps in the right direction. This, I believe, is the context in which we must understand the BBB confessional for the elect.

Another consequence of Mani's teaching was uncertainty about the degree of responsibility for sin which could be borne by the sinner. Again Augustine points to a contradiction. If man's nature is compounded of good and evil, some of his actions must be evil whether he is conscious of it or not. If he commits an evil act of which he is not conscious or over which he has no control, it cannot be a sin in the normal theological understanding of this concept. In his condemnation of the supposedly immoral lives of the Manichaeans, he claims that they commit evil actions and exculpate themselves on the grounds that the sinful origin of such actions lies in the dark elements within them and is not of their free choice. He goes further and states that this belief appeased his own guilty conscience when he led a sinful life at the time that he was a member of the sect.[32] While this may have been true of Augustine and no doubt many of his Manichaean associates, it is a far cry from what we find in BBB. It has long been observed that much of the thrust of this confessional formulary is conditional.[33] 'If I have done this, may I be forgiven.' There are so many possibilities of unconscious as well as conscious 'sin' that in making confession all possible 'occasions of sin' must be thoroughly rehearsed in the examination of conscience. Only in this way can the penitent be sure that nothing has been omitted. The same conditional formulation appears in a text bearing the Parthian title *Xwāstwānīft* 'confession', an extensive confessional for hearers, of which only fragments survive in the original Sogdian,[34] but of which a fairly complete translation exists in Turkish.[35] The ten commandments for hearers to which this confessional refers have only tangential relevance to the five commandments for the elect in BBB, but it is an essential point of reference in view of its length and its its excellent state of preservation. On each Monday elect and hearers alike were required to take part in a service which consisted of prayers and hymns, a sermon, confession and accompanying absolution. Failure to observe the Monday rite is mentioned in BBB as a sin for which the elect must ask forgiveness; the Turkish *Xwāstwānīft* likewise refers to it as a sin if a hearer fails to attend the Monday service and to make confession in the presence of the elect.[36]

The date of BBB

Only an approximate date can be assigned to our text and this depends largely on external evidence. BBB was found in a deposit of many manuscript fragments which were probably part of a Manichaean library in Qočo on the northern rim of the Turfan basin. It belongs to a period when Manichaean scribes were free to ply their trade without hindrance, a period of relative peace in this part of the Silk Road. The Qočo manuscripts mostly consist of texts in MP, Parthian and Sogdian, together with a fair number in Uighur Turkish. The vernaculars of their readers would have been principally Sogdian and Turkish. Most of the text fragments may well date from the time that the Uighurs established a kingdom in that region after they had been driven from Mongolia by the Kirghiz in 840 CE. Before this the Uighurs had possessed a vast kingdom in the Orkhon Valley and had inter-

32 *Confessions*, V.x.18, and *De Moribus Manichaeorum*, XX (74), both cited in Gardner–Lieu 2004, 134–5. Similarly *De Haeresibus*, XLVI.19 (*ibid.*, 191).

33 On this see especially the discussion in BeDuhn 2004, 173–7, citing the seminal ideas found in Puech 1979.

34 Reck 2015.

35 Clark 2013, 7–111.

36 Clark 2013, 92 (§XIII).

vened in China against An Lushan's rebellion in 762–763 CE. A few years earlier their *qaghan* had been converted to the religion of Mani by Sogdian missionaries, as we read in the trilingual inscription at Karabalgasun[37] and in an extensive Manichaean Turkish text.[38] Qočo was therefore in a region controlled by rulers who espoused Manichaeism. Such an environment would have been conducive to the production of high-quality books such as BBB. The crude state in which it was found points to a later time in Qočo when the picture had changed for the worse for the followers of Mani. The Manichaeans and their Uighur rulers were subject to increasing Buddhist influence and the stability of the Manichaean religious establishments was undermined as a result. The site of BBB's discovery in Qočo was probably a Manichaean temple later converted to a Buddhist monastery. If the Buddhist monks retained the Manichaean books but did not maintain them, this could account for the neglect from which BBB so clearly suffered. The date of the conversion of 'Ruin α' at Qočo to a Buddhist monastery has now been established as 25 October 1008 by the correct identification of the Uighur *qaghan* mentioned there in an inscription to commemorate the event.[39] This therefore provides a *terminus ante quem* for BBB. Internal evidence would favour a substantially earlier date, a period when Manichaeism was still strong.

The 'Additional texts'

In an Appendix to his edition of BBB, Henning added six additional Sogdian texts which he designated by the letters *a* to *f*. In all subsequent references including those in *DMT* III/2, they are referred to as BBBa, BBBb etc. It is important to remember, however, that they do not form part of M801a, but are fragments which Henning noticed elsewhere which had relevance to BBB. His purpose in including them was, as he states in the heading to this Appendix, to further our understanding of Manichaean ritual. For the convenience of the reader these texts are also included in this edition on pp. 163–95 below.[40]

Text a. The first text is a fragment of another Sogdian confessional for the elect, covering the end of the second commandment and a substantial part of the third, which is divided into two parts as in BBB. Although much shorter than the equivalent sections of BBB, there are many coincidences in wording, which suggest that the fragment may belong to a condensed version of the same text.

Text b. The second text consists of two double-folios, the second being badly damaged and reconstructed by Henning from two separate fragments. The original order of pages is unknown. In the order adopted by Henning (and accepted here), the first two folios, IA and IIA, belong to another confessional for the elect, this time not arranged to reflect sins against the five commandments but rather sins in thought, word and (presumably) deed. The other two folios, IIB and IB, contain a lament, expressed in highly emotional language, for the fate of the soul, that is, the light imprisoned in matter.

37 For the Sogdian text of the inscription see now Yoshida 2020.

38 Bang–von Gabain 1929. English translation in Klimkeit 1993, 366–8.

39 See Sundermann 1991, 286–8.

40 Klimkeit 1993, 148–5, provides English translations and commentary on most of these texts.

Text c has already been discussed above, p. xi, where the fact is noted that the two sides should be read in the opposite order to that adopted by Henning (with some hesitation, it should be said). In the present edition the order of Recto and Verso is corrected, but Henning's line-numbers are retained, since the text has always been quoted by them. The text is a summary of part of the liturgy for the Bema festival. The rubrical instructions are in Sogdian, but most of the text consists of hymns in Parthian or (in one case) in MP. It is worth noting that the hymn which immediately follows the reading from the Seal Letter is not one of those which occur at this point in BBB.

Text d is a folio containing part of a liturgy for the little-known 'Body-soul rite'. A second folio from the same manuscript, perhaps originally forming a double-folio with the first, contains a MP hymn in a different hand which was not published in BBB, presumably because Henning did not regard it as relevant. However, this second folio has now been published by Enrico Morano, who shows that the hymn which it contains is a dialogue between body and soul, of which further fragments can also be identified in MP, Sogdian and (probably) Parthian, thus strongly suggesting that the hymn forms part of the same ritual.[41] In addition to providing evidence for the 'Body-soul rite', Text d is of interest for its references to the reading in the service of what appear to be a 'Mahāyāna' text and a Buddhist story used as a parable.[42] The full significance of this has been rather underrated, I believe, in the relevant literature.

Text e. Henning here presented two fragments which appear from their shape to have belonged to a double-folio. The first fragment describes explicitly the trans-cendent power of the remission of sins to efface all the evil deeds of which a man may be guilty. The second fragment is not directly relevant to BBB, being a cosmogonic text concerning Adam, Eve, Seth and Šaqlōn.[43]

Text f is a rather large but damaged double-folio. The first folio is concerned with absolution and contains a powerful statement about the effect of a refusal of absolution. The second folio concerns the proper state of mind for participation at meals at the sacred table and throws light on the passage concerning this at the end of BBB.[44]

Walter Bruno Henning and BBB

It is appropriate in concluding this introduction to say something more about the man upon whom so much here depends, the original editor Walter Bruno Henning. In his article on Henning in *Encyclopædia Iranica* XII/2, 188–98, Werner Sundermann does not exaggerate when he says that writing an appreciation of Henning 'would almost amount to writing a history of the study of Middle Iranian languages and cultures in the 20th century. There exists hardly any discovery in this realm of knowledge to which Henning has not made major and fundamental contributions, and the fact that it is precisely this area of Iranian studies which

41 Morano 2017.

42 See Klimkeit 1993, 150–51 with nn. 40 and 42 on p. 154.

43 On this episode see Reeves 1999.

44 On this folio see BeDuhn 2000, 155.

went through an unprecedented evolution in the 20th century underlines the importance of this scholar, who can be without exaggeration considered as one of the leading philologists of the past century'.

Born in Ragnit in East Prussia on 26 August 1908, Walter Henning showed great ability in mathematics in his school days and went on to study this subject at the University of Göttingen. He was fascinated by the contribution made to his subject by the Arabs and determined to learn Arabic. This brought him into contact with F. C. Andreas, who introduced him to Middle Iranian languages and so his great career began. His doctorate was awarded *summa cum laude* in 1931 for his dissertation on the Middle Persian verb in the Turfan texts. Andreas had died in 1930 and Henning was now commissioned by the Prussian Academy of Sciences in Berlin to continue and edit Andreas' incomplete work, which he did in a series of three ground-breaking publications, as has been mentioned above. These were followed by the even more fundamentally important edition of BBB. Between the completion of this work and its publication Henning's life underwent a major change when he decided to leave Germany because of the threat which National Socialism and its anti-semitism posed to his family life. He became engaged to marry Maria Polotsky, sister of the German-Jewish Egyptologist and Semitic scholar Hans Jacob Polotsky, and the couple moved to England in 1936 and were married in London in 1937. According to a well-known anecdote, Harold Bailey, who was strongly supportive of Henning's move to England, was at the train station in London to meet him and, finding him without cash, gave him the fare for his taxi. Henning replaced Bailey as lecturer in Iranian languages in the London School of Oriental Studies when the latter became professor of Sanskrit at Cambridge. Henceforth Henning's publications were almost all in English. There is no inkling of a second language in his impeccable and elegant academic writing. When war broke out in 1939 he suffered the fate of other foreign nationals and was interned on the Isle of Man. During this time Bailey arranged to see his important volume *Sogdica* through the press. After his release Henning was able to resume work and ultimately became Head of the Department of the Languages and Cultures of the Near and Middle East in what had been renamed as the School of Oriental and African Studies. Among his distinguished pupils were Ilya Gershevitch and Mary Boyce. In 1961 he left England for a chair of Iranian Studies at the University of California in Berkeley where he remained active until his death on 8 January 1967 owing to an accidental fall. His health had been fragile throughout his life owing to illness in childhood, but, as Mary Boyce put it, 'his spirit belied his body.' I met him only once in my undergraduate days; it was at a meeting of the Philological Society in Oxford, not long before he departed for America. He seemed very frail and I remember, irrelevantly as one does, that he wore blue-tinted spectacles, which was something I had not seen before. He was given to working through the night in order to be uninterrupted, a habit he is said to have acquired while a student of Andreas.

Henning's work on BBB remains a monument to his scholarship. There is not a word wasted nor a short-cut taken. He presents all evidence with complete accuracy and with absolute scholarly integrity is never tempted to overplay his hand in the supporting material he invokes to substantiate his arguments. In BBB he is quite frank in stating when he had been wrong in his earlier work and he is quite objective about what he proposes, admitting any limitations there might be. There is a touch of humour from time to time, though this will be found more in his later work. Rereading the manuscripts which he published one finds almost nothing which does not seem to be correctly read, and it is only rarely and with great hesitation that one may dare to depart from his interpretation in the slightest detail. Despite three-quarters of a century of progress in Manichaean and Middle Iranian studies, his pioneering work can hardly be bettered: BBB remains forever Henning's book.

Editor’s note

As John Sheldon makes clear in his Introduction above, Henning’s edition of BBB was a brilliant pioneer work. Henning’s interpretation of the text, especially his elaborate commentary on the Sogdian texts, remains of immense value and will continue to be consulted for many years to come. It has therefore seemed useful to indicate specifically in the footnotes to the present edition and translation the more important changes from Henning’s reading or interpretation (even in the case of re-interpretations which are by now well-established), so that those who consult this edition and Henning’s side by side will not be confused by the occasional discrepancies.

The texts below make use of the conventions which are usual in editions of Middle Iranian Manichaean texts:

[xyz] = letters missing in a lacuna or where the surface of the paper is destroyed;
(xyz) = letters which are damaged and therefore not unambiguously legible;
<ʾ> = a letter omitted by the scribe. In general such an omission is indicated by a subscript double point; where the omission mark is not present this is explained in a footnote.

I take this opportunity to express my thanks
• to the Museum für Asiatische Kunst, Berlin, and the Berlin-Brandenburgische Akademie der Wissenschaften, for providing the photographs published in this volume and allowing their publication;
• to John Sheldon for his Introduction;
• to Zsuzsanna Gulácsi for her chapter on the Codicology of BBB;
• to Jason BeDuhn for carefully reading the whole work and saving me from errors in matters of Manichaean doctrine and practice;
• to Sam Lieu and Enrico Morano for inviting me to edit this work as the first volume of the Corpus Fontium Manichaeorum, Series Iranica, and for their helpful advice on the contents.

Nicholas Sims-Williams
Cambridge, November 2020

Bibliography & bibliographical abbreviations

Allberry 1938 = C. R. C. Allberry, *A Manichaean Psalm-book*, Part II, Stuttgart.

Andreas–Henning 1932 = F. C. Andreas & W. B. Henning, *Mitteliranische Manichaica aus Chinesisch-Turkestan I* (SPAW 1932, No. 10), Berlin.

Andreas–Henning 1933 = F. C. Andreas & W. B. Henning, *Mitteliranische Manichaica aus Chinesisch-Turkestan II* (SPAW 1933, No. 7), Berlin.

Andreas–Henning 1934 = F. C. Andreas & W. B. Henning, *Mitteliranische Manichaica aus Chinesisch-Turkestan III* (SPAW 1934, No. 27), Berlin.

APAW = Abhandlungen der Preussischen Akademie der Wissenschaften, Phil.-hist. Klasse.

Asmussen 1965 = J. P. Asmussen, *X^{u}āstvānīft. Studies in Manichaeism*, Copenhagen.

Bang–von Gabain 1929 = W. Bang & A. von Gabain, *Türkische Turfantexte II* (SPAW 1929, No. 22), Berlin.

BeDuhn 2000 = J. D. BeDuhn, *The Manichaean body in discipline and ritual*, Baltimore–London.

BeDuhn 2004 = J. D. BeDuhn, 'The Near Eastern connections of Manichaean confessionary practice', *ARAM* 16, 161–77.

BeDuhn 2013 = J. D. BeDuhn, 'The Manichaean weekly confessional ritual', *Practicing Gnosis: Ritual, magic, theurgy and liturgy in Nag Hammadi, Manichaean and other ancient literature. Essays in honor of Birger A. Pearson* (ed. A. DeConick et al.), Leiden, 271–99.

Benkato 2017 = A. Benkato, *Āzandnāmē. An edition and literary-critical study of the Manichaean Sogdian Parable-book* (Beiträge zur Iranistik 42), Wiesbaden.

Benveniste 1938 = É. Benveniste, 'Notes sogdiennes [IV]', *BSOS* 9/3, 495–518. [Reprinted in Benveniste 1979, 163–86.]

Benveniste 1940 = É. Benveniste, *Textes sogdiens*, Paris.

Benveniste 1959 = É. Benveniste, 'Études sur quelques textes sogdiens chrétiens (II)', *Journal Asiatique* 247, 115–34. [Reprinted in Benveniste 1979, 267–86.]

Benveniste 1979 = É. Benveniste, *Études sogdiennes* (Beiträge zur Iranistik 9), Wiesbaden.

Bi–Sims-Williams 2011 = Bi Bo & N. Sims-Williams, 'Sogdian documents from Khotan, I: Four economic documents', *Journal of the American Oriental Society* 130/4, 2010 [2011], 497–508.

Boyce 1960 = M. Boyce, *A catalogue of the Iranian manuscripts in Manichean script in the German Turfan collection*, Berlin.

Boyce 1975 = M. Boyce, *A reader in Manichaean Middle Persian and Parthian* (Acta Iranica 9), Tehran–Liège.

BSO(A)S = *Bulletin of the School of Oriental (and African) Studies.*

Clark 2013 = L. Clark, *Uygur Manichaean texts* II: *Liturgical texts* (Corpus Fontium Manichaeorum, Series Turcica 2), Turnhout.

Colditz 2005 = I. Colditz, 'Terminological dualism in Middle Persian and Parthian', *Middle Iranian Lexicography* (ed. C. G. Cereti & M. Maggi), Rome, 277–87.

Colditz 2018 = I. Colditz, *Iranische Personennamen in manichäischer Überlieferung* (Iranisches Personennamenbuch II/1), Vienna.

de Blois 2003 = F. de Blois, 'Manes' "Twin" in Iranian and non-Iranian texts', *Religious themes and texts of pre-Islamic Iran and Central Asia. Studies in honour of Professor Gherardo Gnoli on the occasion of his 65th birthday on 6th December 2002* (ed. C. G. Cereti, M. Maggi & E. Provasi), Wiesbaden, 7–16.

de Blois 2006 = F. de Blois, 'Glossary of technical terms and uncommon expressions in Arabic (and in Muslim New Persian) texts relating to Manichaeism', *Texts from Iraq and Iran* (Dictionary of Manichaean Texts II, ed. F. de Blois & N. Sims-Williams), Turnhout, 21–88.

DMT III/1 = Durkin-Meisterernst 2004.

DMT III/2 = Sims-Williams–Durkin-Meisterernst 2012.

Durkin-Meisterernst 2000 = D. Durkin-Meisterernst, 'Erfand Mani die manichäische Schrift?', *Studia Manichaica. IV. Internationaler Kongreß zum Manichäismus, Berlin, 14.–18. Juli 1997* (Berlin-Brandenburgische Akademie der Wissenschaften, Berichte und Abhandlungen, Sonderband 4, ed. R. E. Emmerick, W. Sundermann & P. Zieme), Berlin, 161–78.

Durkin-Meisterernst 2004 = D. Durkin-Meisterernst, *Dictionary of Manichaean Middle Persian and Parthian* (Dictionary of Manichaean Texts III/1), Turnhout. [Cited as *DMT* III/1.]

Durkin-Meisterernst 2014 = D. Durkin-Meisterernst, *Miscellaneous hymns. Middle Persian and Parthian hymns in the Turfan Collection* (Berliner Turfantexte 31), Turnhout.

Gardner–Lieu 2004 = I. Gardner & S. N. C. Lieu, *Manichaean texts from the Roman Empire*, Cambridge.

Gershevitch 1946 = I. Gershevitch, 'Sogdian compounds', *Transactions of the Philological Society* 1945 [1946], 137–49. [Reprinted in Gershevitch 1985, 6–18.]

Gershevitch 1954 = I. Gershevitch, *A grammar of Manichean Sogdian*, Oxford, 1954. [Cited as *GMS*.]

Gershevitch 1962 = I. Gershevitch, 'The Sogdian word for "advice", and some Muγ documents', *Central Asiatic Journal* 7, 77–95. [Reprinted in Gershevitch 1985, 33–51.]

Gershevitch 1979 = I. Gershevitch, 'No Old Persian *spāθmaida*', *Festschrift for Oswald Szemerényi on the occasion of his 65th birthday* (ed. B. Brogyanyi), Amsterdam, 291–5.

Gershevitch 1985 = I. Gershevitch, *Philologia Iranica* (Beiträge zur Iranistik 12, ed. N. Sims-Williams), Wiesbaden.

GMS = Gershevitch 1954.

Gulácsi 2001 = Zs. Gulácsi, *Manichaean Art in Berlin collections* (Corpus Fontium Manichaeorum, Series Archaeologica et Iconographica 1), Turnhout.

Haloun–Henning 1952 = G. Haloun & W. B. Henning, 'The Compendium of the doctrines and styles of Mani, the Buddha of Light', *Asia Major*, N.S. 3/2, 184–212.

Henning 1933 = W. B. Henning, 'Das Verbum des Mittelpersischen der Turfanfragmente', *Zeitschrift für Indologie und Iranistik* 9, 158–253. [Reprinted in Henning 1977, I, 65–160.]

Henning 1936 = W. B. Henning, 'Neue Materialien zur Geschichte des Manichäismus', *Zeitschrift der Deutschen Morgenländischen Gesellschaft* 90, 1–18. [Reprinted in Henning 1977, I, 379–96.]

Henning 1937 = W. B. Henning, *Ein manichäisches Bet- und Beichtbuch* (APAW 1936, No. 10), Berlin. [Reprinted in Henning 1977, I, 417–557. Generally referred to simply as 'Henning'.]

Henning 1943 = W. B. Henning, 'The Book of the Giants', *BSOAS* 11/1, 52–74. [Reprinted in Henning 1977, II, 115–37.]

Henning 1945 = W. B. Henning, 'Sogdian tales', *BSOAS* 11/3, 465–87. [Reprinted in Henning 1977, II, 169–91.]

Henning 1946 = W. B. Henning, 'Two Central Asian words', *Transactions of the Philological Society* 1945 [1946], 150–62. [Reprinted in Henning 1977, II, 259–71.]

Henning 1946a = W. B. Henning, 'The Sogdian texts of Paris', *BSOAS* 11/4, 713–40. [Reprinted in Henning 1977, II, 231–58.]

Henning 1977 = W. B. Henning, *Selected Papers*, I–II (Acta Iranica 14–15), Tehran–Liège.

Klimkeit 1993 = H.-J. Klimkeit, *Gnosis on the Silk Road*, San Francisco.

Le Coq 1923 = A. von Le Coq, *Die manichäischen Miniaturen. Die buddhistische Spätantike in Mittelasien*, Berlin.

Leurini 2017 = C. Leurini, *Hymns in honour of the hierarchy and community, Installation hymns and hymns in honour of church leaders and patrons* (Berliner Turfantexte XL), Turnhout.

MacKenzie 1985 = D. N. MacKenzie, 'Two Sogdian *Hwydgm'n* fragments', *Papers in honour of Professor Mary Boyce* II (Acta Iranica 25), Leiden, 421–8.

MacKenzie 1995 = D. N. MacKenzie, '»I, Mani ...«', *Gnosisforschung und Religionsgeschichte. Festschrift für Kurt Rudolph zum 65. Geburtstag* (ed. H. Preißler & H. Seiwert), Marburg, 1994 [1995], 183–98.

Monier-Williams 1899 = M. Monier-Williams, *A Sanskrit-English dictionary*, Oxford.

Morano 1982 = E. Morano, 'The Sogdian hymns of *Stellung Jesu*', *East and West* 32, 9–43.

Morano 2017 = E. Morano, 'An antiphonal Body and Soul hymn in Manichaean Middle Persian, Parthian and Sogdian', *Zur lichten Heimat. Studien zu Mani-*

chäismus, Iranistik und Zentralasienkunde im Gedenken an Werner Sundermann (Iranica 25), Wiesbaden, 445–52.

Müller 1904 = F. W. K. Müller, *Handschriften-Reste in Estrangelo-Schrift aus Turfan, Chinesisch-Turkistan*, II. Teil (Anhang zu den APAW 1904), Berlin.

Müller 1913 = F. W. K. Müller, *Ein Doppelblatt aus einem manichäischen Hymnenbuch (Maḥrnâmag)* (APAW 1912, No. 5), Berlin.

Nyberg 1932 = H. S. Nyberg, 'Un pseudo-verbe iranien et son équivalent grec', *Symbolae Philologicae O. A. Danielsson octogenario dicatae*, Uppsala, 237–61.

Puech 1979 = Puech, H.-C., *Sur le manichéisme et autres essais*, Paris.

Reck 2004 = C. Reck, *Gesegnet sei dieser Tag. Manichäische Festtagshymnen – Edition der mittelpersischen und parthischen Sonntags-, Montags- und Bemahymnen* (Berliner Turfantexte 22), Turnhout.

Reck 2008 = C. Reck, 'Tage der Barmherzigkeit. Nachträge zu den mitteliranischen manichäischen Montags- und Bemahymnen', *Iranian languages and texts from Iran and Turan. Ronald E. Emmerick memorial volume* (ed. M. Macuch et al.), Wiesbaden, 2007 [2008], 317–42.

Reck 2009 = C. Reck, 'A Sogdian version of Mani's *Letter of the Seal*', *New Light on Manichaeism. Papers from the Sixth International Congress on Manichaeism* (ed. J. BeDuhn), Leiden, 225–39.

Reck 2015 = C. Reck, 'Sogdian Manichaean confessional fragments in Sogdian script in the Berlin Turfan Collection: The fragments of the *Xwāstwānīft*', *Mani in Dublin* (ed. S. G. Richter et al.), Leiden, 289–323.

Reeves 1999 = J. Reeves, 'Manichaica Aramaica? Adam and the magical deliverance of Seth', *Journal of the American Oriental Society* 119/3, 432–9.

Sims-Williams 1982 = N. Sims-Williams, 'Notes on Manichaean Middle Persian morphology', *Studia Iranica* 10/2, 1981 [1982], 165–76.

Sims-Williams 1983 = N. Sims-Williams, 'Indian elements in Parthian and Sogdian', *Sprachen des Buddhismus in Zentralasien. Vorträge des Hamburger Symposions vom 2. Juli bis 5. Juli 1981* (ed. K. Röhrborn & W. Veenker), Wiesbaden, 132–41.

Sims-Williams 1985 = N. Sims-Williams, *The Christian Sogdian manuscript C 2* (Berliner Turfantexte 12), Berlin.

Sims-Williams 1985a = N. Sims-Williams, 'The Manichean commandments: a survey of the sources', *Papers in honour of Professor Mary Boyce* II (Acta Iranica 25), Leiden, 573–82.

Sims-Williams 1986 = N. Sims-Williams, 'Sogdian *''δprm* and its cognates', *Studia grammatica iranica. Festschrift für Helmut Humbach* (ed. R. Schmitt & P. O. Skjærvø), Munich, 407-424.

Sims-Williams 1989 = N. Sims-Williams, 'A new fragment from the Parthian hymn-cycle *Huyadagmān*', *Études irano-aryennes offertes à Gilbert Lazard* (Cahiers de Studia Iranica 7), Paris, 321–31.

Sims-Williams 1991 = N. Sims-Williams, 'The Sogdian fragments of Leningrad III: Fragments of the *Xwāstwānīft*'', *Manichaica Selecta. Studies presented to Professor Julien Ries on the occasion of his seventieth birthday* (Manichaean Studies I, ed. A. van Tongerloo & S. Giversen), Louvain, 323–8.

Sims-Williams 1996 = N. Sims-Williams, 'On the historic present and injunctive in Sogdian and Choresmian', *Münchener Studien zur Sprachwissenschaft* 56, 173–89.

Sims-Williams 2007 = N. Sims-Williams, *Bactrian documents from Northern Afghanistan*, Vol. 2: *Letters and Buddhist texts*, London.

Sims-Williams 2010 = N. Sims-Williams, *Bactrian Personal Names* (Iranisches Personennamenbuch II/7), Vienna.

Sims-Williams 2014 = N. Sims-Williams, *Biblical and other Christian Sogdian texts from the Turfan Collection* (Berliner Turfantexte 32), Turnhout.

Sims-Williams 2015 = N. Sims-Williams, *The Life of St Serapion and other Christian Sogdian texts from the manuscripts E25 and E26* (Berliner Turfantexte 35), Turnhout.

Sims-Williams 2016 = N. Sims-Williams, *A Dictionary: Christian Sogdian, Syriac and English* (Beiträge zur Iranistik 41), Wiesbaden.

Sims-Williams 2017 = N. Sims-Williams, *An ascetic miscellany: The Christian Sogdian manuscript E28* (Berliner Turfantexte 42), Turnhout.

Sims-Williams 2019 = N. Sims-Williams, 'A multilingual Manichean calendar from Turfan (U130)', *Language, Society, and Religion in the world of the Turks: Festschrift for Larry Clark at Seventy-Five* (Silk Road Studies 19, ed. Zs. Gulácsi), Turnhout, 2018 [2019], 251–66.

Sims-Williams 2019a = N. Sims-Williams, *From liturgy to pharmacology: Christian Sogdian texts from the Turfan Collection* (Berliner Turfantexte XLV), Turnhout.

Sims-Williams 2020 = N. Sims-Williams, 'The rediscovery of Sogdian', *Byzantium to China: Religion, History and Culture on the Silk Roads. Studies in honour of Samuel N. C. Lieu at seventy* (ed. P. Edwell, G. Mikkelsen & K. Parry), Leiden–Boston.

Sims-Williams–Durkin-Meisterernst 2012 = N. Sims-Williams & D. Durkin-Meisterernst, *Dictionary of Manichaean Sogdian and Bactrian* (Dictionary of Manichaean Texts III/2), Turnhout. [Cited as *DMT* III/2.]

SPAW = Sitzungsberichte der Preussischen Akademie der Wissenschaften, Phil.-hist. Klasse.

Sundermann 1975 = W. Sundermann, 'Nachlese zu F. W. K. Müllers "Soghdischen Texten I", 2. Teil", *Altorientalische Forschungen* 3, 55–90.

Sundermann 1981 = W. Sundermann, *Mitteliranische manichäische Texte kirchengeschichtlichen Inhalts* (Berliner Turfantexte 11), Berlin.

Sundermann 1991 = W. Sundermann, 'Completion and correction of archaeological work by philological means: the case of the Turfan texts', *Histoire et cultes de l'Asie Centrale préislamique* (ed. P. Bernard & F. Grenet), Paris, 283–8. [Reprinted in Sundermann 2001, I, 427–36.]

Sundermann 1992 = W. Sundermann, *Der Sermon vom Licht-Nous* (Berliner Turfantexte 17), Berlin.

Sundermann 1997 = W. Sundermann, 'Three fragments of Sogdian letters and documents', *La Persia e l'Asia centrale da Alessandro al X secolo* (Atti dei convegni Lincei 127), 1996 [1997], Rome, 99–111. [Reprinted in Sundermann 2001, II, 725–38.]

Sundermann 2001 = W. Sundermann, *Manichaica Iranica. Ausgewählte Schriften*, I–II, Rome.

Sundermann 2005 = W. Sundermann, 'On the identity and the unity of the Parthian language, and on its unknown words', *Middle Iranian Lexicography* (ed. C. G. Cereti & M. Maggi), Rome, 85-100.

Waldschmidt–Lentz 1926 = E. Waldschmidt & W. Lentz, *Die Stellung Jesu im Manichäismus* (APAW 1926, No. 4), Berlin.

Waldschmidt–Lentz 1933 = E. Waldschmidt & W. Lentz, *Manichäische Dogmatik aus chinesischen und iranischen Texten* (SPAW 1933, No. 13), Berlin.

Weber 2000 = D. Weber, *Iranian Manichaean Turfan texts in publications since 1934. Photo edition* (Corpus Inscriptionum Iranicarum, Supplementary Series 4), London.

Wurst 1995 = G. Wurst, *Das Bemafest der ägyptischen Manichäer*, Altenberg.

Wurst 1996 = G. Wurst, *Psalm Book* II/1 (Corpus Fontium Manichaeorum, Series Coptica 1), Turnhout.

Yoshida 1998 = Y. Yoshida, 'The Sogdian Dhūta text and its Chinese original', *Bulletin of the Asia Institute*, N.S. 10, 1996 [1998], 167–73.

Yoshida 2000 = Y. Yoshida, 'First fruits of Ryūkoku-Berlin joint project on the Turfan Iranian manuscripts', *Acta Asiatica* 78, 71–85.

Yoshida 2019 = Y. Yoshida, *Three Manichaean Sogdian letters unearthed in Bäzäklik, Turfan*, Kyoto.

Yoshida 2020 = Y. Yoshida, 'Studies of the Karabalgasun Inscription: Edition of the Sogdian version', *Modern Asian Studies Review* 11, 1–139.

Part 1:

A Middle Persian and Parthian Bema liturgy

M801a (III 53) fol. I/r

P. 1 (BBB 1–18)

Photograph (III 53_32) reproduced by permission
© Staatliche Museen zu Berlin, Museum für Asiatische Kunst / Lina Wällstedt

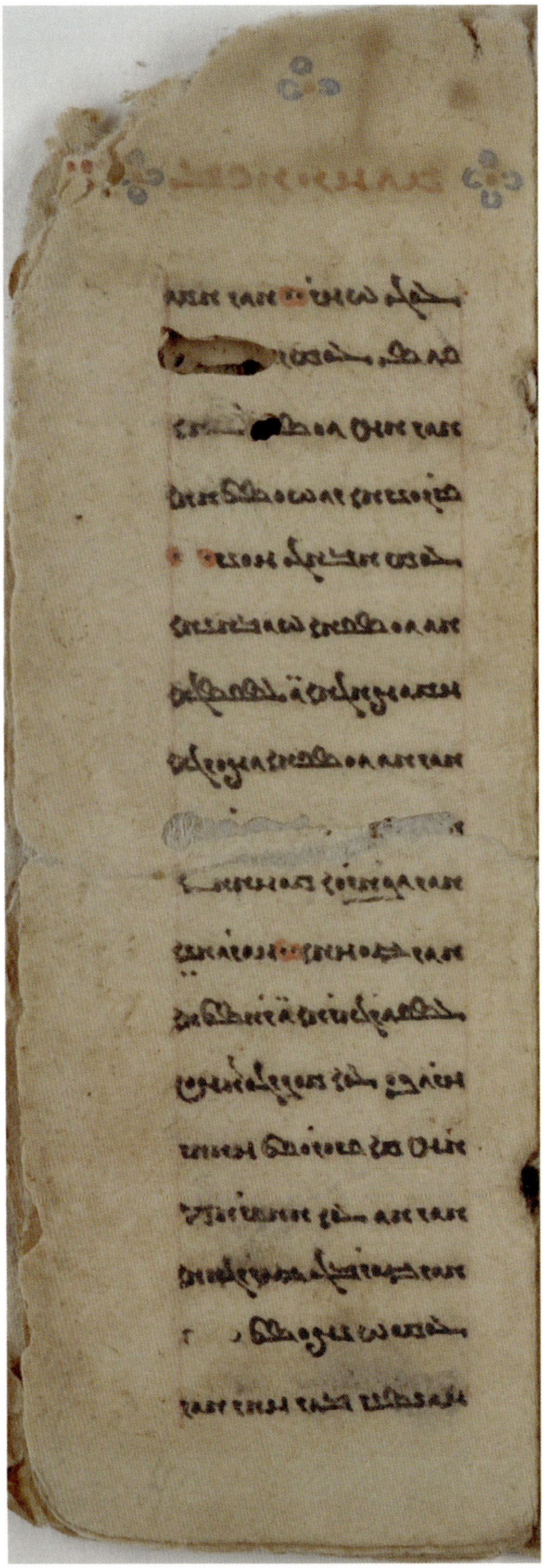

M801a (III 53) fol. I/r

P. 1 (BBB 1–18)

hdl. [?–]1/ {*red*} [nwyst] | mwhr dyb[1]
'[Here begins] the Seal Letter'

hdl. 1/ mwhr dyb

1 1/ {MP} ʿyg šhr ◦◦ ʾwd ʾmw
2 2/ pws ʿym d[wšysṭ]
3 3/ ʾwd ʾc wys[p]ʾn
4 4/ przyndʾn dwšysṭʾʾn
5 5/ ʿym ʾbʾg hynd ◦◦
6 6/ ʾw wyspʾn šwbʾnʾn
7 7/ hmwcʾgʾn ẅ ʿspsgʾn
8 8/ ʾwd ʾw wyspʾn wcydgʾn
9 9/ ʾ[wd nywšʾgʾn brʾd](r)[ʾn][2]
10 10/ ʾwd wxʾryn[3] myhʾʾn
11 11/ ʾwd qyhʾn ◦◦ hwrwʾn<ʾ>n
12 12/ ʿspwrgʾrʾn ẅ rʾsṭʾn
13 13/ hrw ky ʿyn myzdgtʾcy
14 14/ ʾc mn pdyrypṭ hʾʾd
15 15/ ʾwd ʾw ʿyn ʾʾprʾẖ
16 16/ ʾwd qyrbg qyrdgʾʾn
17 17/ ʿymyš ncysṭ[4]
18 18/ hwnsnd bwd hʾd ʾwd

{MP} [(From) Mani, the apostle of Jesus Aryaman, the persecuted, whose name is spurned by the rulers][5] (1) of the world, and (from) Ammo my [most beloved] son, and from all the most beloved children (5) who are with me.[6] To all pastors, teachers and bishops, and all the elect [and hearers, brothers] (10) and sisters, old and young, the pious, the perfect and the righteous, all you who have received this gospel from me, (15) and have found contentment in these precepts and good works which I have taught, and

---

[1] This restoration of the headline on the missing page is made likely by the fact that the text on that page will have included the very first words of Mani's 'Seal Letter' (see n. 5 below).

[2] Thus restored by Henning (in Haloun–Henning 1952, 207 n. 6), now confirmed by the additional copies edited in Reck 2009 (see n. 5 below).

[3] Pa. form in MP context (as also in lines 225, 231). The parallel text in M1313 (Reck 2009, 230) has the expected MP spelling *xwʾryn*.

[4] + line-filler.

[5] The text of the opening of the Seal Letter is attested in several fragmentary MP manuscripts and a Sogd. translation, all of which are now edited in Reck 2009, 228–31. The words preceding line 1 of BBB can be reconstructed as follows on the basis of other copies of the Seal Letter: *mʾny frystg yyšwʿ ʾryʾmʾn mwrzydg ʿyrpʾy nʾm ʾc šhryʾrʾn* [beginning of BBB] *ʿyg šhr* ...

[6] In the Sogd. translation, the list of addressees which follows is preceded by the verb *nyštyʾm* 'I send word'.

M801a (III 53) fol. I/v

P. 2 (BBB 19–26)

Photograph (III 53_21) reproduced by permission

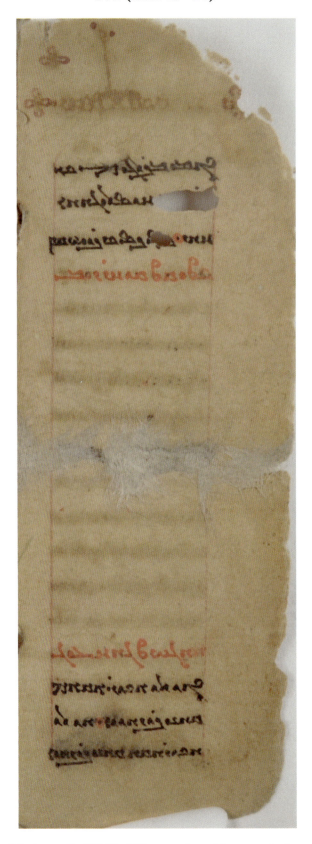

M801a (III 53) fol. I/v

P. 2 (BBB 19–26)

hdl. 2–3/ {*green*} nwyst mhr | ʿ[y]g gʾh̲
‘Here begin the hymns of the Bema’

hdl. 2/ nwyst mhr

19 1/ ʾbybxtgyh̲ pd	are undivided[7] in (20) (your) firm
20 2/ [w](r)[wyšn]hwstygʾʾn	[belief]. To each one in his own name.
21 3/ hʾd ° (k)s ks pd xwyš nʾm	
22 4/ {*red*}{Sogd.} pṭymṭ mwhr dyb	{Sogd.} Here ends the Seal Letter.[8]
{*ten lines left blank*}	{*ten lines left blank*}
23 15/ {*red*}{Sogd.} ʾʾγšṭ gʾhʿyg	{Sogd.} Here begin the Bema (hymns).
24 16/ {MP} ʾw tw ʾpwrʾmʾh̲	{MP}{Hymn 1} Let us bless you, (25)
25 17/ mʾny xwdʾwwn ° ʾw tw	Mani, lord; let us bless you, Mani, lord,
26 18/ ʾpwrʾmʾ mʾny xwdʾwn	

[7] The meaning of *ʾbybxtgyh̲* is clarified by the Sogd. translation *](p)w δβmʾnkyʾ* ‘without doubt’.

[8] This marks the end of the excerpt appointed to be read on this occasion, which is in fact the very beginning of the Seal Letter, not the end of the letter as this wording might be thought to imply. Regarding other copies of the passage which ends here see above, p. 3 n. 5.

M801a (III 53) fol. H/r

P. 3 (BBB 27–44)

Photograph (III 53_21) reproduced by permission
© Staatliche Museen zu Berlin, Museum für Asiatische Kunst / Lina Wällstedt

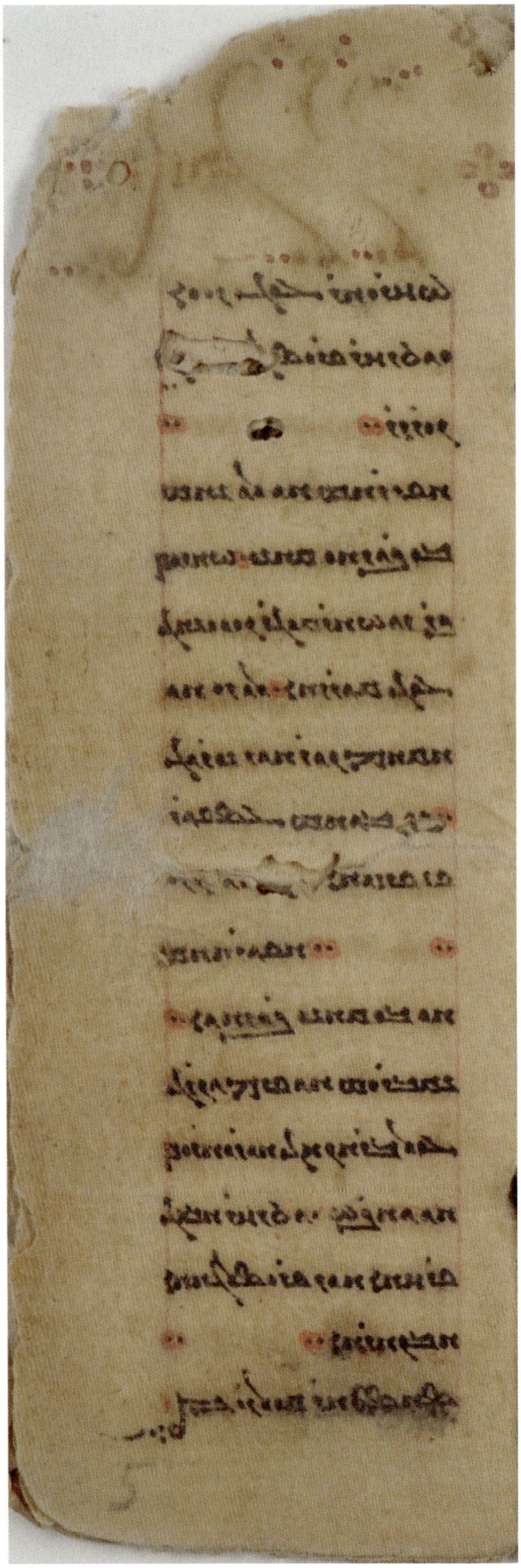

M801a (III 53) fol. H/r

P. 3 (BBB 27–44)

hdl. 2–3/ {*green*} nwyst mhr | ʿ[y]g gʾh̲
'Here begin the hymns of the Bema'

hdl. 3/ ʿ[y]g gʾh̲

27 1/ šhryʾr ʿyg dyn	ruler of the holy religion, most wise of
28 2/ ywjdhr prys(tg)[ʾn wzr](g<ʾ>n)	the great apostles.
29 3/ zyrdr ◦◦ ◦◦	
30 4/ ʾpwrʾm ʾw tw nʾm	(30) {Hymn 2} Let us bless your name,
31 5/ by xwdʾy mʾny ◦ šʾdwm	god, lord Mani. Make me happy, loving
32 6/ kr[9] dwšʾrmygr zywynʾg	one, who gives life to the dead. Give us
33 7/ ʿyg mwrdʾn ◦ tw dy ʾw	power and strength (35) so that we may
34 8/ ʾmʾh̲ zwr ʾwd nyrwg	be perfect according to your command,
35 9/ ◦◦ (kw) bwʾm ʿspwr	O god.
36 10/ pd p(r)mʾn [ʿy](g t)w (y)zd	
37 11/ ◦◦ ◦◦ ʾpwrʾʾm	{Hymn 3} Let us bless god Mani, the
38 12/ ʾw by mʾny xwdʾwn ◦◦	lord. (39) We revere your great radiant
39 13/ nmbrym ʾw p(r)h̲ wzrg	majesty, we adore the Holy Spirit
40 14/ ʿyt brʾzʾg ʾwrwʾrym	together with the Glories and mighty
41 15/ ʾw wʾxš ywjdhr ʾbʾg	angels.[10]
42 16/ prhʾn ʾwd prystgʾʾn	
43 17/ ʾbzʾrʾn ◦◦ ◦◦	
44 18/ {Pa.} sʾsṭʾr mytrq	{Pa.}{Hymn 4} Commander Maitreya,

9 Pa. form in MP context.

10 Other copies of this short hymn are found in M4b, iR16–21 (ed. Müller 1904, 58) and in M341a, R2–7 (ed. Reck 2004, 146). In the latter it is followed by the same hymn as here (no. 4). M341a, V, ends with hymn no. 7, but the intervening hymns are different.

M801a (III 53) fol. H/v

P. 4 (BBB 45–62)

Photograph (III 53_22) reproduced by permission
© Staatliche Museen zu Berlin, Museum für Asiatische Kunst / Lina Wällstedt

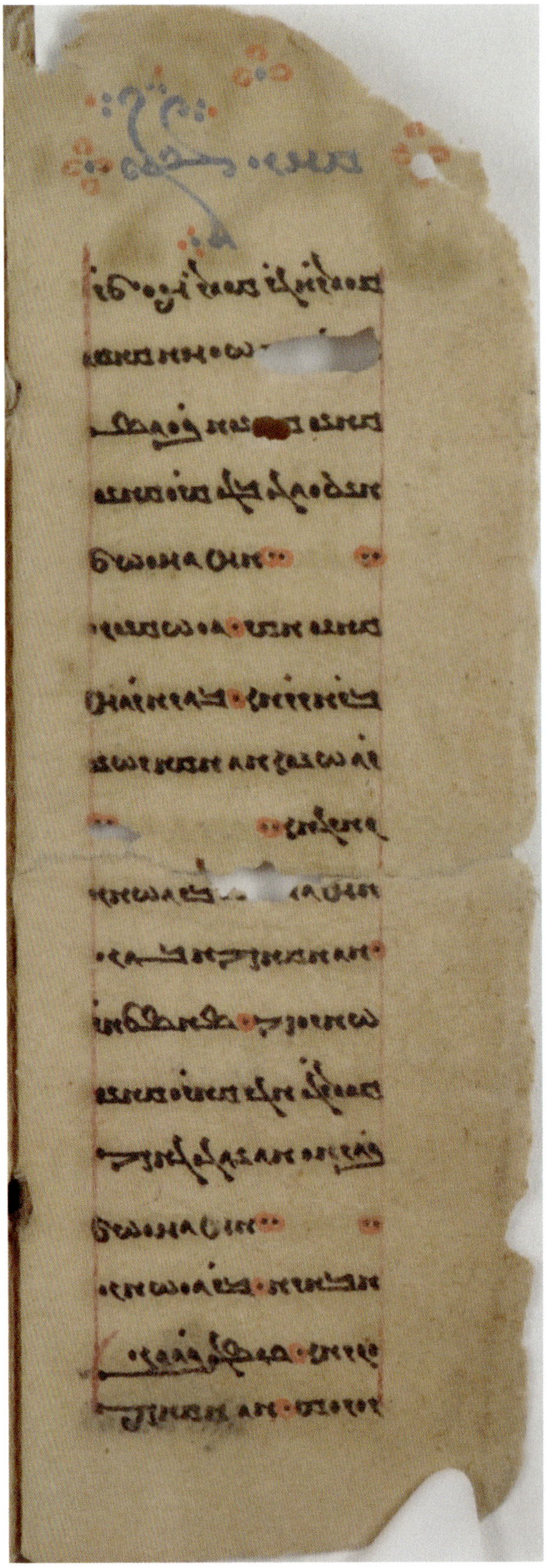

M801a (III 53) fol. H/v

P. 4 (BBB 45–62)

hdl. 4[–?]/ {*blue*} mhr ʿyg | [gʾẖ rʾy]
'Hymns [for the Bema]'

hdl. 4/ mhr ʿyg

45 1/ mytrʾgr mytr cyṭr	(45) Maitrāgar, Maitr Čaitr, [god]
46 2/ [b](g)[ ](m)šyhʾ mʾnyw	Messiah, Mānī'ū, Mānī'ī, Mānī'ā-
47 3/ mʾny (m)[ʾ]nyʾ xyws	chaios, life-giving god Mar Mani.[12]
48 4/ ʾnjywg bg myrmʾny	
49 5/ ◦◦ ◦◦ {MP/Pa.}[11] ʾc whyšṭ	{MP/Pa.}{Hymn 5} From paradise (50)
50 6/ mʾny ʾmd ◦ wyšmnyd	has Mani come. Be glad, brethren; it
51 7/ brʾdrʾn ◦ bwdʾ rwc	has been a shining day for us children
52 8/ rwšnyn ʾw ʾmʾ dšny	of the right hand.[13]
53 9/ zʾdgʾn ◦◦ ◦◦	
54 10/ ʾc w(h)[y](št)b(r) wšʾd	{Hymn 6} The door of[14] paradise has
55 11/ ◦ ʾw ʾmʾẖʾ bwd	opened; (55) joy has come to us. The
56 12/ šʾdyẖ ◦ sʾsṭʾr	commander Maitreya, Mar Mani the
57 13/ mytrg ʾgd mʾry mʾny	lord, has come to a new Bema.
58 14/ xwdʾy ʾw nwg gʾẖ	
59 15/ ◦◦ ◦◦ {Pa.} ʾc whyšṭ	(59) {Pa.}{Hymn 7} The gods have
60 16/ ʾbʾdʾ ◦ br wyšʾd	opened the door of[14] the prosperous
61 17/ yzdʾn ◦ pwsg xwwd	paradise. The garland, crown (and) dia-
62 18/ dydym ◦ ʾw ʾmʾẖ	dem [have become visible] to us [all].[15]
{*some pages missing*}	{*some pages missing*}

---

[11] Following Henning, the notation 'MP/Pa.' is used to denote passages where the two languages are mixed (as opposed to passages in one language with no more than the occasional use of a form or spelling which properly belongs to the other).

[12] This short hymn, of which another poorly-preserved copy is found in M341a, R7–10 (ed. Reck 2004, 146), consists chiefly of cabbalistic variants of the names of Maitreya and Mani, remarkably including a form derived from the Greek Μανιχαῖος (Henning 1936, 6). The ingenious interpretation of *mʾny* here as standing for Mānīʾī (beside Mānī'ū and Mānī'ā[-chaios]) is due to Henning. (For a different interpretation of these forms see de Blois 2006, 75 n. 9.)

[13] Cf. the phrase *ʾabnāʾu l-yamīni* 'sons of the right hand', i.e. 'those who will stand at the right hand of Jesus at the last judgement', in Arabic sources on Manichaeism (de Blois 2006, 88).

[14] Lit. 'from'.

[15] M341a, V6–9 (ed. Reck 2004, 146) contains another copy of this short hymn, ending with the words *[hrwyn](?) bwd p(y)[dʾ](g)*. M341a indicates that the hymn is to be sung to the tune *ʿjgnd ʾgd ʾc whyšt* 'A messenger has come from paradise'.

M801a (III 53) fol. G/r

P. 5 (BBB 63–80)

Photograph (III 53_22) reproduced by permission
© Staatliche Museen zu Berlin, Museum für Asiatische Kunst / Lina Wällstedt

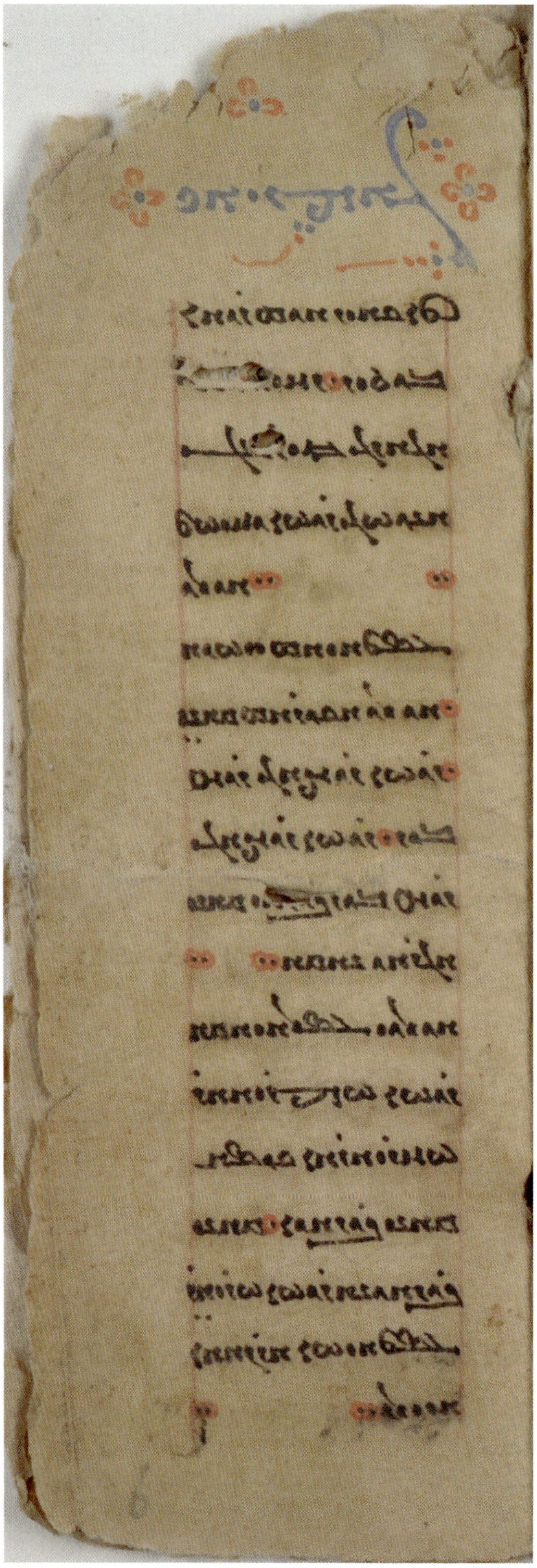

M801a (III 53) fol. G/r

P. 5 (BBB 63–80)

hdl. [?–]5/ {*blue*} [mhr ʿyg] | g’ẖ r’y
‘[Hymns] for the Bema’

hdl. 5/ g’ẖ r’y

63 1/ ṭn p’yd ’wm rw’n
64 2/ bwjyd ◦ dhy(d)[w](m)
65 3/ ’g’dg qyr(b)g
66 4/ ’nwšg rwšn whyšṭ

{Hymn 8} Protect (my) body and save my soul. Grant my pious wish, (66) the immortal paradise of light.

67 5/ ◦◦ ◦◦ {MP} ’w tw
68 6/ ʿsṭ’y’m yyšw’ ◦◦
69 7/ ◦ ’w tw ’pwr’m m’ny<’>
70 8/ ◦ rwšn rwc’g rwc
71 9/ bwd ◦ rwšn rwc’g
72 10/ rwc bwd (xwd’)y m’ny
73 11/ ’gr’w n’m’ ◦◦ ◦◦

{MP}{Hymn 9} Let us praise you, Jesus; let us bless you, Mani. (70) Brightly shining was the day; brightly shining was the day, lord Mani, noble in name.

74 12/ ’w twy[16] ʿsṭ’y’m’
75 13/ rwšn šẖry’’r[17]
76 14/ šhry’r’n pws’
77 15/ m’ny xwd’wn ◦ m’ny
78 16/ xwd’wn’ rwšn š<h>ry’r[18]
79 17/ ʿsṭ’yšn ’rz’’n
80 18/ ’yy tw ◦◦ ◦◦

{Hymn 10} Let us praise you, (75) bright ruler, son of rulers, lord Mani; lord Mani, bright ruler, worthy of praise (80) are you.[19]

---

[16] Scribal error for *tw* according to Henning. Durkin-Meisterernst, *DMT* III/1, 330a, implies that the *y* may be interpreted as a hiatus filler before the initial palatal vowel of the following *ʿst’y’m’*.

[17] Sic. A calligraphically expanded form of the usual *šhry’r*. Other examples in this manuscript of *ẖ* in non-initial position include *pdwẖn* (line 289), *šẖr* (lines 385, 477), *zyẖr* (line 406), *ẖrw* (line 413) and perhaps *xrwẖx[w’n]* (line 708).

[18] Although the omission points are placed under the last letters of the word, they are surely intended to indicate the omission of *h* as Henning assumed.

[19] A copy in Sogd. script of this short hymn is attested in So 14152, iiV2–7 (ed. Reck 2008, 327–8).

M801a (III 53) fol. G/v

P. 6 (BBB 81–98)

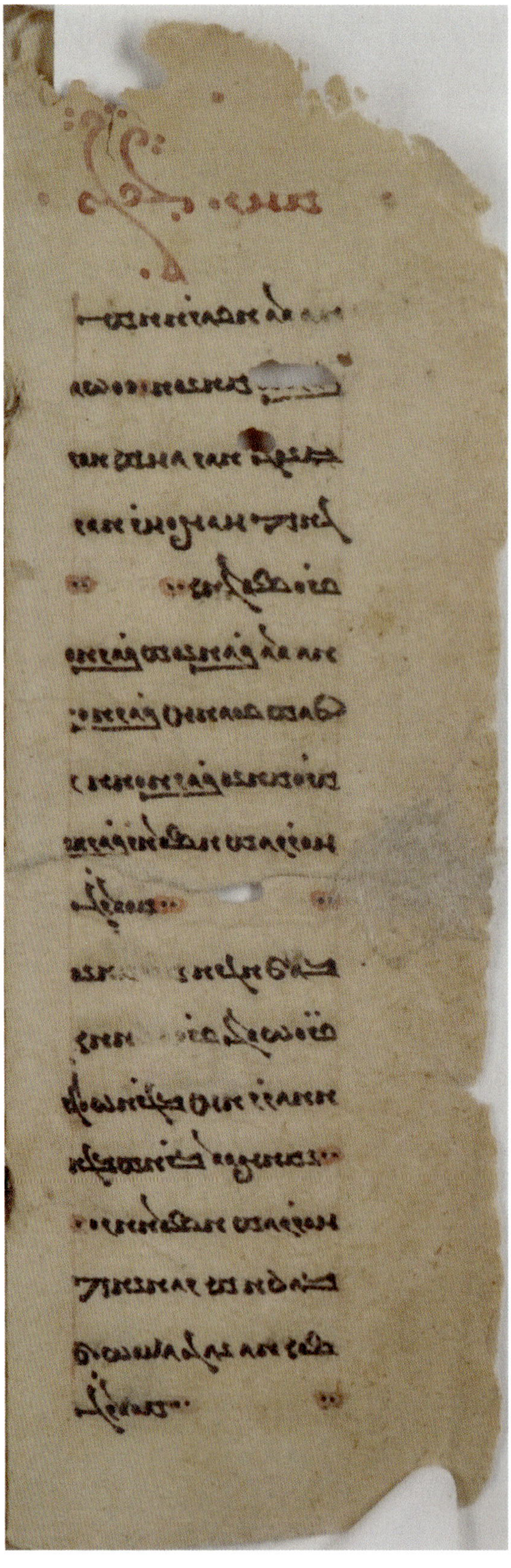

Photograph (III 53_23) reproduced by permission

M801a (III 53) fol. G/v

P. 6 (BBB 81–98)

hdl. 6[–?]/ {*violet*} mhr ʿyg | [gʾẖ rʾy]
'Hymns [for the Bema]'

hdl. 6/ mhr ʿyg

81 1/ ʾw tw ʾpwrʾʾm	{Hymn 11} To you let us give praise,
82 2/ (x)[wdʾy] mʾnyʾ ◦ yyšw	lord Mani, (and to) Jesus, the Maiden,
83 3/ qnyg ʾwd whmn ʾwd	and Wahman, and the beautiful Bema
84 4/ gʾẖ hwcyhr ʾwd	and (85) the apostles.[21]
85 5/ prystgʾn ◦◦ ◦◦	
86 6/ ʾw tw xwʾnym xwdʾy	{Hymn 12} I call to you, lord. Answer
87 7/ ṭwm pywʾc xwdʾy ◦	me, lord, Mar Mani, lord. {Pa.} Forgive
88 8/ mrymʾny xwdʾyʾʾ[20]	my sins, lord.
89 9/ {Pa.} hyrzwm ʾstʾr xwdʾy	
90 10/ ◦◦ ◦◦ mytrg	(90) {Hymn 13} Maitreya Buddha has
91 11/ bwṭ ʾgdʾ (mrym)ʾny	come, Mar Mani the apostle; he has
92 12/ fryštg pry(wj)ʾʾn	brought victory from the righteous god.
93 13/ ʾʾwrd ʾc bgrʾštgr	I pay homage to you, O god; (95)
94 14/ ◦◦ nmʾcwt brʾm bgʾ	forgive my sins; save my soul; raise (it)
95 15/ hyrzwm ʾstʾʾ(r) ◦	up to the New Paradise.[22]
96 16/ bwjʾ mn rwʾnʾẖ	
97 17/ syn ʾw nwg whyšṭ	
98 18/ ◦◦ ◦◦ mytrg	{Hymn 14} Maitreya ...
{*some pages missing*}	{*some pages missing*}

[20] + line-filler.

[21] A fragmentary copy in Sogd. script of this short hymn is found in So 14155 (ed. Reck 2008, 325).

[22] Another copy of this short hymn is found in M486, R3–7 (ed. Reck 2004, 148). The first words may also be attested in Sogd. script in TM 406b = So 20208b, R8–9 (ed. Sims-Williams 1989, 330–31).

M801a (III 53) fol. g/r

P. 7 (BBB 99–116)

Photograph (III 53_7) reproduced by permission
© Staatliche Museen zu Berlin, Museum für Asiatische Kunst / Lina Wällstedt

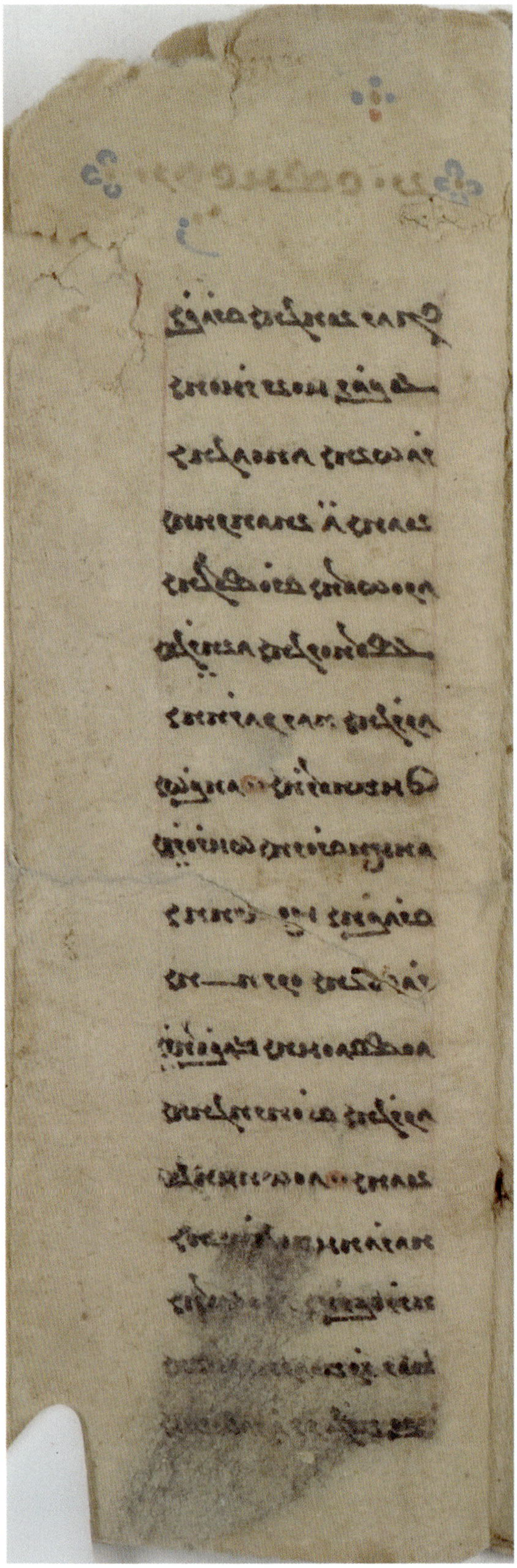

M801a (III 53) fol. g/r

P. 7 (BBB 99–116)

hdl. [?–]7 {*red*} [’pwryšn ‘yg] | nryshyzd
‘[Hymn of praise to] Narisah-yazad’

hdl. 7/ nryshyzd

99 1/ {MP} ’wd ny’g’n prwx<’>n[23]
100 2/ ‘y xwd hynd rhy’n
101 3/ rwšn’n w’ywg’n
102 4/ nyw’n ẅ n’w’z’’n
103 5/ wzyšt’n prystg’n
104 6/ ‘st’ydg’n wn’r<’>g’n
105 7/ wzrg’n ’wd zwr’’n
106 8/ ṭhm’tr’n °° w’xš<’>n[24]
107 9/ w’c’pryd’n šhry<’>r’n
108 10/ prwx’n cy(hr)’’n
109 11/ rw(šn)’n yzd’’n
110 12/ wyspwyh’n bwxt’r<’>n
111 13/ wzrg’n pry’d’g’’n
112 14/ nyw’n °° wyš’h’g’n
113 15/ ’wrw’hm(y)g(r’)’n
114 16/ ’rdykr’n (wzyš)t’n
115 17/ ’wd rzmywz’(n thm’)n
116 18/ °° ky mrg zd ẉ dwšm(nw)n

{MP} ... and blessed ancestors, (100) who are themselves the bright chariots, valiant hunters[25] and zealous[26] helmsmen, praised angels, great disposers and very strong powers, spirits[27] (107) created by the (divine) word, blessed rulers, beings of light, supreme gods, great redeemers, valiant helpers, joy-giving saviours, (114) zealous combatants and mighty warriors, who have struck down death, and conquered (their) enemies,

---

23 Written *prwxn*, without subscript points to indicate the omission of a letter.

24 Written *w’xšn*, without subscript points.

25 On *w’ywg* ‘hunter’ (not ‘charioteer’) see Henning 1943, 68 n. 2.

26 On *wzyšt* ‘zealous’ (not ‘greatest’ as in some early publications) see Gershevitch 1979, 292–3.

27 As noted by Henning *apud* Boyce 1960, 44, another copy of lines 101–6 is found in M629b, R. This provides *inter alia* the following variants: 102 om. *ẅ*; 103 (after *wzyšt’n*) + *’wd*; 104 *‘st’yd’n wn’r’g’n*.

M801a (III 53) fol. g/v

P. 8 (BBB 117–134)

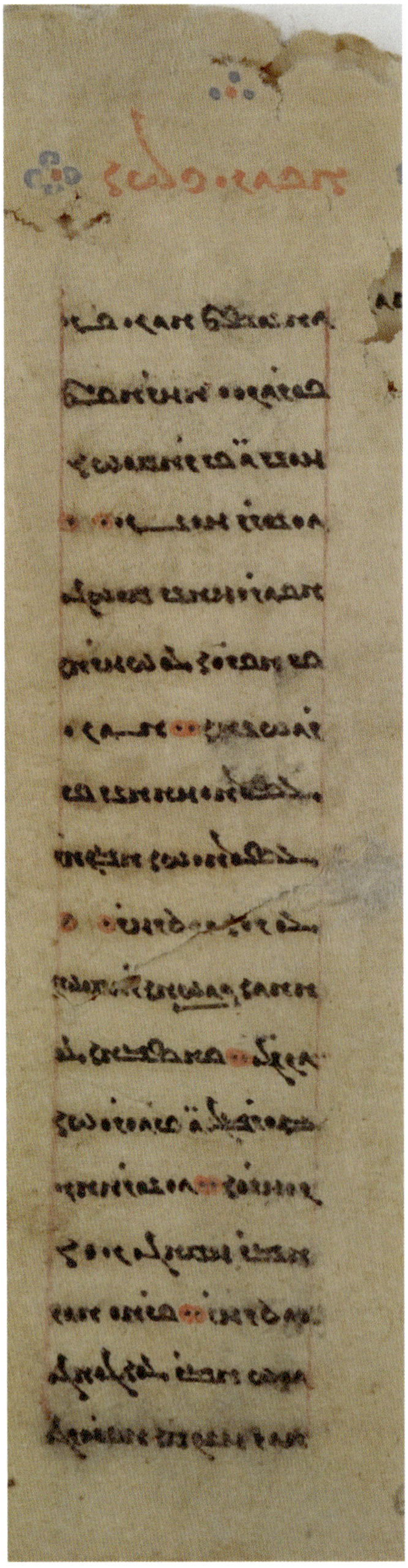

Photograph (III 53_8) reproduced by permission

M801a (III 53) fol. g/v

P. 8 (BBB 117–134)

hdl. 8[–?]/ {*red*} ʾpwryšn | [ʿyg nryshyzd]
‘Hymn of praise [to Narisah-yazad]’

hdl. 8/ ʾpwryšn

117 1/ wʾnysṭ ʾwd pd
118 2/ pyrwzyy ʾhrʾpṭ
119 3/ hynd ẅ pd rʾmyšn
120 4/ wynyrd hynd ◦ ◦
121 5/ ʾpwryhʾnd myšg
122 6/ pd ʾpryn ʿy šhrʾn
123 7/ rwšnʾn ◦◦ ʾwd
124 8/ ʿsṭʾyhʾʾnd pd
125 9/ ʿsṭʾyšn ʾbzʾr
126 10/ ʿy dy(n yw)jdhr ◦ ◦
127 11/ ʾʾwn kwšʾn r(ʾ)myšn
128 12/ wzrg ◦◦ pʾsbʾn ʿy[28]
129 13/ qyrbg ẅ prwyryšn
130 14/ zyhryn ◦◦ wynyrʾʾd
131 15/ ʾbr hmʾg dyn
132 16/ ywjdhr ◦◦ prʾy ʾwd
133 17/ wyš ʾbr ʿyn gyʾg
134 18/ ʾwd hnzmn ʾprydg
{*some pages missing*}

and have been exalted in victory and have been established in peace; (121) may they always be blessed with the blessing of the light Aeons and may they be praised with the mighty praise of the holy church, (127) so that their great peace, (their) virtuous protection and (their) life-giving nurture[29] may be established (131) for the entire holy church, especially for this place and blessed community ...[30]
{*some pages missing*}

---

[28] Henning already pointed out that *pʾsbʾn ʿy*, written as two words, is an error for the abstract noun *pʾsbʾnyy* or *pʾsbʾnyẖ*, which could also be written *pʾsbʾnʿy* (as one word). This is now confirmed by the variant *pʾsbʾ(nyẖ)* in M629b (see n. 30 below).

[29] It is not clear why Henning translated *prwyryšn* here as ‘growth’. The meaning of the underlying verb *prwr-* ‘to nurture, foster’ was well known to him (cf. Henning 1933, 175; 1937, 114).

[30] As noted by Henning *apud* Boyce 1960, 44, another copy of lines 126–34 is found in M629b, V. This ends as follows, diverging somewhat from the text in BBB: *ʾwd pʾsbʾ(nyẖ) kyrbg ʾwd prwryšn (ʿy zy)hryn* ◦◦ *wynyrʾd [ʾbr hm](ʾg d)ynywjdhr [... z](y)ndg ẅ*. See also Durkin-Meisterernst 2014, 3, where the divergence is discussed.

M801a (III 53) fol. h/r

P. 9 (BBB 135–150)

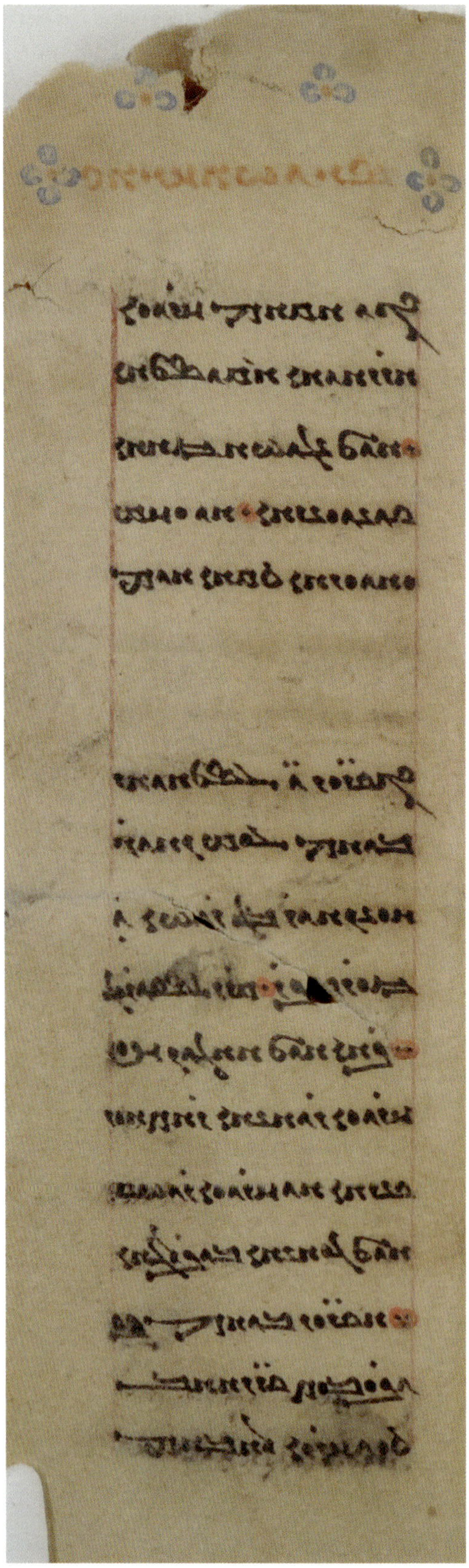

Photograph (III 53_8) reproduced by permission

M801a (III 53) fol. h/r

P. 9 (BBB 135–150)

hdl. [?–]9/ {*red*} [ʾpwryšn ʿyg] | srwšhrʾy
‘[Hymn of praise to] Srōšahrāy’

hdl. 9/ srwšhrʾy

135 1/ {Pa.} ʾw ʾmʾh̲ hrwyn
136 2/ ʾrdʾwʾn ʾmwsṭʾn
137 3/ ◦ ʾwṭ ngwšʾqʾʾn
138 4/ pwnwyndʾn ◦ ʾw yhm
139 5/ yʾwydʾn jmʾn ʾwh̲[31]
{*two lines left blank*}

(135) {Pa.} ... to us all, faithful[33] electi and virtuous hearers. For ever and ever, so (be it).

{*two lines left blank*}

140 8/ ʾfryd ẅ ʿsṭʾwʾd
141 9/ bwʾh̲ ʿym zʾwr
142 10/ hynzʾwr bg r(w)šn ẉ
143 11/ qyr(b)kr ◦ mrd ʿspwryg
144 12/ ◦◦ xʾn ʾwṭ ʾʾγwz[32] cy
145 13/ hrwyn rwʾnʾn rʾh̲ ʾwd
146 14/ pndʾn ʾw hrwyn rwšn(ʾn)
147 15/ ʾwṭ gyʾnʾn bwxtgʾn
148 16/ ◦◦ ʾfryd bwʾh̲ kw
149 17/ wxybyh̲ frdʾʾb
150 18/ jywhryn tʾbʾh̲

(140) Blessed and praised be this mighty power, (this) light and beneficent god, (this) perfect man, a house and shelter for (145) all souls, a way and path for all lights and redeemed spirits. May he be blessed so that (149) his life-giving brightness may shine

---

31 *ʾwh̲* ‘so’ (also in line 161) is an abbreviation for the phrase *ʾwh̲ bwyndyy* ‘So be it’, ‘Amen’.

32 *ʾʾγwz* = *ʾʾgwz*. Other examples of the occasional use of the letter *γ* instead of *g* (to indicate its pronunciation as a fricative) are *bwγ* (line 300) and *swγlyy* (line 462).

33 On the meaning of *ʾmwst* ‘faithful’ (not ‘mournful’, ‘monk’) see Henning 1943, 74 n. 2.

M801a (III 53) fol. h/v

P. 10 (BBB 151–165)

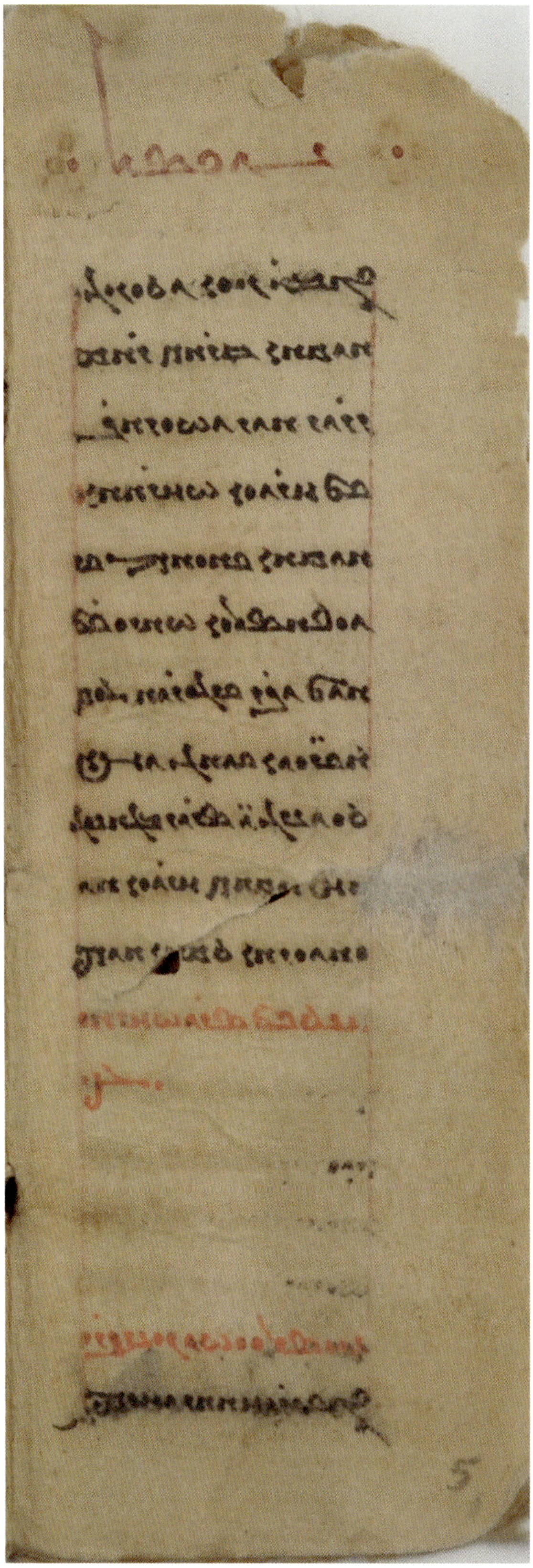

Photograph (III 53_9) reproduced by permission

M801a (III 53) fol. h/v

P. 10 (BBB 151–165)

hdl. 10–11/ {*violet*} nwyst | yyšwʿzyndkry
'Here begin (the hymns of praise) to Jesus the life-giver'

hdl. 10/ nwyst

151 1/ ʾbr dyn wjydg	upon the chosen religion, and he may
152 2/ ʾwmʾn qrʾẖ rʾm	create for us peace, health and security
153 3/ drwd ʾwd wšydʾx	in all lands. (155) May he protect us in
154 4/ pṭ hrwyn šhrʾʾn ◦	wonderful joy and may he himself
155 5/ ʾwmʾn pʾyʾẖ pd	accept this pure blessing, (this) living
156 6/ wylʾstyn šʾdyfṭ	word and divine song (160) from us
157 7/ ʾwṭ wxd pdgyrwʾ ʿym	all. For ever and ever, so (be it).
158 8/ ʾfrywn pwʾg wcn	
159 9/ jywndg ẅ srwd bgʾnyg	
160 10/ (ʾ)c (ʾ)mʾẖ hrwyn ʾw	
161 11/ yʾwydʾn jm(ʾ)n ʾwẖ	
162 12/ {*red*} (h)njpṭ srwšh(r)ʾy	Here end the Srōšahrāy (hymns).
163 13/ {*red*} ◦ VI ◦	Six (hymns).
{*three lines left blank*}	{*three lines left blank*}
164 17/ {*red*}{MP} nwyst yyšwzyndkry[34]	{MP} Here begin (the hymns of praise to) Jesus the life-giver. (165)
165 18/ ʾpwryhʾʾd whyẖ	May the sacred wisdom be blessed,

[34] As noted by Henning, this is an abbreviated spelling (so also in the headline to p. 11) for an adjective **yyšw(ʿ)zyndkryg* 'concerning Jesus the life-giver', the noun 'hymn' being understood from the context.

M801a (III 53) fol. i/r

P. 11 (BBB 166–183)

Photograph (III 53_9) reproduced by permission
© Staatliche Museen zu Berlin, Museum für Asiatische Kunst / Lina Wällstedt

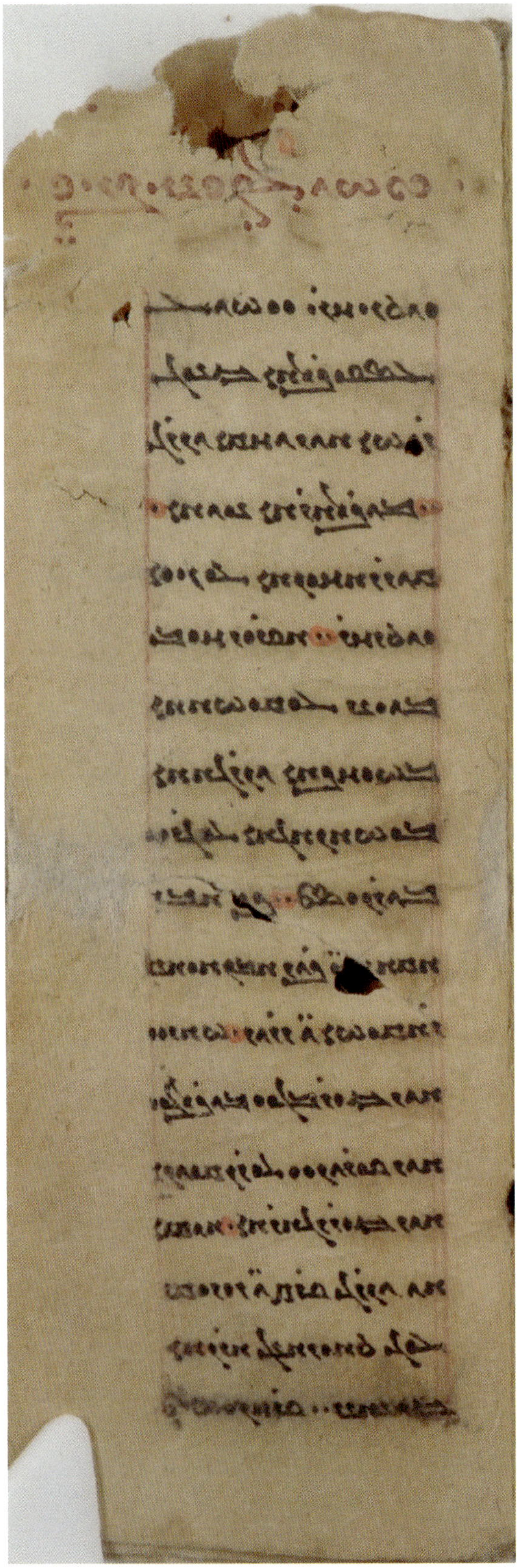

M801a (III 53) fol. i/r

P. 11 (BBB 166–183)

hdl. 10–11/ {*violet*} nwyst | yyšwʿzyndkry
‘Here begin (the hymns of praise) to Jesus the life-giver’

hdl. 11/ yyšwʿzyndkry

166 1/ ywjdhr yyšwʿ
167 2/ ʿspyxtʾn qnyg
168 3/ r(w)šn ʾwd whmn wzrg
169 4/ ◦◦ bwxtʾrʾn nywʾn ◦
170 5/ mwrdʾhyzʾn ʿy dyn
171 6/ ywjdhr ◦◦ ʾpryd hyb
172 7/ bwynd ʿymyšʾʾn
173 8/ bšyhkʾn wzrgʾʾn
174 9/ byšʾzʾgʾn ʿy gryw[35]
175 10/ bwrzysṭ ◦◦ k(w) ʾb(r)
176 11/ ʾmʾ(h)[y]ž[36] xwd ʾbzʾyʾnd
177 12/ rʾmyšn ẅ drwd ◦ šʾdyy
178 13/ ʾwd qyrbgyy bwxtgyy
179 14/ ʾwd pyrwzyy ʿy rzmywz<ʾ>n
180 15/ ʾwd qyrdgʾrʾn ◦ ʾwmʾn
181 16/ ʾw wzrg prẖ ẅ dydym
182 17/ ʿyg jʾydʾng ʾrzʾn
183 18/ qwnʾnd ◦◦ prʾzy(š)ṭ

Jesus the Splendour, the Maiden of Light and great Wahman, the valiant redeemers, (170) the holy church’s raisers of the dead. May these great physicians be blessed, those who heal the highest self, so that for (176) us too they themselves may increase peace and health, joy and piety, salvation and victory for the heroes (180) and champions. May they make us worthy of great glory and the eternal crown. For ever

35 The final *w* is clear in Weber 2000, Pl. 106.

36 Pa. form in MP context (*DMT* III/1, 3b).

M801a (III 53) fol. i/v

P. 12 (BBB 184–199)

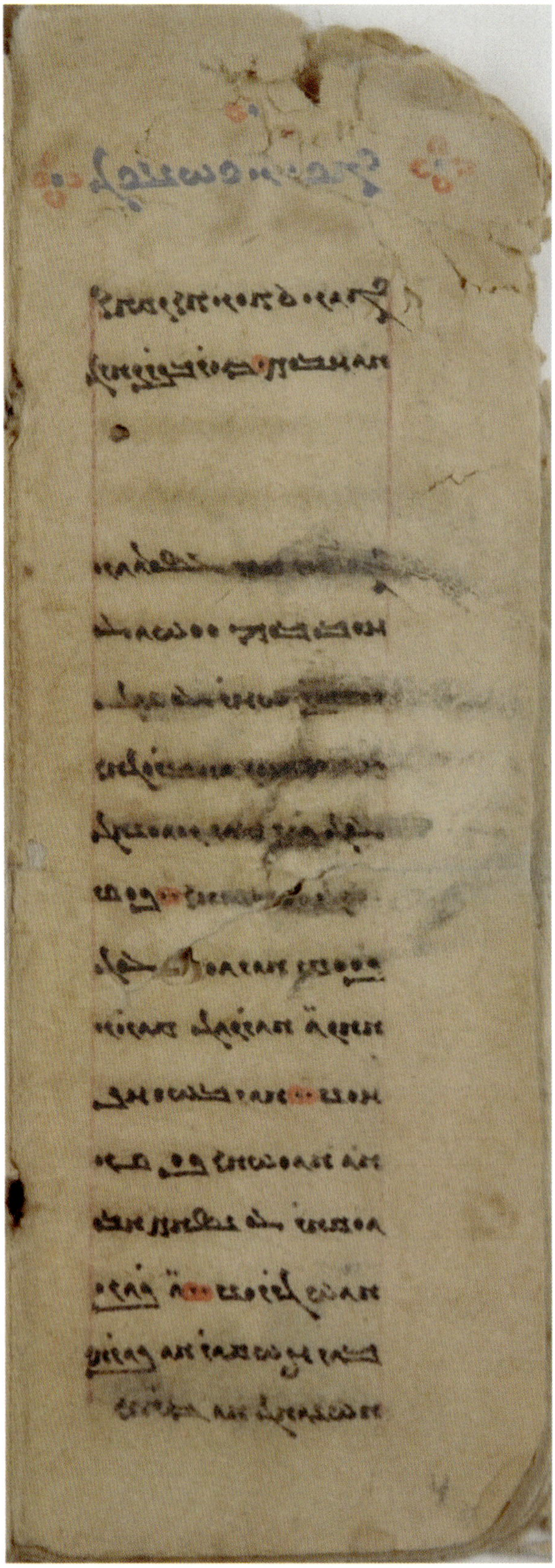

Photograph (III 53_10) reproduced by permission

M801a (III 53) fol. i/v

P. 12 (BBB 184–199)

hdl. 12[–?]/ {*blue*} ʾp(w)ryšnʿyg | [yyšwʿzyndkr]
‘Hymns of praise to [Jesus the life-giver]’

hdl. 12/ p(w)ryšnʿyg[37]

184 1/ ʾwd jʾydʾn zmʾn	and ever, (185) so be it.
185 2/ ʾwhbyh̠[38] ◦ qyrbkrzʾdg	Kirbakkarzādag.[40]
{*two lines left blank*}	{*two lines left blank*}

186 5/ ʾ(pryd ʾwd) ʿstwwd	Blessed and praised be Jesus the life-
187 6/ hyb byh̠ yyšwʿ	giver, the New Aeon, the true raiser
188 7/ (zyndk)r šhr ʿy nwg	from the dead, (190) who is himself a
189 8/ (mwrdʾ)hyz wʾbrygʾn	life-giving mother to those who have
190 9/ ʿyg xwd (mʾ)d zywynʾg	died of injuries and wounds caused by
191 10/ (ʿy)g(ʾwyš)ʾn ◦◦ ky pd	greed and lust and a physician (195) for
192 11/ xyym ʾwd wy[r][39] ʿyg	those who become unconscious through
193 12/ ʾʾz ẅ ʾwrzwg mwrd	a sickness of the body. He himself was
194 13/ hynd ◦◦ ʾwd bšyhk	a seer for the blind and a hearer for the
195 14/ ʾw ʾwyšʾn ky pd	deaf ...
196 15/ wymʾr ʿy nsʾh̠ ʾby	
197 16/ ʾwš grdynd ◦◦ ẅ xwd	
198 17/ bwd cšmwr ʾw kwrʾn	
199 18/ ʾšnwʾg ʾw qrʾn	
{*some pages missing*}	{*some pages missing*}

---

[37] Written as one word, but evidently for *ʾpwryšn* + ezafe *ʿyg*.

[38] Sic, written as one word.

[39] Restored thus by Henning *apud* Boyce 1960, 54, comparing Armenian *vēr* ‘sore, wound’. Perhaps rather *wy[yr]*?

[40] Personal name of an author (thus Henning) or patron (thus Colditz 2018, 335). The same two interpretations are proposed with regard to the names mentioned in lines 427 (Colditz 2018, 235) and 461 (*ibid.*, 269).

M801a (III 53) fol. d/r

P. 13 (BBB 200–217)

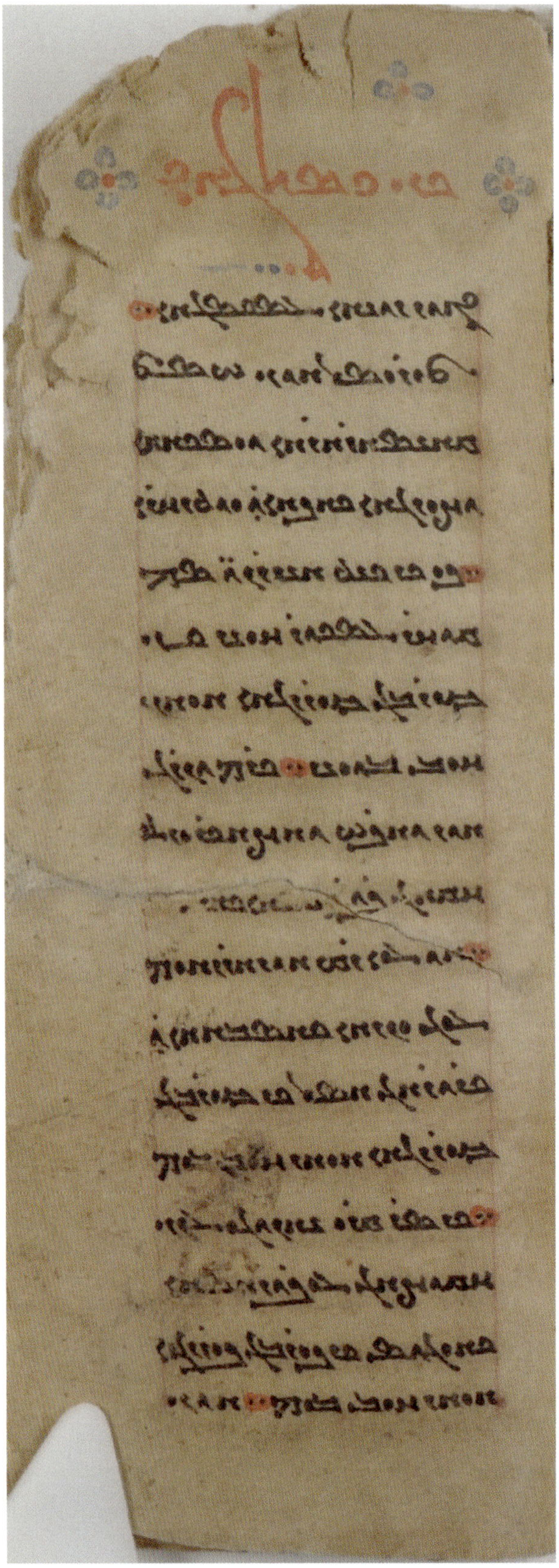

Photograph (III 53_4) reproduced by permission

M801a (III 53) fol. d/r

P. 13 (BBB 200–217)

hdl. [?–]13/ {*red*} [ʾpwryšn ʿyg] | prystgʾn
‘[Hymns of praise to] the messengers’

hdl. 13/ prystgʾn

200 1/ ʾwd dwnʾn ʿspsgʾn ◦◦	... [the seventy] (200) and two bishops,
201 2/ t̤yryst ʾwd ššṭ	the three hundred and sixty heads of
202 3/ mʾnsʾrʾrʾn wyspʾʾn	(religious) houses, all the pure and holy
203 4/ wcydgʾn pʾkʾn ẉ̇ ywjdhr<ʾ>n[41]	electi who are perfect in (observing) the
204 5/ ◦◦ ky pd pnj ʾndrz ẅ sẖ	five commandments and the three (205)
205 6/ mwhr ʿspwr hynd pd	seals, may they be remembered for
206 7/ qyrbg qyrdgʾn ʾyʾd	(their) pious works.
207 8/ hyb bwynd ◦◦ prẖ wzrg	The great Glory and word-created
208 9/ ʾwd wʾxš wʾcʾpryd ʿy	Spirit of the entire province of the east,
209 10/ hmʾg xw(rʾsʾ)n pʾ(yq)[ws][42]	(210) (which)[44] is the guardian and nur-
210 11/ ◦◦ ʾw ʿyn rm ʾwd ʾrdʾyẖ	turer of this flock and (of) the order of
211 12/ ʿyg yzdʾn pʾsbʾʾn ẉ̇	the elect of the gods: may it be remem-
212 13/ prwrʾg ʾst pd qyrbg	bered for (its) pious works.
213 14/ qyrdgʾn ʾyʾd hyb byẖ	
214 15/ ◦◦ pd sr mry nʾzwgyʿzd[43]	At the head (of all) Mar Nāzugyazad,
215 16/ hmwcʾg ʿy xwrʾsʾn	(215) the Teacher of the province of the
216 17/ pʾygws pd kyrbg kyrdgʾn	east: may he be remembered for (his)
217 18/ ʾyʾd hyb byẖ ◦◦ ʾwd	pious works. And

[41] The MS has *ywjdhrn*, without subscript points to indicate the omission of a letter.

[42] Henning read *pʾ(y)[g](w)[s]*, but with great hesitation, as his note makes clear. More likely is *pʾ(yq)[ws]*, a form found in M7351 (see Leurini 2017, 103), or perhaps even *pʾ(dq)[ws]* (which would be a Pa. form, attested as *pʾdgws*).

[43] Sic. The position of the superfluous ʿ (after rather than before the *y*) is unusual.

[44] According to Henning, *ky* ‘which’ was probably omitted by mistake.

M801a (III 53) fol. d/v

P. 14 (BBB 218–235)

Photograph (III 53_5) reproduced by permission
© Staatliche Museen zu Berlin, Museum für Asiatische Kunst / Lina Wällstedt

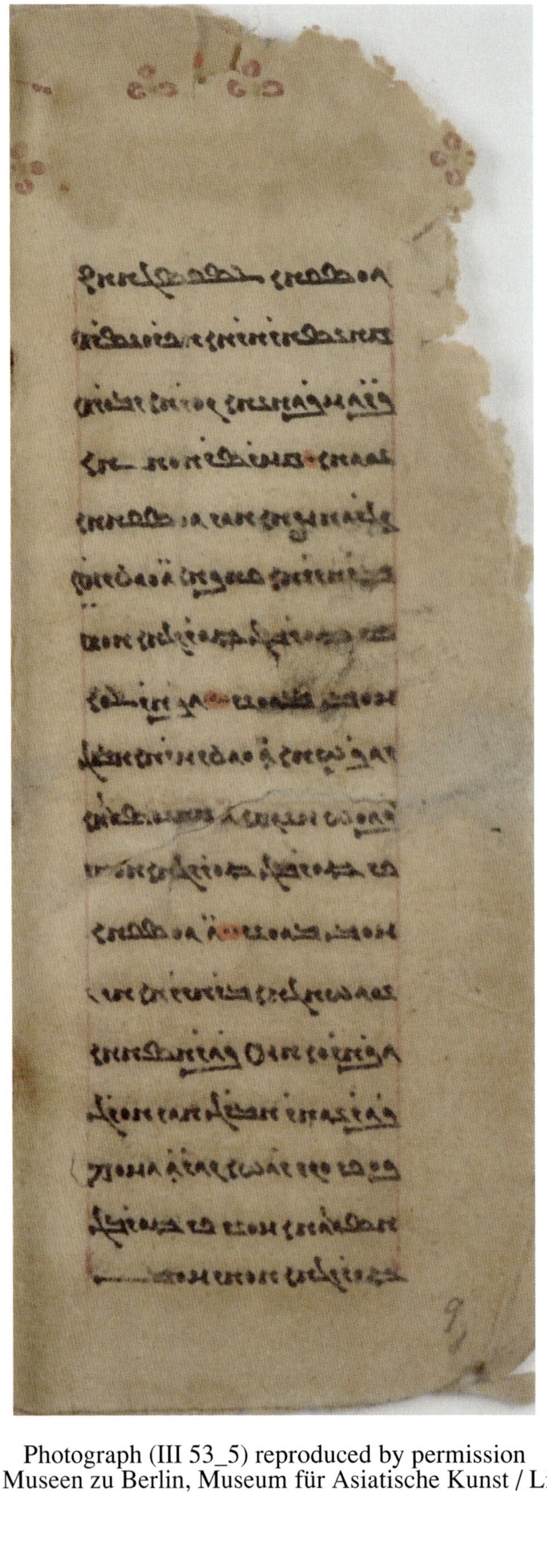

M801a (III 53) fol. d/v

P. 14 (BBB 218–235)

hdl. 14–15/ {*green*} [ʾpwryšn ʿyg] | [prystgʾn]
‘[Hymns of praise to the messengers]’

hdl. 14/ [ʾpwryšn ʿyg][45]

218 1/ wyspʾn ʿspsgʾʾn
219 2/ mʾnsʾrʾn ʾprynsrʾn
220 3/ xrwhxwʾnʾn zyrʾn dbyrʾn
221 4/ nywʾn ◦ mhrsrʾyʾʾn
222 5/ zgrwʾcʾn ʾwd wyspʾʾn
223 6/ brʾdrʾn pʾkʾn ẅ ywjdhr<ʾ>n
224 7/ pd qyrbg qyrdgʾn ʾyʾd
225 8/ hyb bwynd ◦◦ wxʾrʿyn[46]
226 9/ dwxšʾn ẉ ywjdhrʾn ʾbʾg
227 10/ xwyš hnzmn ẅ mʾnystʾn
228 11/ pd qyrbg qyrdgʾn ʾy(ʾ)d
229 12/ hyb bwynd ◦◦ ẅ wyspʾn
230 13/ nywšʾgʾn brʾdrʾn ʾ(wd)
231 14/ wxʾryn ʾc xwrʾsʾʾn
232 15/ xwrnwʾr ʾbrg ʾwd ʾyrg
233 16/ ky pd yzd rwšn zwr ẉ whyẖ
234 17/ ʾstwʾn hynd pd qyrbg
235 18/ qyrdgʾn ʾyʾd hyb

all bishops, heads of (religious) houses, prayer-leaders, (220) wise preachers, doughty scribes, melodious cantors and all the pure and holy brethren: may they be remembered for (their) pious works.

The virginal and holy sisters, with (226) their communities and *mān-istāns*:[47] may they be remembered for (their) pious works.
And all (230) the hearers, brothers and sisters from east, west, north and south, who believe in God, Light, Power and Wisdom: may they be remembered for (their) pious works.

---

45 Only illegible traces of the headline to p. 14 are visible.

46 Pa. form in MP context (also in line 231). See n. 3 on p. 3 above.

47 The common translation of *mānistān* as ‘monastery’ is misleading, since it seems that it was not (at least initially) a communal dwelling-place for the elect but a building used for ritual activities (BeDuhn 2013, 285 n. 69). Since there is no convenient English equivalent, I follow the advice of Jason BeDuhn to leave the word untranslated.

M801a (III 53) fol. k/r

P. 15 (BBB 236–253)

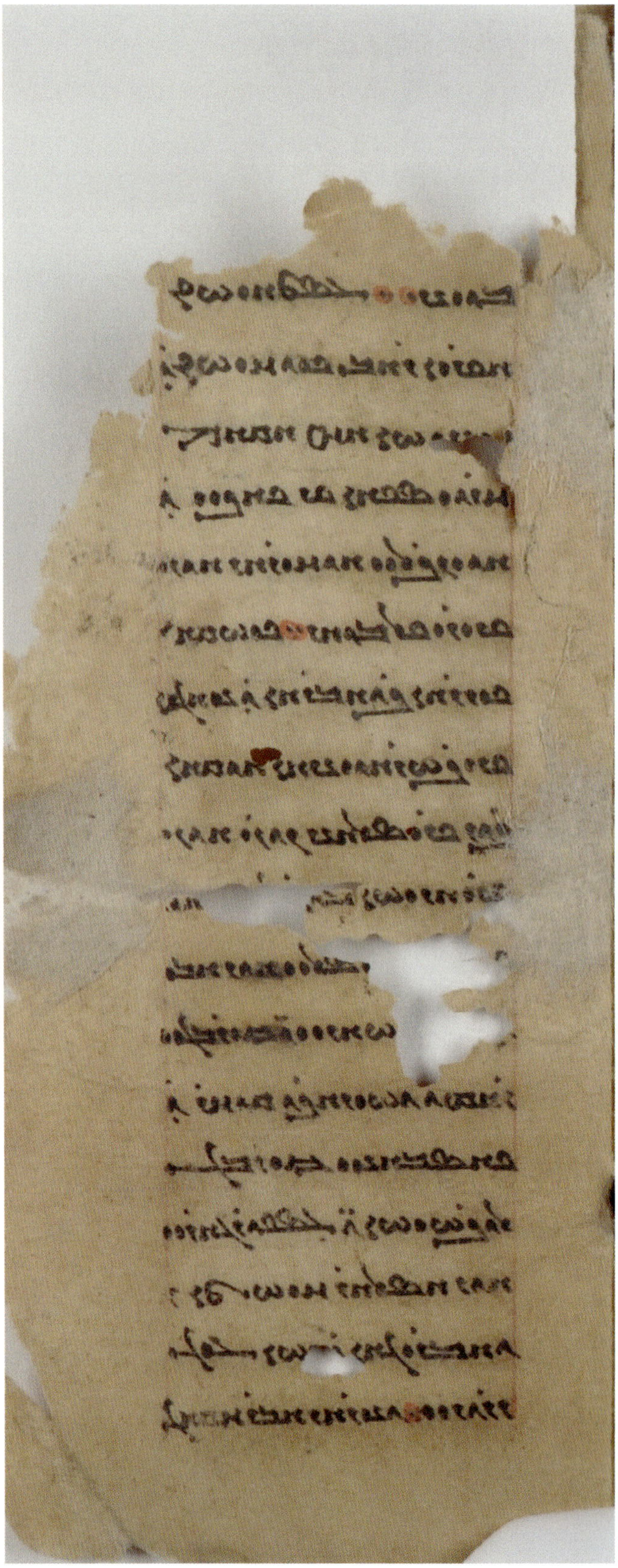

Photograph (III 53_11) reproduced by permission

M801a (III 53) fol. k/r

P. 15 (BBB 236–253)

hdl. 14–15/ {*green*} [ʾpwryšn ʿyg] | [prystgʾn]
ʻ[Hymns of praise to the messengers]ʼ

hdl. 15/ [prystgʾn][48]

236 1/ bwynd ◦◦ ʿsṭʾyšn
237 2/ ʾpryn rʾb pywhyšn ẉ̇
238 3/ (wyndy)šn ʾc ʾmʾẖ
239 4/ hrwyspʾn pd pʾkyy ẉ̇
240 5/ ʾwyzxtyy ʾwhyrʾd ʾwd
241 6/ pdyrypt bwʾd ◦◦ pyšmʾn
242 7/ pydrʾn xwʾbrʾn ẉ̇ nyʾgʾn
243 8/ pdyxšrʾwyndʾn ʾwmʾn
244 9/ xwd prystʾnd zwr ʾwd
245 10/ pryʾdyšn b(wxt)[gyy](ʾwd)
246 11/ (p)[yrwzyy dr](y)styy ʾwd ʾby
247 12/ (wz)[yndyy]šʾdyy ẅ qyrbgyy
248 13/ rʾm (ẅ) wšydʾxw m(y)hr[49] ẉ̇
249 14/ pʾsbʾnyy qyrbg
250 15/ twxšyšn ẅ ʿspwrgʾryy
251 16/ ʾwd ʾstʾr hyšṭn[50]
252 17/ wʾbrygʾn (rw)šn ʿyg
253 18/ drwdyy ◦ wnyrʾd ʾbr hmʾg

May praise, blessing, entreaty, prayer and supplication ascend from us all in purity and forgiveness and (241) be accepted in the sight of our beneficent fathers and honoured forbears; and may they themselves send us support and (245) aid, salvation and [victory], health and freedom from [harm], joy and piety, peace and security, friendship(?) and protection, pious (250) zeal and striving for perfection, and forgiveness of sins, the true light of salvation. May (all this) be established for the whole

[48] The headline to p. 15 is torn away.

[49] Henning leaves open the choice between the readings *myhr* ʻfriendshipʼ and *mwhr* ʻsealʼ.

[50] + line-filler.

M801a (III 53) fol. k/v

P. 16 (BBB 254–269)

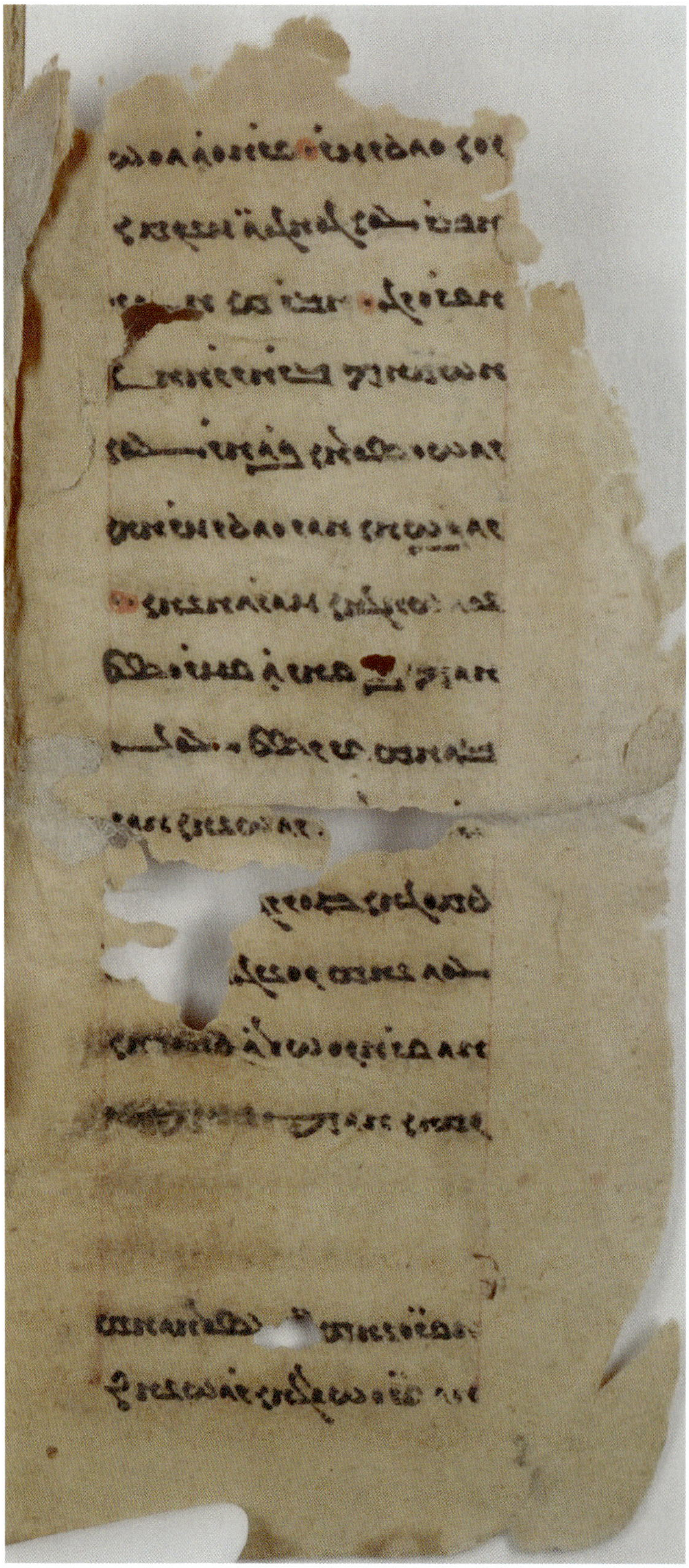

Photograph (III 53_12) reproduced by permission

M801a (III 53) fol. k/v

P. 16 (BBB 254–269)

hdl. 16[–?]/ [ʾpwryšn ʿyg] | [prystgʾn]
‘[Hymns of praise to the messengers]’

hdl. 16/ [ʾpwryšn ʿyg][51]

254 1/ dyn ywjdhr ° prʾy ẉ wyš
255 2/ ʾbr ʿyn gyʾg ẅ hnzmn
256 3/ ʾprydg ° ʾbr mn ʾ(w)d
257 4/ ʾšmʾẖ brʾdrʾʾn
258 5/ dwšystʾn xwʾrʿyn
259 6/ dwxšʾn ʾwd ywjdhrʾʾn
260 7/ nywšʾgʾn hwrwʾnʾn °°
261 8/ ʾwẖ (kw) pʾd ẉ phrysṭ
262 9/ bwʾm pd dsṭ ʿyg
263 10/ (pr)[ys](t)[gʾn][52] (r)wšnʾn ʾw(d)
264 11/ jmygʾn qy(r)dg[ʾrʾn pd]
265 12/ ʿyw nʾm zyndg [ẅ ywjdh](r)
266 13/ ʾw prʾzyšt ẉ j(ʾyd)ʾn
267 14/ zmʾn ʾwẖ (by)ẖ
{*two lines left blank*}

holy church, especially (255) for this place and (this) blessed community, for me and (for) you, (my) dearest brothers, virginal and holy sisters (and) (260) pious hearers, so that we may be guarded and protected by the hands of the [messengers] of light and (their) mighty ‘twins’.[53] [In] (265) the one living [and holy] name, for ever and ever, so be it.
{*two lines left blank*}

268 17/ {Pa.} (ʾ)frynʾm (ẅ)ʿstʾwʾm
269 18/ ʾw fryštgʾn rwšnʾn
{*one folio missing*}

{Pa.}[54] We bless and praise the messengers of light ...
{*one folio missing*}

[51] The headline to p. 16 is torn away.

[52] The tip of a letter above the lacuna probably belongs to *t* (rather than to *g* with Henning).

[53] That MP *jmyg* means ‘twin’ (rather than ‘church leader, ἀρχηγός’), was established by de Blois 2003.

[54] The Pa. hymn partly preserved in lines 268–307 is to a large extent a translation of the MP hymn of which the end is preserved in lines 200–267.

M801a (III 53) fol. e/r

P. 17 (BBB 270–287)

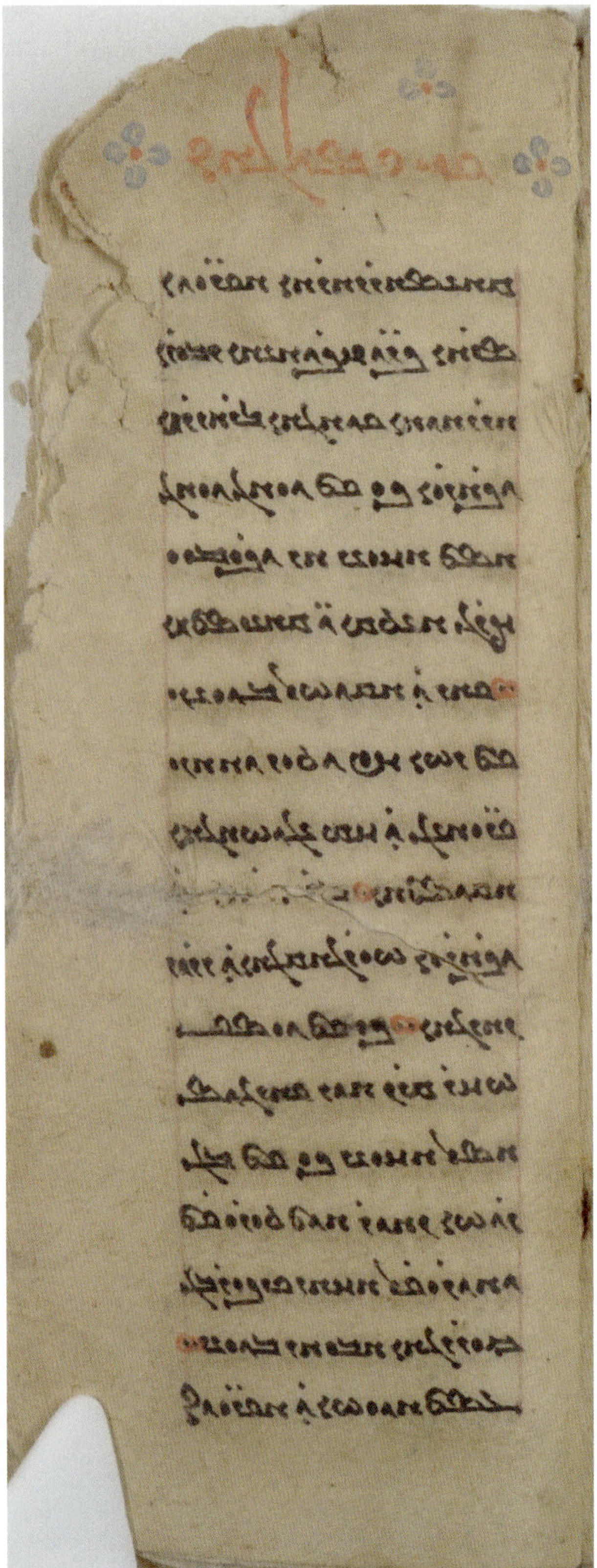

Photograph (III 53_5) reproduced by permission

M801a (III 53) fol. e/r

P. 17 (BBB 270–287)

hdl. [?–]17/ {*red*} [ʾpwryšn ʿyg] | prystgʾn
‘[Hymns of praise to] the messengers’

hdl. 17/ prystgʾn

270 1/ mʾnsʾrdʾrʾn ʾfrywn
271 2/ srʾn xrwhxwʾnʾn dbyr<ʾ>n[55]
272 3/ ʾrdʾwʾn pwʾgʾn brʾdrʾn
273 4/ wxʾryn ky pṭ wyʾg wyʾg
274 5/ ʾsṭ ʾhynd ʾd wxybyy
275 6/ crg ʾnjmn ẅ mʾnysṭʾn
276 7/ °° pʾd ẉ̇ ʾmwšt bwynd
277 8/ pṭ dšn cy wjyd wʾʾd
278 9/ fryʾng ẉ̇ hm ngwšʾgʾn
279 10/ ʾmwsṭʾn ° (br)[ʾd](rʾn ẉ̇)
280 11/ wxʾryn šyrgʾmgʾn ẉ̇ drwd
281 12/ zʾdgʾn °° ky pṭ wysp
282 13/ šhr mrz ʾwd pʾdgws
283 14/ ʾst ʾhynd ky pṭ bg
284 15/ rwšn zʾwr ʾwṭ jyryfṭ
285 16/ wʾwryft ʾhʾd pd kyrbg
286 17/ qyrdgʾn ʾbyʾd bwynd ° °
287 18/ ʿsṭʾwyšn ẉ̇ ʾfrywn

... [And all bishops],[56] (270) heads of (religious) houses, prayer-leaders, preachers, scribes, pure electi, brothers (and) sisters who dwell[57] in various places, together with their (275) parishes, communities and *mānistāns*; may they be protected and united by the right hand of the Holy Spirit, the friend. And also the faithful hearers, brothers and (280) sisters, friends and children of salvation who dwell in all lands, borderlands and provinces, who believe in God, Light, Power and Wisdom: may they be remembered for (their) pious works. (287)

May praise and blessing,

---

[55] Written *dbyrn*, without subscript points to indicate the omission of a letter.

[56] Restored on the basis of the MP parallel text in lines 217–18 (see n. 54 on p. 33 above).

[57] The Pa. expression *ʾst ʾh-* ‘to dwell’ is discussed, rather inconclusively, in *DMT* III/1, 55b.

M801a (III 53) fol. e/v

P. 18 (BBB 288–305)

Photograph (III 53_6) reproduced by permission
© Staatliche Museen zu Berlin, Museum für Asiatische Kunst / Lina Wällstedt

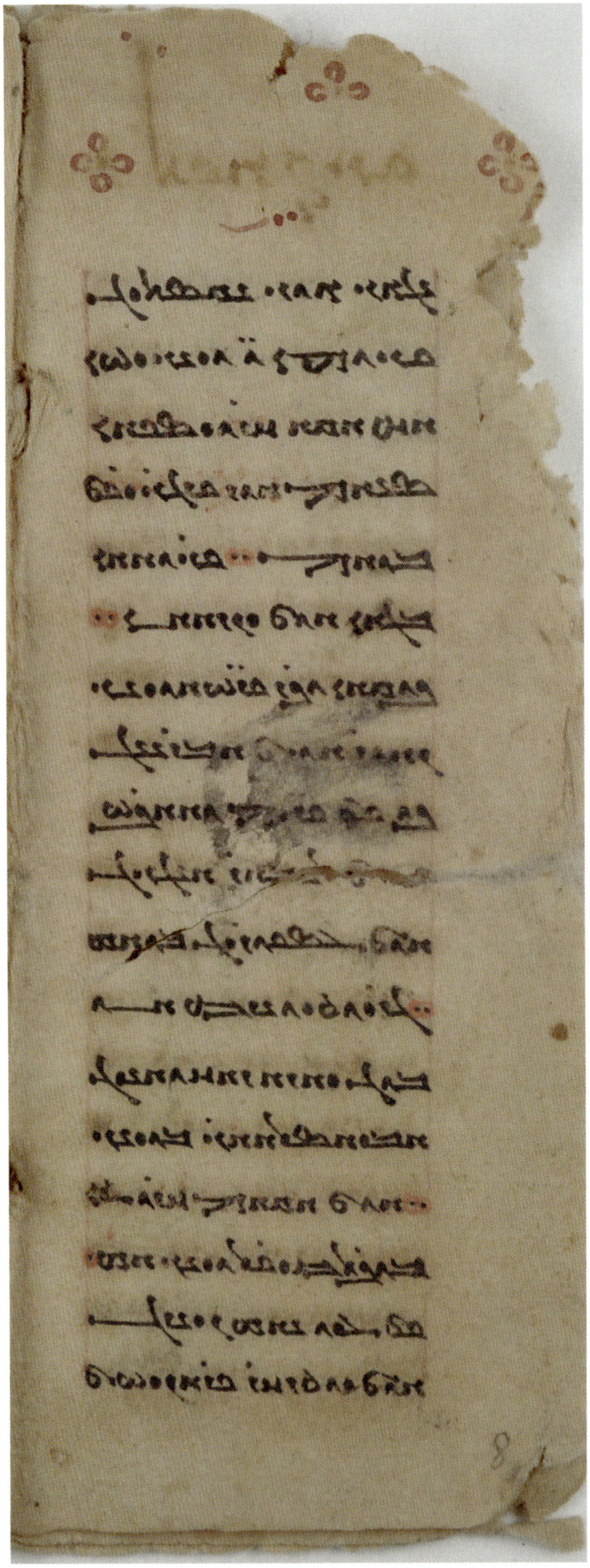

M801a (III 53) fol. e/v

P. 18 (BBB 288–305)

hdl. 18–19/ {*green*} prz'pt | prystg'nyg
'Here end (the hymns of praise) to the messengers'

hdl. 18/ prz'pt

288 1/ ng'd 'wd nmstyg
289 2/ pdwh̠n ẅ wyndyšn
290 3/ 'c 'm' hrwysp'n
291 4/ sn'h̠ 'wd pdgryfṭ
292 5/ bw'h̠ ◦◦ prw''n
293 6/ bg'n 'wṭ yzd''n ◦◦
294 7/ kwm'n wxd frš'wynd
295 8/ z'wr 'wṭ 'brnng
296 9/ kw pṭ fr(y)h̠[58] w''xš
297 10/ ['w](ṭ t)[n]b'r 'ngdg
298 11/ 'wṭ ʿspwryg bw'm
299 12/ ◦◦ gryw jywndq 'w
300 13/ bwγ y'd' d'hw'nyg
301 14/ 'by'st''r bwynd
302 15/ ◦◦ 'wṭ 'm'h̠ hrwʿyn
303 16/ bwxtqyft wynd'm ◦
304 17/ {MP} pṭ ʿyw n'm zyndg
305 18/ 'wṭ ywjdhr pr'zyšṭ

entreaty and petition, prayer and supplication (290) ascend from us all and be accepted in the sight of the gods and divine beings: may they themselves send us (295) support and zeal[59] so that we, (both) spirits [and] bodies, may become whole and perfect in love.[60] May the Living Self (300) attain salvation. May the donors be absolved from their sins. And may we all find redemption.

(304) {MP}[61] In the one living and holy name, for ever

[58] If taken as the abstract *friyīh* 'love', with Henning, a MP word in Pa. context.

[59] On *'brn(n)g* 'eagerness, zeal' (not 'chastity', nor 'splendour') see Henning 1946, 154 n. 2.

[60] Boyce 1960, 106, notes that M5225 contains a fragment of another copy of lines 292–8 and 305–7, including the following variants: 294 *'wm'n*, 297 *'wd tnw'r* (a MP form) and 307 *byh̠* (also a MP form, as expected here in a mostly MP context).

[61] For its concluding formula this Pa. hymn switches into MP (with the exception of the characteristic Pa. word *bwyndyh̠* in line 307, cf. the preceding note). The wording is thus almost identical with that of its MP counterpart in lines 264–7.

M801a (III 53) fol. f/r

P. 19 (BBB 306–313)

Photograph (III 53_6) reproduced by permission

M801a (III 53) fol. f/r

P. 19 (BBB 306–313)

hdl. 18–19/ {*green*} przʾpt | prystgʾnyg
'Here end (the hymns of praise) to the messengers'

hdl.19/ prystgʾnyg

306 1/ ʾwṭ jʾydʾn zmʾn	and ever, so be it.
307 2/ ʾwẖ bwyndyẖ[62]	
308 3/ {*red*} hnzpṭ ʾpwryšn ʿy	Here end the hymns of praise to the
309 4/ {*red*} prysṭgʾn pd m̈r[63] II	messengers, two in number.
{*ten lines left blank*}	{*ten lines left blank*}

310 15/ {*red*} nwyst ʾpwryšn ∘∘	(310) Here begin the hymns of praise to
311 16/ {*red*} gʾhʿyg	the Bema.[64]
312 17/ ʿšnwg ngwcym pd	We genuflect in deep reverence, we
313 18/ zwpr nyzʾyšn nmbrym	revere

[62] For the variant *byẖ* in M5225 see p. 37 n. 60 above.

[63] The writing *m̈r* with superscript points seems to be an abbreviation for MP *mrg* 'number'. See Sims-Williams 2019, 263 with n. 15.

[64] The series of hymns which are referred to both here and at the end of the sequence (lines 388–9) as 'Bema hymns' are described in the headlines as 'hymns of praise to the Apostle (i.e. Mani)'. Since Mani was envisaged as returning to earth to occupy the Bema (cf. lines 335–8 below), there is no contradiction between the two descriptions. See Boyce 1975, 153, 157; Reck 2004, 163–4; and above, p. x.

M801a (III 53) fol. f/v

P. 20 (BBB 314–331)

Photograph (III 53_7) reproduced by permission
© Staatliche Museen zu Berlin, Museum für Asiatische Kunst / Lina Wällstedt

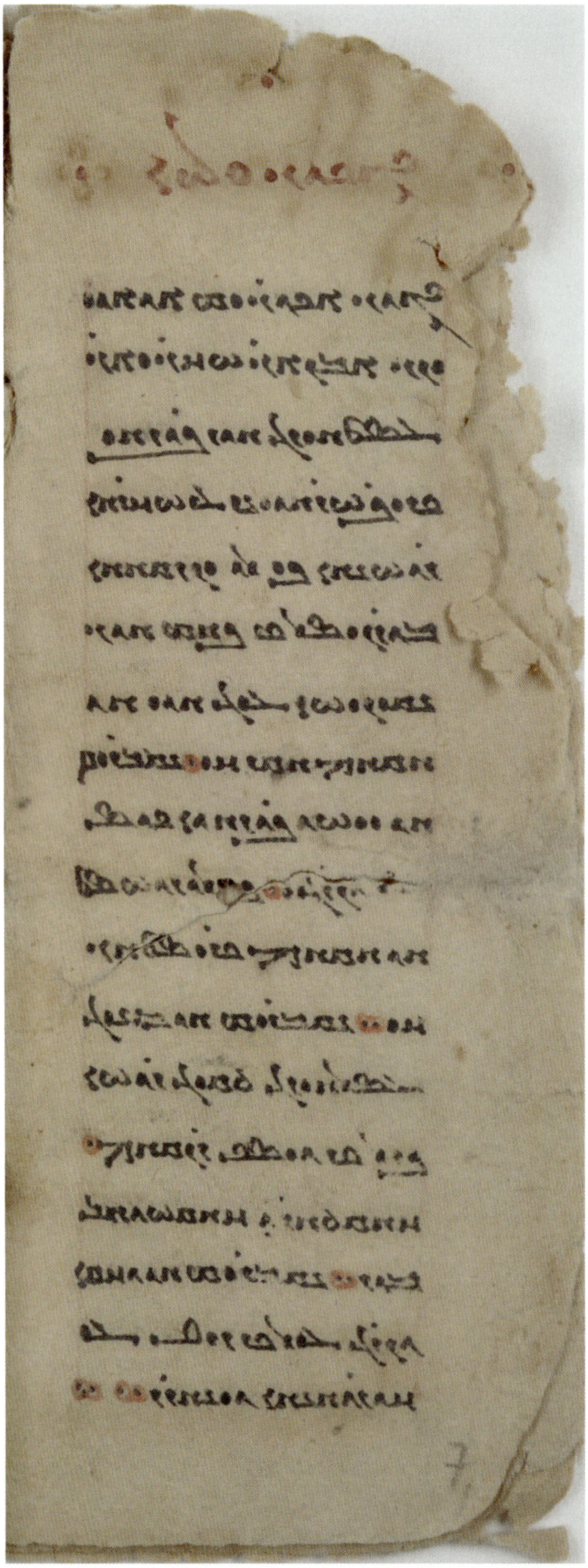

M801a (III 53) fol. f/v

P. 20 (BBB 314–331)

hdl. 20–21/ {*violet*} ʾpwryšn | pry[stgyg]
'Hymns of praise to the Apostle'

hdl. 20/ ʾpwryšn

314 1/ ʾwd ʾpwrym ʾw ʾwy	and bless the (315) mighty God, the
315 2/ yzd ʾbzʾr šhryʾr	praised ruler and worshipful lord of the
316 3/ ʿsṭʾydg ʾwd xwdʾy	Aeons of light, according to whose
317 4/ pdyxšrʾwynd ʿy šhrʾn	wish and urging you, our most exalted
318 5/ rwšnʾn ky tw yzdmʾʾn	god, have come to us.
319 6/ bwrzyst pd kʾm ʾwd	
320 7/ nmyzyšn ʿyg ʾwy ʾw	
321 8/ ʾmʾẖ ʾmd hy ◦ nmbrym	We revere (322) Jesus, the lord, the Son
322 9/ ʾw yyšw xwdʾwn pws	of Greatness, who has sent us you, our
323 10/ (ʿy) wzrgyy ◦ k[y]tw dwšsṭ[65]	best beloved.
324 11/ ʾw ʾmʾẖ prysṭʾd	
325 12/ hy ◦◦ nmbrym ʾw qnyg	We revere the praised Maiden, the
326 13/ ʿstʾydg jmyg rwšn	radiant twin, (327) who was your com-
327 14/ kyt pd wysp rzmʾẖ ◦	panion and comrade in every conflict.
328 15/ hʾmjʾr ẉ hʾmšwdʾb	
329 16/ bwd ◦◦ nmbrym ʾw whmn	We revere great Wahman, whom you
330 17/ wzrg ʿyt pd dyl ʿy	implanted in the heart of the pious.
331 18/ hwrwʾnʾn wynʾrd ◦◦ ◦◦	

[65] An unusual, perhaps unique, spelling for *dwšyst*, evidently as a result of lack of space at the end of the line.

M801a (III 53) fol. j/r

P. 21 (BBB 332–349)

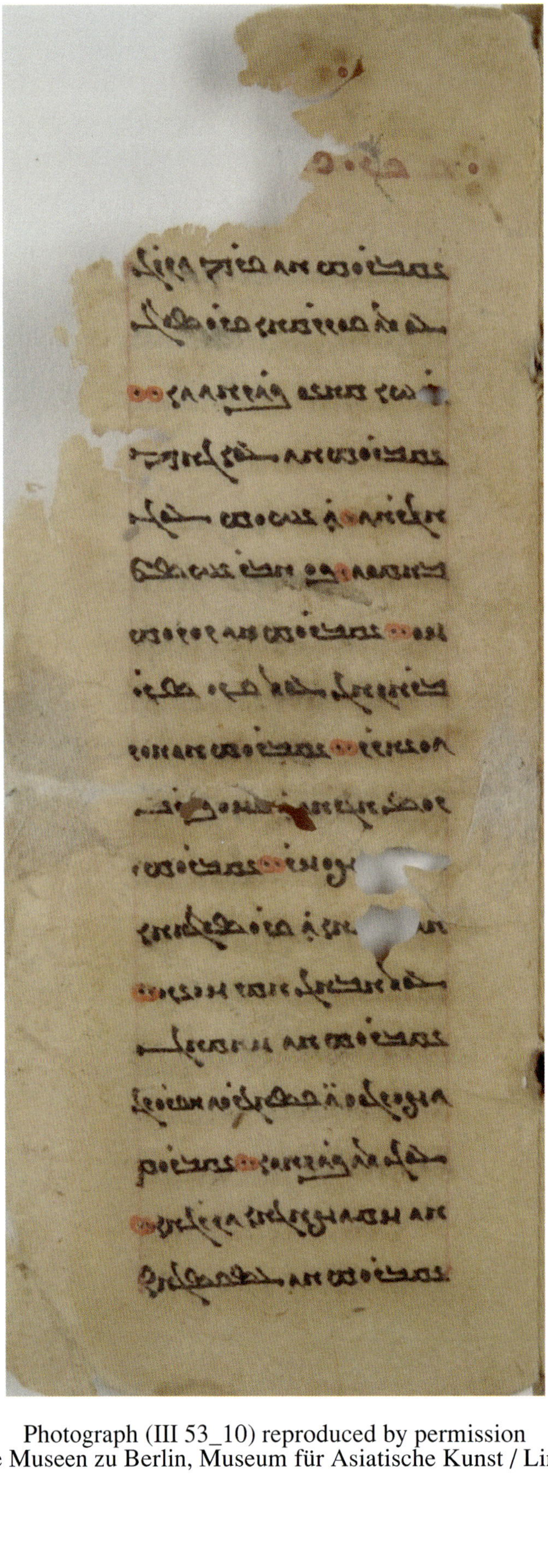

Photograph (III 53_10) reproduced by permission

M801a (III 53) fol. j/r

P. 21 (BBB 332–349)

hdl. 20–21/ {*violet*} ʾpwryšn | pry[stgyg]
‘Hymns of praise to the Apostle’

hdl. 21/ pry[stg]

332 1/ nmbrym ʾw prh̲ wzrg	We revere your great majesty, our
333 2/ ʿy tw pydrmʾn prystg	father, Apostle of light, lord Mani.
334 3/ (r)[w]šn mʾny xwdʾwwn ∘∘	
335 4/ nmbrym ʾw ʿyn gʾh̲	(335) We revere this noble Bema and
336 5/ ʾgrʾw ∘ ẉ̇ nšym ʿyg	splendid seat upon which you have sat.
337 6/ bʾmyw ∘ ky ʾbr nšsṭ	
338 7/ hy ∘∘ nmbrym ʾw dydym	We revere the shining diadem which
339 8/ brʾzʾg ʿyt pd sr	you have placed upon (your) head.
340 9/ wynʾrd ∘∘ nmbrym ʾw ʾyd	We revere this noble image and beauti-
341 10/ dys ʾgrʾ(w ẉ̇ p)hyk[y]rb	ful portrait.
342 11/ [ʿy hw]cyhr ∘∘ nmbrym[66]	We revere (343) the gods and angels
343 12/ ʾ(w)[bʾ]ʾn ẉ̇ prystgʾʾn	who have come with you.
344 13/ ʿyt ʾbʾg ʾmd hynd ∘∘	
345 14/ nmbrym ʾw hʾmʾg	We revere the whole community of the
346 15/ wcydgyy ẅ psʾgryw ʾprydg	elect and your blessed representative, O
347 16/ ʿyg tw xwdʾwn ∘∘ nmbrym	lord.
348 17/ ʾw hmwcʾgʾn wzrgʾn ∘∘	We revere (348) the great Teachers.
349 18/ nmbrym ʾw ʿspsgʾn	We revere the potent bishops.

66 + line-filler.

M801a (III 53) fol. j/v

P. 22 (BBB 350–367)

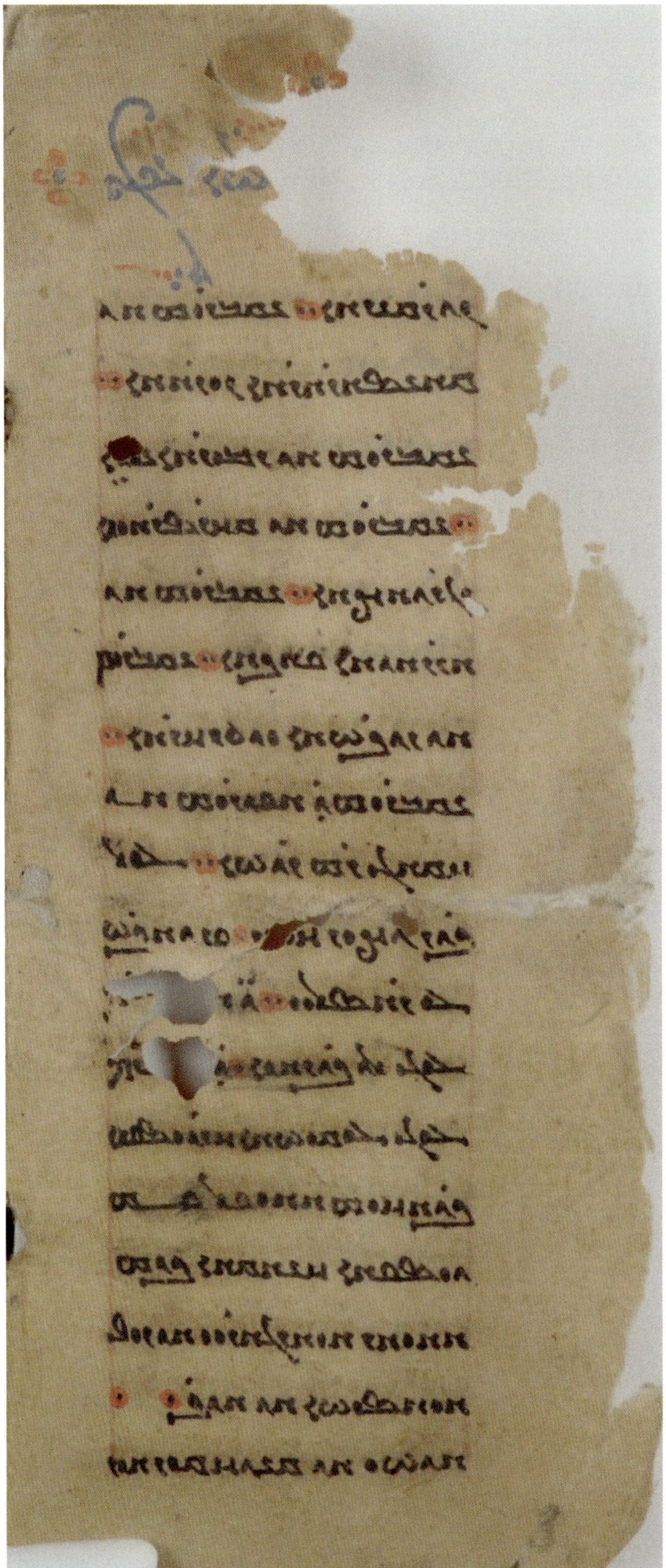

Photograph (III 53_11) reproduced by permission

M801a (III 53) fol. j/v

P. 22 (BBB 350–367)

hdl. 22[–?]/ {*blue*} [’pw](r)[y]šn ‘yg | [prystg]
‘Hymns of praise to [the Apostle]’

hdl. 22/ [’pw](r)[y]šn ‘yg

350 1/ zwrmnd’n °° nmbrym ’w	We revere the wise heads of (religious)
351 2/ m’ns’r’r’n zyr’’n °°	houses.
352 3/ nmbrym ’w dbyr’n nyw<’>n	We revere the doughty scribes.
353 4/ °° nmbrym ’w mhrsr’y’n	We revere the melodious cantors.
354 5/ zgrw’c’n °° nmbrym ’w	We revere the (355) pure elect.
355 6/ ’rd’w’n p’k’n °° nmbrym	We revere the holy virgins.
356 7/ ’w dwxš’n ywjdhr’n °°	
357 8/ nmbrym ẉ̇ ’pwrym ’w	We revere and bless the whole flock of
358 9/ hm’g rm rwšn °° ‘yt	light, whom you yourself have chosen
359 10/ xwd wcyd h(ynd) ° pd w’xš	through the spirit (360) of truth.
360 11/ ‘y r’styy °° ẅ (’)[c p](rẖ)	And [from] your majesty, O lord, and
361 12/ ‘yg tw xwd’wn ° ẉ̇[’c p]rẖ	[from] the majesty of all these (afore
362 13/ ‘yg ‘ymyš’n hrwysp’n	mentioned), I beg (as) a boon for all my
363 14/ xw’hym ’’ypt pm	limbs that remembrance may come to
364 15/ wysp’n hn’m’n kwm	my heart, (366) recollection to (my)
365 16/ ’’y’d ’y’dg’ryy ’w dyl	mind, awareness to (my) thinking, and
366 17/ ’y’syšn ’w ’wx ° °	...
367 18/ ’wšy ’w mnwhmyd ’wd	
{*at least one folio missing*}	{*at least one folio missing*}

M801a (III 53) fol. 1/r

P. 23 (BBB 368–375)

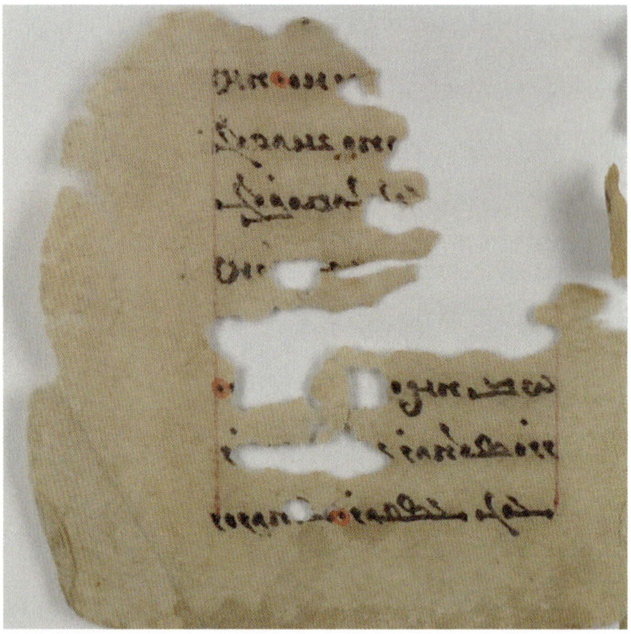

Photograph (III 53_12) reproduced by permission

M801a (III 53) fol. 1/v

P. 24 (BBB 376–383)

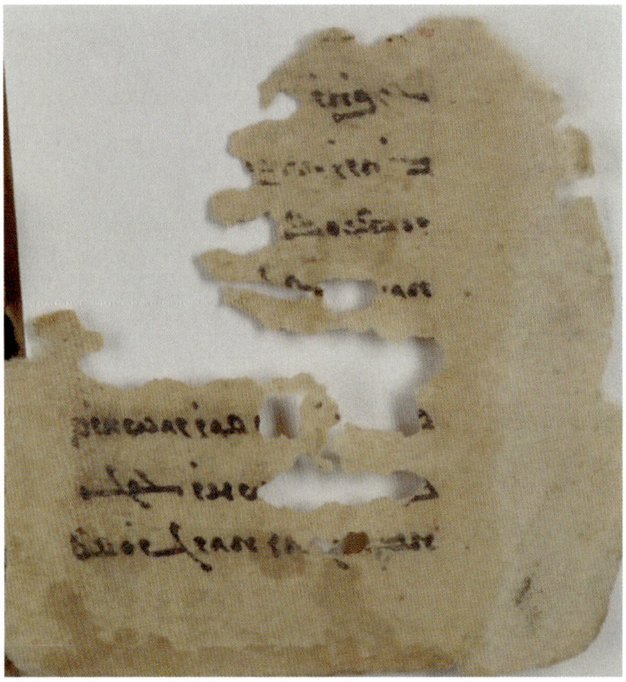

Photograph (III 53_13) reproduced by permission

M801a (III 53) fol. 1/r

P. 23 (BBB 368–375)

{*headline and ten lines torn off*}	{*headline and ten lines torn off*}
368 11/ [ ](.d) hy ° ʾc	... you were, from
369 12/ [ ](z)ʾy nhwptg	... hidden
370 13/ [ ](ʿyg)gwmyxtg	... mixed
371 14/ [ ]..[ ](rw)c[67]	... day(?)
372 15/ [ ]	...
373 16/ šb ʾcy[š] °	night from ...
374 17/ dryst ʾwr n[m](r)d	Welcome[68] ...
375 18/ ʿyg ʿspwr ° ʿ(y)ʾwzyd	perfect man, who went out ...

M801a (III 53) fol. 1/v

P. 24 (BBB 376–383)

{*headline and ten lines torn off*}	{*headline and ten lines torn off*}
376 11/ ʿ(y)xʾr [ ]	of thorns ...
377 12/ b(r)ʾdrʾ(n ky)[ ]	brothers who ...
378 13/ dyswys [ ]	garment(?)[69] ...
379 14/ ʾw.[ ]s(t)[ ]	...
380 15/ [ ]	...
381 16/ (p)[ ]. pwr dwšʾrm	... full of love,
382 17/ k[y]šhr ʿyg	w[ho came into](?) the world of
383 18/ ʾb[dʾ]g(ʾ)n ʾwd grypṭ	the assailants and was seized ...
{*at least one folio missing*}	{*at least one folio missing*}

---

67 Uncertain reading.

68 On *ʾwr*, an adverb ‘hither’ reinterpreted as an imperative ‘come!’, see Nyberg 1932.

69 The meaning of this word is debated. See *DMT* III/1, 152b, with references.

M801a (III 53) fol. c/r

P. 25 (BBB 384–389)

Photograph (III 53_3) reproduced by permission
© Staatliche Museen zu Berlin, Museum für Asiatische Kunst / Lina Wällstedt

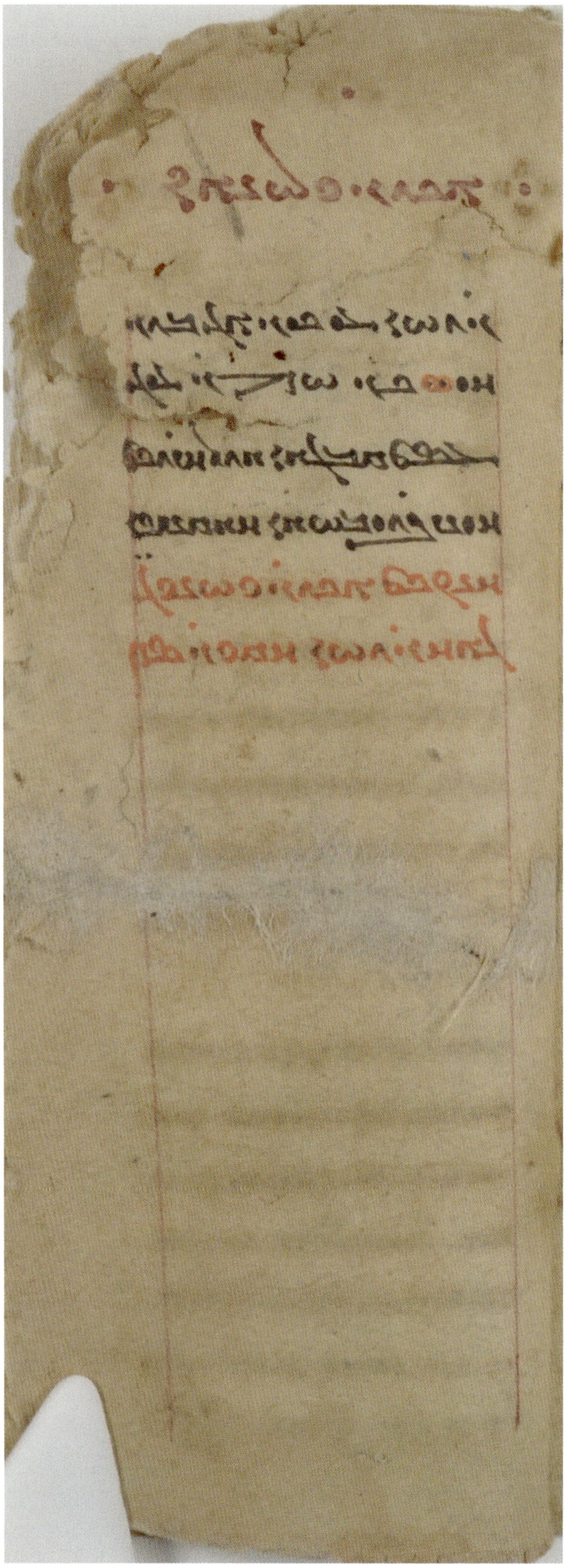

M801a (III 53) fol. c/r

P. 25 (BBB 384–389)

hdl. [?–]25/ {*violet*} [hnzpṭ](?) | ʾpwryšnʾn
'[Here end](?) the hymns of praise'

hdl. 25/ ʾpwryšnʾn

384 1/ rwšn ʿy pydʾg bwd	... light, you who appeared in the world
385 2/ hy °° pd šẖr ʿyg	of (385) tyrants and gathered together
386 3/ ʿsṭmbgʾn ʾwt hrwpṭ	your kinsfolk.
387 4/ hynd xwybšʾn hʾmnʾp<ʾ>n	
388 5/ {*red*} hnzpṭ ʾpwryšnyg[70]	Here end the hymns of praise of the
389 6/ {*red*} gʾhrwšn hmyr[71] sẖ	Bema of Light, three in total.
{*rest of the page left blank*}	{*rest of the page left blank*}

[70] As Henning noted, this must stand for *ʾpwryšn ʿyg* (noun + ezafe).

[71] Pa. form in a MP context.

M801a (III 53) fol. c/v

P. 26 (BBB 390–406)

Photograph (III 53_4) reproduced by permission
© Staatliche Museen zu Berlin, Museum für Asiatische Kunst / Lina Wällstedt

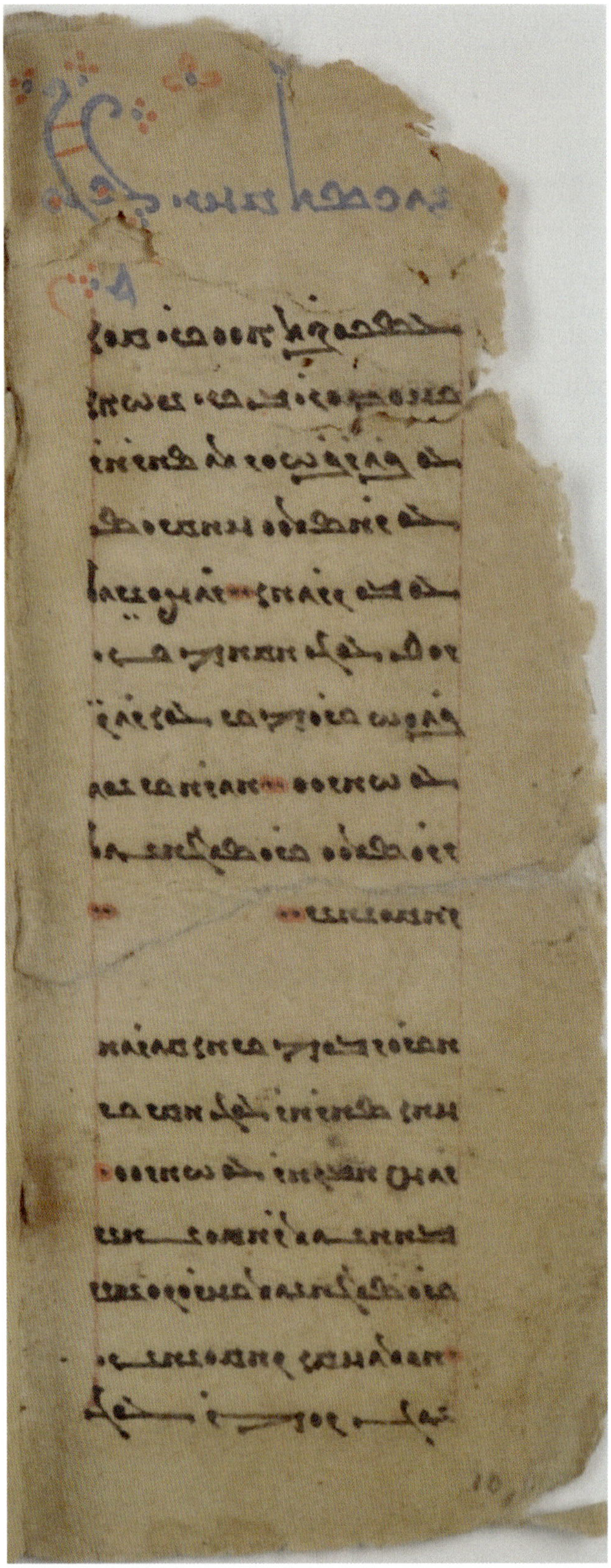

M801a (III 53) fol. c/v

P. 26 (BBB 390–406)

hdl. 26–27/ {*blue*} nwyst mhr ʿyg | š’dcn’n
‘Here begin the hymns of the joyful ones’

hdl. 26/ nwyst mhr ʿyg

390 1/ ʿspyxt ’yy prmyn
391 2/ phyqyrb pd nyš’n
392 3/ ʿy xwrxšyd tw s’r’r
393 4/ ʿy r’styy h’mdys
394 5/ ʿy by zrw’n °° rwcyn<’>dwt
395 6/ dyl ʿyg ’m’ẖ pd
396 7/ xwyš pryẖ pd ʿyn rwž
397 8/ ʿy š’dyy °° ’wr’ pd nyw
398 9/ drystyy prystg’nwt
399 10/ r’myn’nd °° °°
{*one line left blank*}
400 12/ ’pryd byẖ pd ’n[72] mwrw’
401 13/ h’n s’r’r ʿyg ’md pd
402 14/ rwc ’bz’r ʿy š’dyy °
403 15/ b’’nwt r’myn’nd
404 16/ prystg’nwt phryzyn’nd
405 17/ ° ’wt whmn z’myn’nd[73]
406 18/ nwg zyẖr ʿyg

(390) {Hymn 1}[74] You are shining, happy form, like the sun, you leader of truth, likeness (395) of god Zurwan. Our hearts shall irradiate you with their love on this day of joy. Come hither in good health; may the angels give you peace.

{*one line left blank*}

(400) {Hymn 2} May that leader who has come on a great day of joy be blessed with another (propitious) omen. May the gods give you peace, may the angels protect you (405) and may Wahman bring you new (and)

---

[72] Late form of *’ny* ‘other’ (*DMT* III/1, 43, following Henning).

[73] Henning notes that the pl. form -*’nd* is a mistake for sg. -*’d* (caused by the preceding pl. forms).

[74] This hymn is in MP, apart from the Pa. forms *’yy* (390) and *rwž* (396).

M801a (III 53) fol. a/r

P. 27 (BBB 407–424)

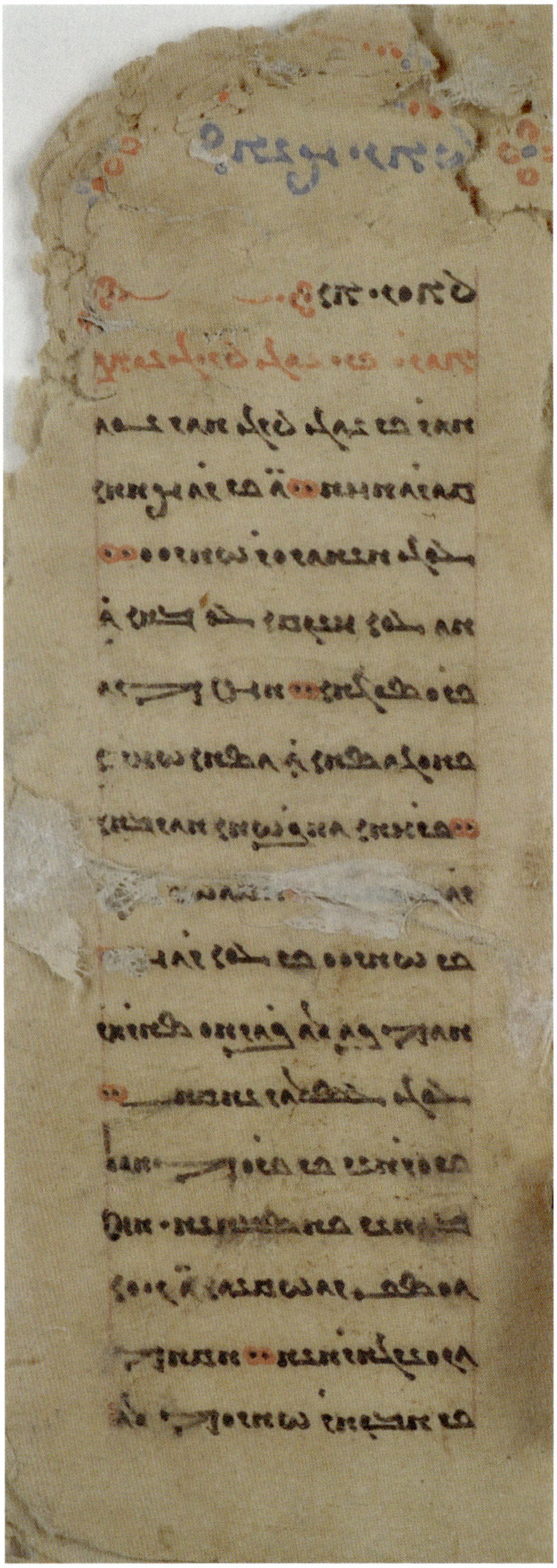

Photograph (III 53) reproduced by permission

M801a (III 53) fol. a/r

P. 27 (BBB 407–424)

hdl. 26–27/ {*blue*} nwyst mhr ʿyg | š'dcn'n
'Here begin the hymns of the joyful ones'

hdl. 27/ š'dcn'n

407 1/ j'yd'n ○○ ○○
408 2/ {*red*} 'wr pd nwg jdg nw'k[75]
409 3/ 'wr pd nwg jdg 'wd nyw
410 4/ mwrw'h' ○○ ẅ pd rwc''n
411 5/ ʿyg 'n'wdyr š'dyy ○○
412 6/ 'w ʿyn hnzmn ʿy b'n ẉ
413 7/ prys(t)g'n ○○ 'c h̲(r)w
414 8/ p'ygws'n ẉ ws'n šh(r')n
415 9/ ○○ prh'n w'xš'n 'wd b'n
416 10/ r(wšn'n' ○○ ')mw(št)[hynd]
417 11/ pd š'dyy pd ʿyn rw(c ○○)
418 12/ 'wh̲ kw tw xwd'y s'r'r
419 13/ ʿyg ʿstwdn'm' ○○
420 14/ pdyr'nd pd pryh̲ 'wt
421 15/ bw'nd p'sb'n' ○[76] 'c
422 16/ wysp dwšmnwn ẅ dyn
423 17/ wzyndg'r'n' ○○ 'm'h̲
424 18/ pd 'bz'r š'dyh̲ tw

eternal life.
{Hymn 3}[77] (To) the tune 'Come hither to new fortune'.—Come hither to new fortune[78] and a good (410) omen, and to days of abiding joy for this gathering of gods and angels. From all provinces and (from) many lands, (415) Glories, Spirits and light gods [have] gathered in joy on this day, so that they may receive you in love, lord, leader whose name is praised, and be your protectors from (422) all enemies and destroyers of the church. In mighty joy let us

[75] The form *nw'k* (rather than *nw'g*) is probably Sogdian. As noted in *DMT* III/1, 246b, in a case like this the whole caption, the rest of which consists solely of the quoted title, can be regarded as Sogdian. This explanation does not apply in cases where the caption includes other MP words, e.g. *pd ... nw'k* 'to the tune ...' or *ʿyn pd ... nw'k* 'this one to the tune ...' (see lines 428 and 446 below).

[76] The punctuation point is not circled in red ink as usual. Other examples of the same omission are found in lines 437, 490(?), 529, 651 and 732.

[77] M7351, lines 1–10 (Leurini 2017, 101–2), a student exercise, is another copy of this hymn. Apart from mistakes and normal spelling variants this provides the readings: 410 *mwrw'h̲* (without -'), 411 om. *ʿyg* , 412 om. *ʿy*, 414 *p'ygws*, 416 *rwšn'n'n'm*[sic] *'mwšt hynd*, 418 *hmwc'g* 'Teacher' (for *s'r'r*; this variant, for which cf. p. 59 n. 89 below, is surely deliberate, implying that the hymn could be used on various occasions to welcome different members of the hierarchy), 423 *wzyndg'r'*, 424 *pyš tw* and 426 *š'dyy* (for *prwxyh̲*).

[78] See MacKenzie 1985, 421 n. 2. MP *jdg* has sometimes been translated as 'fame', but it is often paired (as here) with *mwrw'h̲* 'omen'.

M801a (III 53) fol. a/v

P. 28 (BBB 425–440)

Photograph (III 53_2) reproduced by permission
© Staatliche Museen zu Berlin, Museum für Asiatische Kunst / Lina Wällstedt

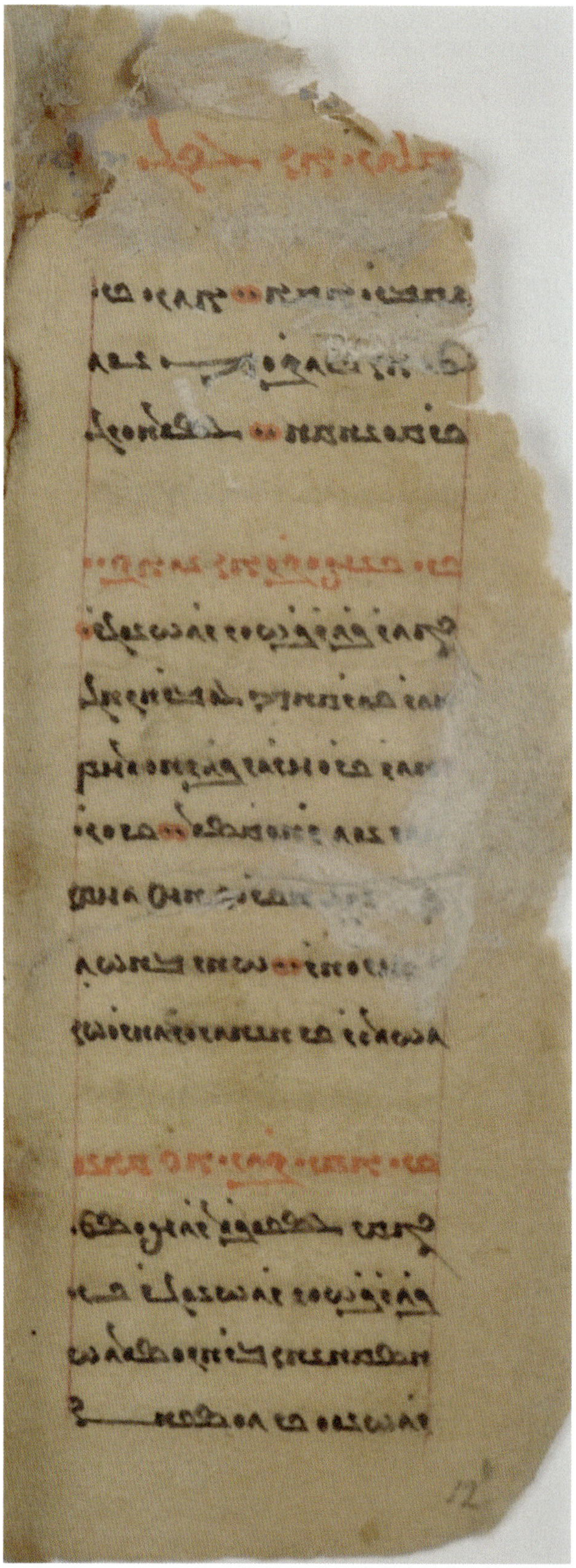

M801a (III 53) fol. a/v

P. 28 (BBB 425–440)

hdl. 28–29/ {*red*} mhr'n 'yg | š'dyh'n[79]
'Hymns of joy'

hdl.28/ mhr'n 'yg

425 1/ nmbr('m)' ◦◦ 'wd pd	(425) revere you and let us rejoice
426 2/ ṭ(w)'n[80] (pr)wxyẖ nyw	greatly in your good fortune.
427 3/ prmyn'm' ◦◦ 'st'ydg	Istāyīdag.
{*one line left blank*}	{*one line left blank*}
428 5/ {*red*} pd pncyxz'n nw'k ◦◦	{Hymn 4} To the tune *pncyxz'n*.[81]
429 6/ 'wr xwrxšyd rwšnygr ◦	Come hither, illuminating sun; (430)
430 7/ 'wr pwrm'ẖ 'y br'z'g	come hither, shining full-moon; come
431 8/ [◦]'wr pryhrwd xwd'y thm	hither, compassionate lord, strong and
432 9/ ('w)d nyw r'ymst ◦◦ pdyr	richly endowed with insight;[82] receive
433 10/ [nwg](nw)g 'pry(n) 'c whmn	[ever] new blessing from Wahman the
434 11/ (šhr)y'r ◦◦ š'd b'š ẉ	king; be joyful and (435) prosper in
435 12/ wštyr pd 'n'wdyr w'ryšn	lasting happiness.[83]
{*one line left blank*}	{*one line left blank*}
436 14/ {*red*} pd 'md xwd'y m'ny	{Hymn 5} To (the tune) 'Lord Mani has
437 15/ 'md 'spyxt rwcysṭ ◦	come'.—The illuminating sun has
438 16/ xwrxšyd rwšnygr pd	come, has shone, has brightened in
439 17/ 'sm'n'n br'zystwš	(439) the heavens, his radiance has
440 18/ rwšnyy pd wysp'n	beamed on all

[79] The plural *š'dyh'n* 'joys' is somewhat unexpected. Is it a mistake for *š'dcn'n* 'the joyful ones' as in the headlines to pp. 27 and 30?

[80] The form *ṭw'n* 'your' is Pa., here used in a MP context. It is worth considering the possibility of interpreting it as a genuine (though rare) MP word meaning 'strong' (Sims-Williams 1989, 331).

[81] The meaning of *pncyxz'n* is unknown.

[82] The meaning of *r'ymst* is debated. For a convenient summary see Colditz 2018, 434.

[83] Another copy of this short hymn is found in M7421, referred to as T II T 22 by Henning, who notes its variant readings, most importantly: 432 *pd* (for *pdyr*, probably by mistake), 433 *nwg nwg* clear. In M7421 the caption, which follows the text of the hymn, reads: *'yn pd pncyyxz'n nw'g*. (Regarding *nw'k* and *nw'g* see above, p. 53 n. 75.)

M801a (III 53) fol. b/r

P. 29 (BBB 441–457)

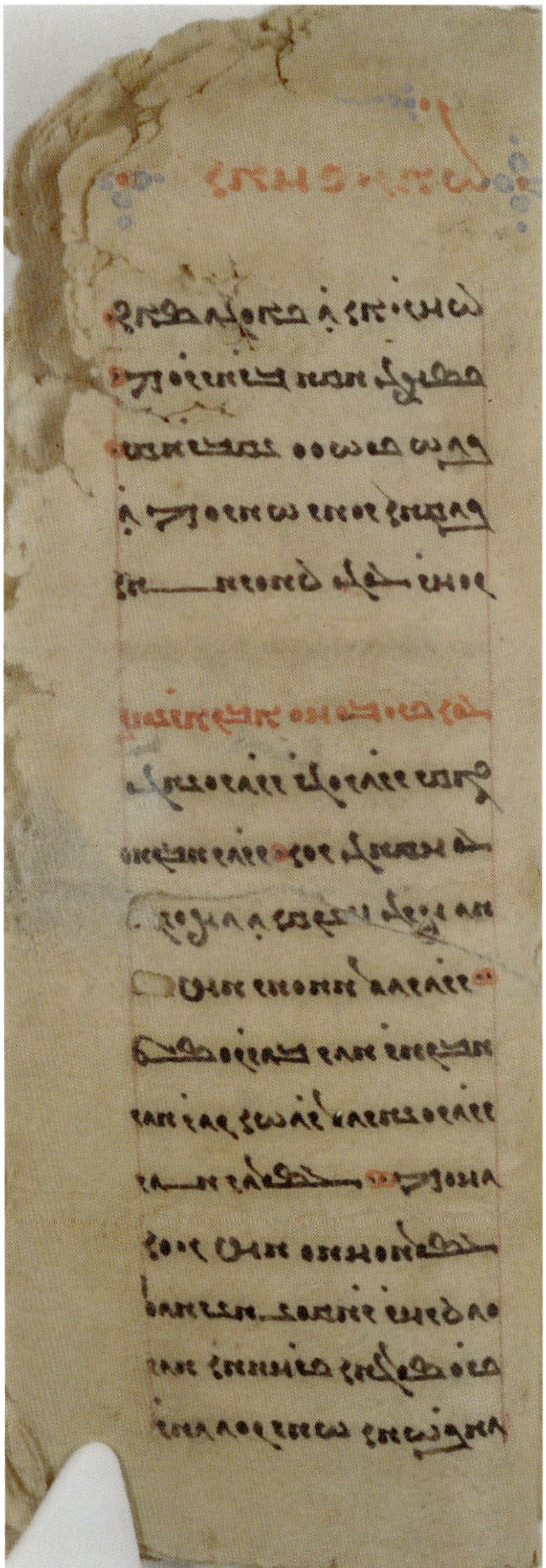

Photograph (III 53_2) reproduced by permission

M801a (III 53) fol. b/r

P. 29 (BBB 441–457)

hdl. 28–29/ {*red*} mhr'n 'yg | š'dyh'n[84]
'Hymns of joy'

hdl. 29/ š'dyh'n

441 1/ šhr'n ẇ p'ygws'n °
442 2/ pscg 'm' br'dryẖ °
443 3/ kwš pyšyy nmbr'm °
444 4/ kwm'n dy'd š'dyẖ ẇ
445 5/ zyhr 'yg j'yd''n
{*one line left blank*}
446 7/ {*red*} 'yn pd by hy 'bz'r nw'k
447 8/ 'md drwdygr drwdyn'g
448 9/ 'y hm'g dyn ° drwd 'bz'y
449 10/ 'w crg (h)nzmn ẇ wcydg[yy]
450 11/ °° drwdwt ''y'd 'c [by]
451 12/ 'bz'r 'wd bwrzysṭ
452 13/ drwdyn'dwt rwšn zwr 'wd
453 14/ whyẖ °° 'stwd 'wd
454 15/ 'st'yh'y 'c dyn
455 16/ ywjdhr r'myn'nd 'wt[85]
456 17/ prystg'n prh''n 'wd
457 18/ w'xš'n š'd zyw w'r

lands and provinces; (it is) fitting (for) us, the brotherhood, to bow down before him, so that he may give us joy and (445) eternal life.

{*one line left blank*}

{Hymn 6} This (one) to the tune 'You are the powerful god'.—He has come, the bringer of salvation, the saviour of the whole church; increase salvation for the flock, the community and [the company of] the elect. (450) May salvation come to you from the mighty and most high [God]; may (his) Light, Power and Wisdom grant you salvation. <You are>[86] praised and (454) you shall be praised by the holy church. May the angels, Glories and Spirits give you peace. Live happily, rejoice

---

[84] On the form *š'dyh'n* 'joys' see above, p. 55 n. 79.

[85] Mistake for *r'myn'ndwt* (3 pl. subjunctive + 2 sg. enclitic pronoun). Boyce 1975, 159, notes that the parallel text M1368 (see the preceding note) has *[r'myn](' n)dwd*. (On the two forms of the 2 sg. enclitic pronoun, *-wt* and *-wd*, see Sims-Williams 1982, 172.)

[86] An auxiliary verb, 2 sg. subjunctive **bw'y* according to Henning but perhaps rather 2 sg. present **hy*, seems to have been omitted after *'stwd*. One may compare the repeated phrase *'stwd 'wd 'st'yhyd* 'She/He has been praised and is praised ...' in the exordium to Mani's 'Living Gospel' (MacKenzie 1995, 186–7), with regular omission of the auxiliary in the third person. — As noted in Boyce 1960, 70, another poorly-preserved copy of lines 454–61 is found in M1368. At the beginning of this fragment *'c d(y)[n* is preceded by a word ending in *](w)d*. Whether this is restored as *'st](w)d* or as *'](w)d*, the text of M1368 clearly differs here from that of BBB.

M801a (III 53) fol. b/v

P. 30 (BBB 458–475)

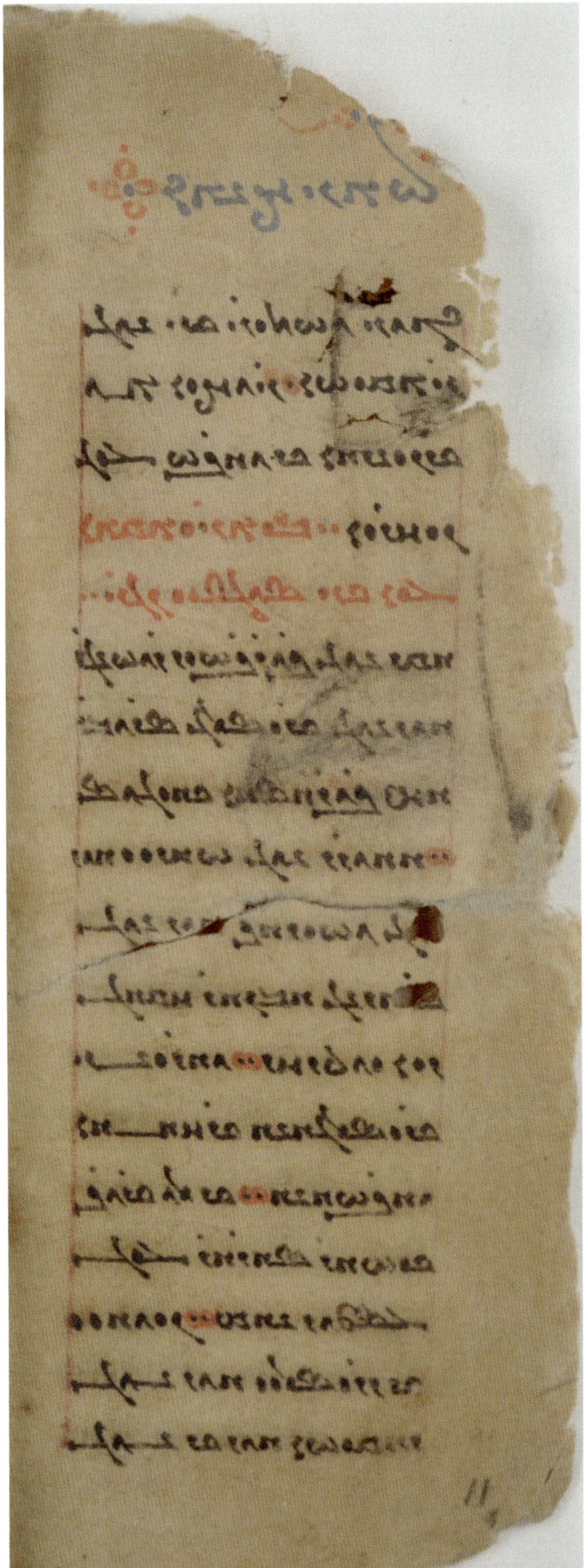

Photograph (III 53_3) reproduced by permission

M801a (III 53) fol. b/v

P. 30 (BBB 458–475)

hdl. 30[–?]/ {*blue*} š'dcn'n | [...]
'The joyful ones ...'

hdl. 30/ š'dcn'n

458 1/ 'wd wštyr pd nwg
459 2/ r'myšn ° rwcyn 'w
460 3/ przynd'n pd w'xš 'yg
461 4/ zyhryn °° {*red*} by 'ry'm'n
462 5/ {*red*} 'yn pd swγlyy[87] zgr °°
463 6/ 'md nwg xwrxšyd rwšngr[88]
464 7/ 'wd nwg prystg srwbr
465 8/ 'c xwr's'n p'ygws
466 9/ °° ''wrd nwg š'dyy 'wd
467 10/ [n](w)g wšyd'(x) (')wd nwg
468 11/ (pr')dng 'bz'r hm'g
469 12/ dyn ywjdhr °° w'rynd
470 13/ prystg'n' prh''n
471 14/ (w)'xš'n' °° pd tw prwx
472 15/ pyš'r s'r'r 'yg
473 16/ 'sṭwdn'm °° zyw'yy
474 17/ pd drystyy 'wd nwg
475 18/ (r')myšn 'wd pd nwg
{*some pages missing*}

and prosper in new peace; enlighten (460) (your) children with the living word. Bay-Aryāmān. {Hymn 7} This (one) to the Sogdian melody.—A new illuminating sun has come, and a new apostle, a teacher (465) from the province of the east. He has brought new joy, and new confidence and powerful new progress (to) the whole (469) holy church. Angels, Glories (and) Spirits rejoice in you, glorious guide, leader whose name is praised. May you live in health and new (475) peace and as a new [auspicious omen and as a valiant guide. May the gods be your protectors and may the angels always give you peace].[89]
{*some pages missing*}

---

[87] Apparently a Bactrian form, which is probably attested as *σογολιγο in the place-name βονοσογολιγο 'the Sogdian settlement' (P. Lurje *apud* Sims-Williams 2010, 87).

[88] Shortened from *rwšnygr* (see the next note) due to lack of space at the end of the line.

[89] As noted by Henning, another copy of part of this hymn (lines 463-72) is found in M276, now edited in Leurini 2017, 140–42, which attests several variants, the most significant being: 463 *rwšnygr*, 467 *nwg* clear, 468 *pr('dnn)g*, 470 *prystg'n* (without final -'), 472 *hmwc['g* 'Teacher' (for *s'r'r*, cf. above, p. 53 n. 77). The headline to M276 may be reconstructed as *'mdyšn 'yg s'l'r'n* 'The coming of the leaders', which suits the content of this hymn.—In addition, M7351, lines 24–31 (Leurini 2017, 103–4), a student exercise, is another copy of lines 463–5 and 469ff. Apart from mistakes and normal spelling variants this gives the readings 463 *rwšnygr*, 470 *frystg'n* and 471 *w'xš'n* (both without -'), 475 *wšyd'x 'wd'* (for *r'myšn 'wd*). After the words preserved in BBB, this copy continues: *mwrw'ẖ 'wd' pd nyw pyš'r °° bw'dwd b'sb'n b''nwd ° ° frystg'n myšyqyt r'ymyn'nd* (read: *bw'ndwd p'sb'n b''n 'wd frystg'n myšyqyt r'myn'nd*).

Part 2:

A Sogdian Confessional

M801a (III 53) fol. B/r

P. 31 (BBB 476–493)

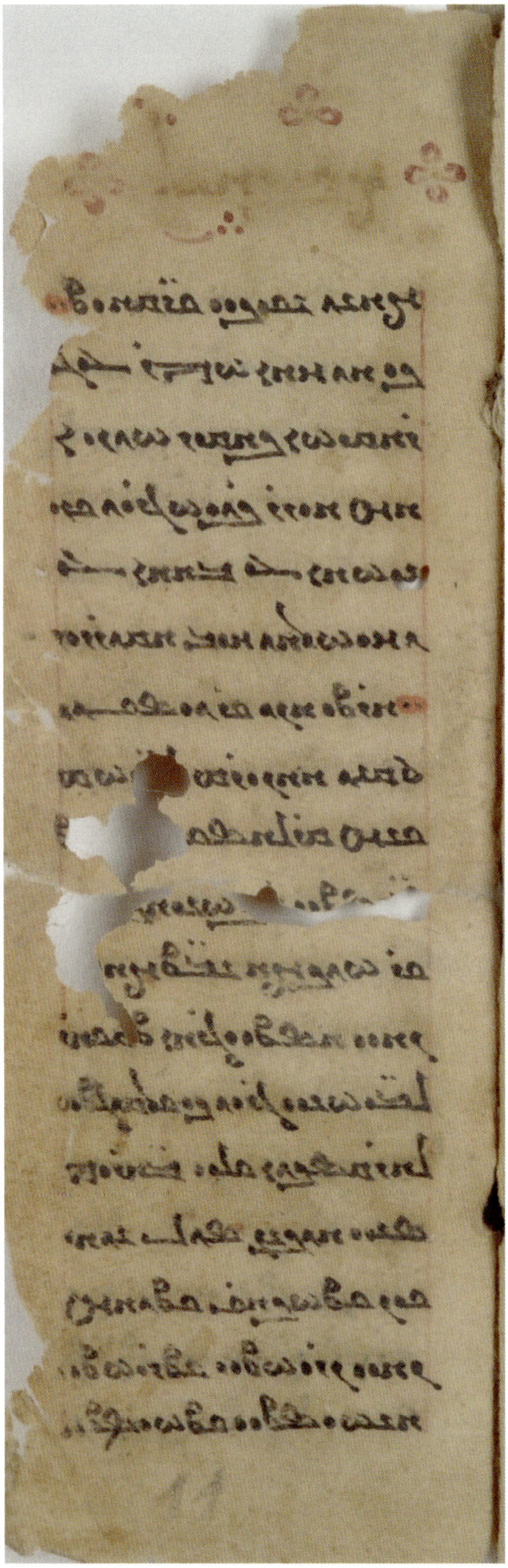

Photograph (III 53_28) reproduced by permission

M801a (III 53) fol. B/r

P. 31 (BBB 476–493)

hdl. [?–]31/ {*green*} [pw ʾzrmyʾẖ] | cxšʾ(p)δ
'The commandment [Non-injury]'

hdl. 31/ cxšʾ(p)δ

476 1/ {Sogd.} cʾnw npykyy frmʾyṭ °°
477 2/ {MP} ky ʾw hʾn šẖr ʿyg
478 3/ rʾmyšn kʾmyd šwdn
479 4/ ʾc ʾydr xwyš gryw pd
480 5/ (n)yšʾn ʿy bʾʾn ʿy
481 6/ whyštʾw hyb ʾmwrdyd
482 7/ °° {Sogd.} ʾrṭy ʾzw pr wyspww
483 8/ jmnw ʾʾzyrm (δβy)šm
484 9/ pnc mrδʾsp[ndṭ]ṭ
485 10/ (β)[y](s)ṭyy (r)[w](x)šnyʾ(k)[kyy]
486 11/ pr šwkcʾ nβṭcʾ[ẖ]
487 12/ zʾyy ʾsṭyy γrʾn ṭmpʾr
488 13/ δβyšnyy γryw ky ptmwγṭyy
489 14/ δʾrmskwn pδyy βʾryẖ
490 15/ snyy ʾw(x)nz swδ nwʾ(y)[1]
491 16/ pyz pṭškʾf pṭwʾc
492 17/ zʾyy zryšṭyy pṭryšṭy(y)
493 18/ ʾnšysṭyy pṭšysṭyy

{Sogd.} ... As (Mani) says in scripture: {MP} 'Whoever desires to go to that land of peace should henceforth collect his soul in the manner of the gods of paradise'. (482) {Sogd.} And at every moment I pain (and) injure the five elements, the fettered light [which] is in the dry (or) moist earth. (If)[2] the heavy body, (488) the injurious self in which I am clad[3]—on foot[4] (or) mounted, going up (or) going down,[5] hurrying (or) dawdling,[6] (491) striking (or) hitting the dried-up earth, tearing (or) ripping, breaking (or) smashing,[7]

---

[1] Or *nwʾ* followed by a punctuation point which is not circled in red ink (cf. p. 53 n. 76).

[2] The conjunction *cw* 'if' is finally reached in line 501.

[3] Henning, followed by *GMS* §855, treated the expression *ptmwγṭyy δʾr* as a rare type of present perfect (past participle + auxiliary 'to have'), but it is also possible that *δʾr* here has the meaning 'to wear', a sense which is well established (see Sims-Williams 1985, 106; 2016, 67).

[4] The passage beginning with *pδyy* 'on foot' has an interesting parallel in the Avesta: 'If the Mazda-worshippers, walking or running, riding or driving, should come upon a corpse in running water ...' (*Vendidad* 6.26).

[5] Here begins a long series of verbal nouns (often described as infinitives or, if they end in *-ty*, as past participles), usually in pairs which are either opposites or near-synonyms. Many pairs consist of two words from the same root (etymological hendiadys, on which see Yoshida 2019, 141–2).

[6] Neither *nwʾy* nor *nwʾ* (cf. n. 1 above) is easily compatible with Christian Sogd. *wynʾw* 'to linger' (Sims-Williams 2014, 122), although the meaning of this verb fits the context perfectly.

[7] On the words *ʾnšysṭyy pṭšysṭyy*, not recognized by Henning, see *DMT* III/2, 13a and 158a.

M801a (III 53) fol. B/v

P. 32 (BBB 494–511)

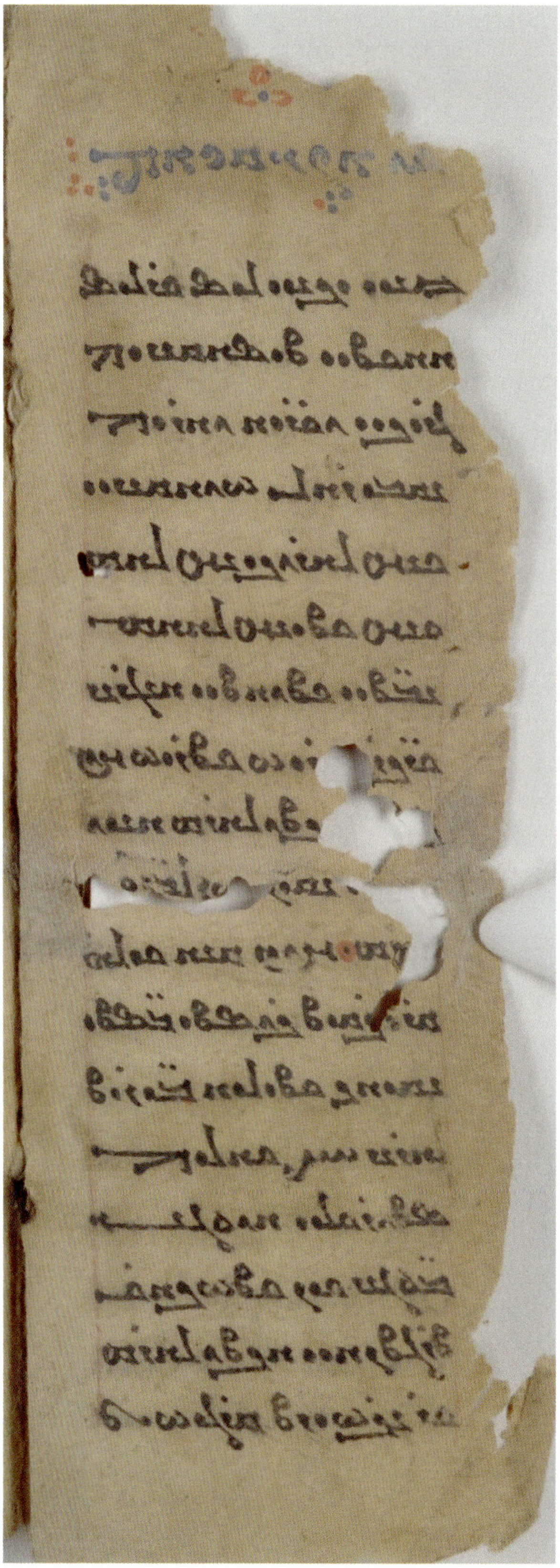

Photograph (III 53_31) reproduced by permission

M801a (III 53) fol. B/v

P. 32 (BBB 494–511)

hdl. 32–33/ {*blue*} pw ’zrmy’ẖ | cxš’pδ
‘The commandment Non-injury’

hdl. 32/ pw ’zrmy’ẖ

494 1/ qnyy yknyy δys prδys
495 2/ ’’pṭyy ṭys’mndyẖ
496 3/ γrykyy wfry’ w’ryẖ
497 4/ nmby r’δ šw’mndyy
498 5/ pnc δ’rwkync δ’m
499 6/ pnc pṭync δ’’m
500 7/ nβṭyy pṭw’ṭyy ’ngrnd
501 8/ frkr[nd z]ryš pṭryš cw
502 9/ (x)[w](ṭ)[yy ’]kṭwδ’rm ’nyw
503 10/ [’’δ](y)[8] nmyz[y](š)n δβ(r)ṭ[ṭ][9]
504 11/ [δ](’)rm[10] ° cww mn’ pyδ’r
505 12/ mr(ṭ)xmyṭ xwsṭy βsṭy
506 13/ nmy’k pṭyδy’ βyrṭ
507 14/ δ’rnd IIII p’δyẖ
508 15/ sṭwrpδyy ’wjγnd
509 16/ βjγnd pyz pṭšk’f
510 17/ ṭrγṭz’yy ’kṭwδ’rm
511 18/ pr nxšyrṭ mrγyšṭ

digging (or) excavating, building (or) constructing, (495) going into water, travelling[11] in mud, snow, rain (or) dew, cutting (or) chopping, tearing (or) ripping the five (types of) vegetable creation (or) the five (types of) fleshly creation, (be they) moist or dry —if (502) I have done (such things) [myself] or have provoked [anyone] else (to do them); if people (have been) beaten (or) bound on my account (506) (or) have suffered scorn (or) contempt; (if) I have oppressed four-footed animals (by) dismounting (or) mounting, (by) beating or hitting (them); (511) (if) I have planned evil against wild animals, birds,

---

[8] Henning restored *[’’δyẖ]*, describing it as ‘uncertain’, but there seems to be room only for *[’’δ](y)*. One might expect to see the top of *δ*, but there is a lacuna at just this point, as one can see more clearly from the photo in Weber 2000, Pl. 99.

[9] Restored thus in *GMS* §879 n. 1.

[10] Thus Henning. The edge of the paper is now folded over so that only *[δ’](r)m* can be seen.

[11] *r’δ šw-* ‘to travel’, lit. ‘to go (one’s) way’, is a fixed expression (*DMT* III/2, 166a).

M801a (III 53) fol. A/r

P. 33 (BBB 512–529)

Photograph (III 53_30) reproduced by permission
© Staatliche Museen zu Berlin, Museum für Asiatische Kunst / Lina Wällstedt

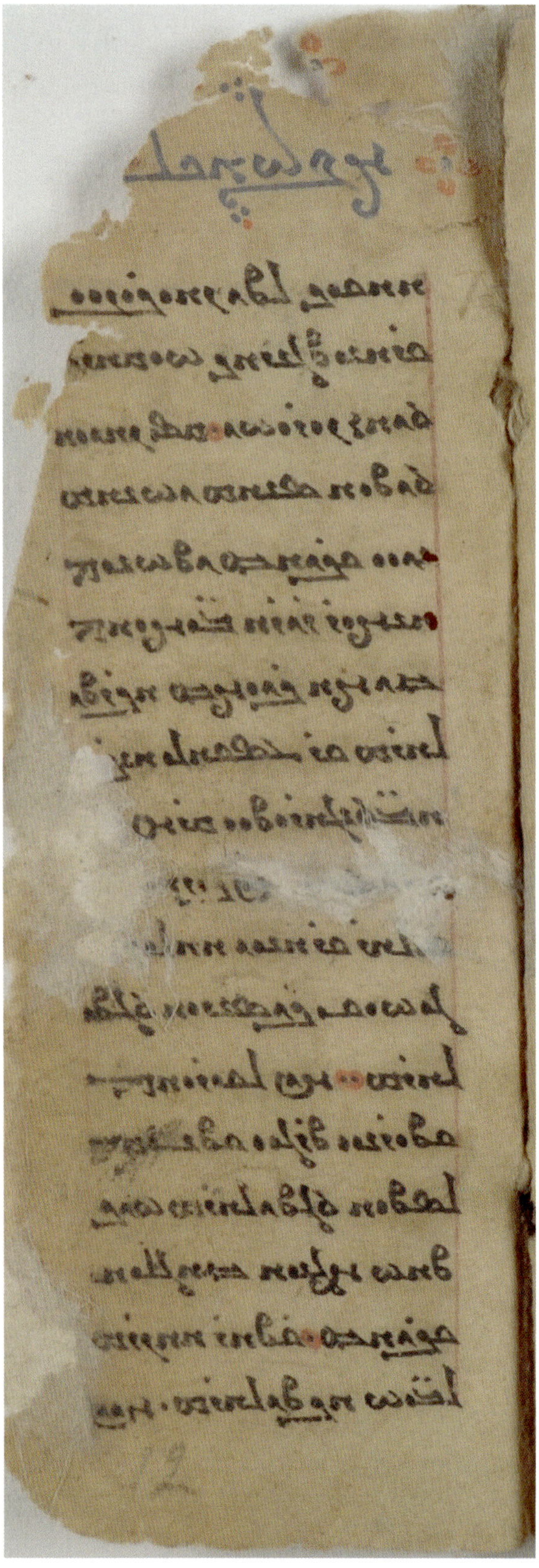

M801a (III 53) fol. A/r

P. 33 (BBB 512–529)

hdl. 32–33/ {*blue*} pw ʾzrmyʾẖ | cxšʾpδ
'The commandment Non-injury'

hdl. 33/ cxšʾpδ

512 1/ ʾʾpyk δṭw zʾyxyzyy	creatures of the water or worms[15] that
513 2/ prʾnyṭ γndʾk šymʾrw(w)[12]	crawl on the earth, (or) have destroyed
514 3/ jwʾn zyryšw ◦ ms zʾwyʾ	(their) life; also (if), (while) filter-
515 4/ jwṭyʾ snʾm wšnʾm	ing(?) (or) chewing(?),[16] bathing (or)
516 5/ (n)wyy pxwʾq wṭšnyẖ	washing, have opened my mouth (for)
517 6/ ʾncyr rwrʾ βycyʾẖ	a new piece or an old (one), a fig, a
518 7/ qwcʾ xwycq ʾkrṭw	remedy (or) a medicine; (519) (if I
519 8/ δʾrm pr ʿspʾδy ʾnx[wnc]	have taken pleasure in) an army's
520 9/ ʾβjngʾryṭyy mrc [ʾty]	bat[tles], (in) the death [and] destruc-
521 10/ (q)ṭ(sndy) ◦ c(w) (xyrʾ)[qyʾ][13]	tion(?) of sinners, if through stupid-
522 11/ (py)δʾr pr ʾnyw ʾʾδy(ẖ)[14]	ity(?) I have taken pleasure in another
523 12/ γyšyp xwsndyʾ jγṭw	person's misfortune; (524) if for the
524 13/ δʾrm ◦◦ cw δpyryʾẖ	sake of[17] writing I have held in my
525 14/ pṭyrnyy ṭrγyy pṭn(ym)	hand a sharp implement,[18] a pen, a
526 15/ δsṭyʾ jγṭwδʾrm šwk	(writing) tablet(?),[19] a piece of silk
527 16/ ṭʾš cγnyʾ qʾγδyʾ	(or) paper, (and) have (thereby)
528 17/ pxwʾq ◦ fṭʾr ʾʾzrm	caused much pain (and) injury; if
529 18/ δβyš ʾkṭwδʾrm ◦ cww	

[12] The end of the word can be seen more clearly in Weber 2000, Pl. 99.

[13] Although **xyrʾqyʾ* 'stupidity' is not otherwise attested, it is a regular and expected formation from *xyry* 'stupid'. Henning restored *(xwrʾ)[ṭyʾ]*, supposedly meaning 'arrogance', but see *DMT* III/2, 221b.—Little can now be seen at the beginning of this line; the reading given is Henning's.

[14] Part of the final *ẖ* can be seen in Weber 2000, Pl. 99.

[15] Contra Henning, both *prʾny* 'insect, worm' and *βyc* 'physician' (whence *βycyʾẖ* 'medicine' in line 517) are now recognized as Indian loanwords: see Sims-Williams 1983, 141.

[16] Neither *zʾwyʾ* 'filtering'(?) nor *jwṭyʾ* 'chewing'(?) is attested elsewhere. The meanings given are proposed in *DMT* III/2, 231b and 94a respectively, largely on etymological grounds.

[17] For *pṭyrnyy* 'because of, for the sake of' (not 'hostile, opposing') see Sundermann 1975, 84 n. 139, and Sims-Williams 1985, 98.

[18] For *pṭnym* 'gear, implement' see Sims-Williams 1985, 179. In the similar passage M133, Rii, 30–33 (ed. Sundermann 1992, 128) one may perhaps translate: 'She placed in his hands two kinds of cruel, sharp implements'. Gershevitch 1962, 79–80, translated *ṭrγyy pṭnym* 'sharply inclined'.

[19] The noun *ṭʾš* 'tablet' (thus Henning) occurs only here. Cf. perhaps the verb *tʾš* 'to hew (wood)'.

M801a (III 53) fol. A/v

P. 34 (BBB 530–547)

Photograph (III 53) reproduced by permission
© Staatliche Museen zu Berlin, Museum für Asiatische Kunst / Lina Wällstedt

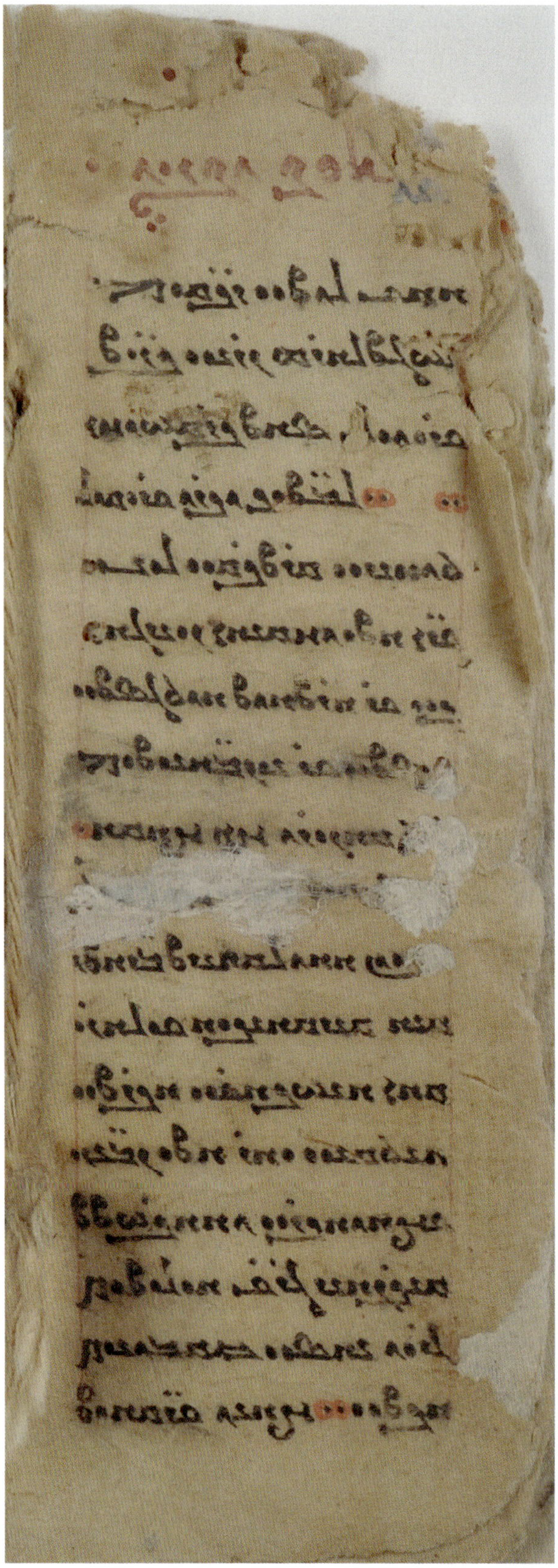

M801a (III 53) fol. A/v

P. 34 (BBB 530–547)

hdl. 34–35/ {*violet*} [δβ]tyk wkrw | pw ʾzrmyʾh̲
‘The second part (of the commandment) Non-injury’

hdl. 34/ [δβ]tyk[20] wkrw

530 1/ ʾʾp δwṭyy rxmyh̲
531 2/ (p)šγṭδʾrm zrnyy xrṭ
532 3/ prywyδ sʾṭ krmšwhn
533 4/ °° °° δβṭyk wkrw prymyδ
534 5/ jwʾndyy mrṭxmyy δyny(y)
535 6/ frn ʾṭy whmnʾn zyndgʾ(n)
536 7/ kyy pr ʾrṭʾwṭ ʾwjγsṭyy
537 8/ (ʾ)sṭyy pr nyzβʾnyṭyh̲
538 9/ (r)[y](j) mʾzyrw cn cʾmʾ °
539 10/ [ ](nyy wrcyʾ ʾkt)[y][21]
540 11/ [°]c(w)w ʾʾwδmʾndṭ βrʾṭ[22]
541 12/ mnʾ mndmʾnkyʾ pyδʾr
542 13/ mʾn ʾnškʾfyy ʾkrṭyy
543 14/ ʾnjmnyy yʾr ʾṭy zβnd
544 15/ pcʾwʾkryy wʾʾxšṭṭ
545 16/ mnxzʾnd γrf ʾyδyṭyh̲
546 17/ (γ)ryw nʾsyy qmbwnyh̲
547 18/ ʾkṭyy °° cʾnw frmʾyṭ

I have poured filth[23] into a water jug,[24] (so that the water) went to waste: for all that (I ask) absolution! (533) The second part (of the commandment Non-injury), concerning the ‘Glory of the Religion’ of the living man and the Living Wahmans, who have settled upon the elect: (if) I have harmed (them) through the desire of the passions (so that) ... was not satisfied(?)[25] with me; (540) if the brothers who live in the same house[26] have had a difference of opinion because of my thoughtlessness, (so that) quarrels and strife[27] arose in the community, (and) provocative words, (whereby) many people (546) have suffered (spiritual) diminution which corrupts the soul[28]—as (Mani) says:

---

[20] The first two letters, apparently still visible to Henning, are now broken off.

[21] Hardly anything can be seen in this line. Henning’s reading, given here, is characterized by him as ‘very uncertain’.

[22] + line-filler? Possibly an incomplete(?) *r*, the scribe having begun to write the pl. *βrʾṭrṭ*.

[23] For *rxmyh̲* ‘filth’ (not ‘remnant’) see Yoshida 1998, 171.

[24] The interpretation of *δwṭyy* as ‘jug’ is just Henning’s guess (with some etymological support).

[25] For *wrcyʾ* ‘soothed, calm, etc.’ (not ‘strengthened’) see Gershevitch 1946, 145 n. 1. However, the reading is uncertain.

[26] Contra Henning, *ʾʾwδmʾndṭ* ‘cohabiting’ is surely a pl. form (*DMT* III/2, 34a). The construction of the sentence is unclear, however.

[27] For *zβnd* ‘quarrel, strife’ (rather than ‘neighbour’) see Henning 1945, 470 with n. 5.

[28] On *γryw-nʾsyy* ‘soul-corrupting’ see *DMT* III/2, 89a.

M801a (III 53) fol. C/r

P. 35 (BBB 548–565)

Photograph (III 53_27) reproduced by permission
© Staatliche Museen zu Berlin, Museum für Asiatische Kunst / Lina Wällstedt

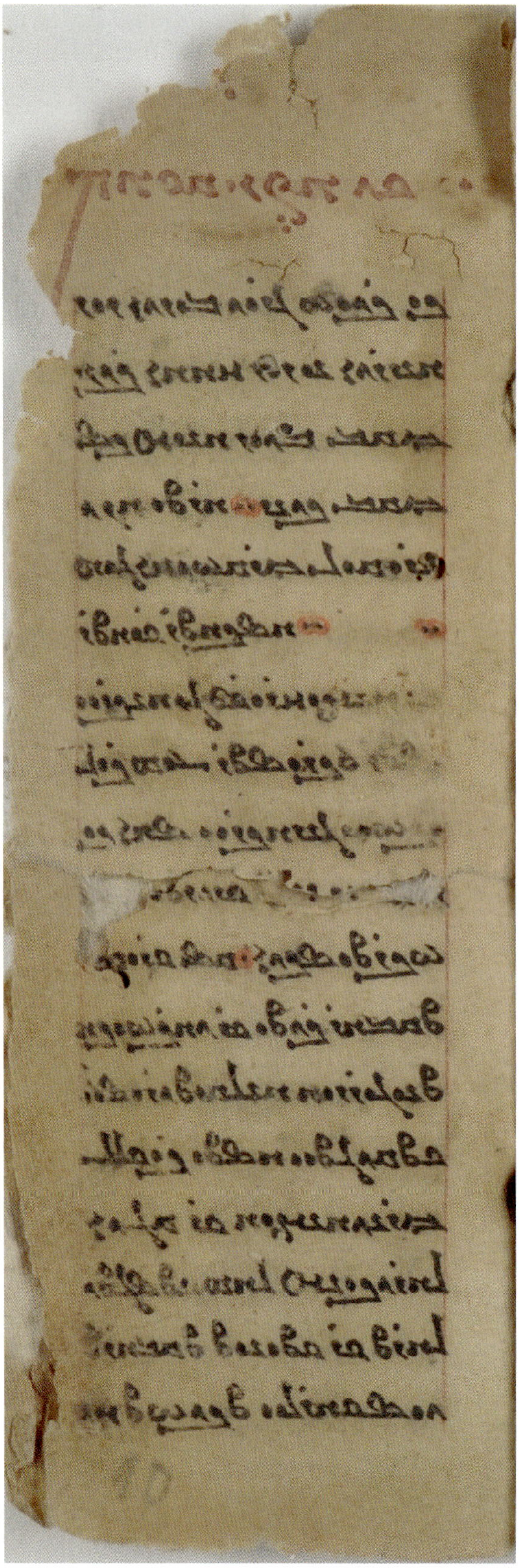

M801a (III 53) fol. C/r

P. 35 (BBB 548–565)

hdl. 34–35/ {*violet*} [δβ]tyk wkrw | pw ʾzrmyʾẖ
‘The second part (of the commandment) Non-injury’

hdl. 35/ pw ʾzrmyʾẖ

548 1/ {MP} ky xwyš gryw by(r)wn dyd
549 2/ ʾndrwn ny dyd hʾʾn xwd
550 3/ qmb bwyd ʾnyc ks
551 4/ qmb kwnd °° {Sogd.} ʾrṭy ʾzw
552 5/ (p)rymyδ qrmšwhn γwʾn[29]
553 6/ °° °° ʾskʾṭr fyʾṭr
554 7/ (pr dy)ncyhryfṭ γwʾnkryy
555 8/ (sṭr) jkrysṭr ʿym xyδ
556 9/ (yk)šyy γndʾkryy sʾn ky
557 10/ (r)[ʾmʾn](d zwrṭ) prwrṭ(y)[y mnʾ]
558 11/ škrṭyskwn ° ms pry(m)[yδ]
559 12/ ṭmbʾr xwṭy pr wʾxšykʾ[30]
560 13/ ṭnygyrdyʾ ʾnδmyṭ wryst(y)
561 14/ pṭmwγṭyy ʾsṭy xypδδ
562 15/ qrnwʾncyʾ pr mγwn
563 16/ δʾrwkync δʾm (p)ṭsγṭw
564 17/ δʾrṭ pr pṭynyṭ ṭmbʾr(ṭ)
565 18/ wyspʾrδyy ṭkwšṭ (cw)

{MP} ‘He who has seen himself outside (but) has not seen himself inside, he becomes less himself and diminishes others’—{Sogd.} for this I (ask) absolution, (forgiveness of) sins! (553) Furthermore, I am very sinful (and) very harmful[31] in respect of (the commandment) Purity.[32] That *yakṣa*, the maleficent enemy, who (557) constantly leads[33] [me] to (and) fro—he himself is clothed with this body, spiritually and physically mixing (himself) with (its) limbs, (and) has deployed his arts in the whole vegetable creation (and) in (all) fleshly bodies (and) (565) is looking everywhere for what

---

[29] Abbreviation (rather than scribal error as suggested in *DMT* III/2, 89b) for *qrmšwhn γwʾnwʾcyy pṭškwyʾm* ‘I ask absolution, forgiveness of sins’, which is easily understood from the context. Cf. above, p. 19 n. 31, for the omission of words at the end of a standard closing formula.

[30] Mistake for *wʾxšykyʾ* (*DMT* III/2, 199b)? For a similar case see below, p. 171 n. 25.

[31] On *jkrysṭr* ‘very harmful’ see *DMT* III/2, 92a.

[32] Lit. ‘behaviour according to the religion’. Cf. p. 73 n. 36.

[33] Or ‘pursues’.

M801a (III 53) fol. C/v

P. 36 (BBB 566–583)

Photograph (III 53_28) reproduced by permission
© Staatliche Museen zu Berlin, Museum für Asiatische Kunst / Lina Wällstedt

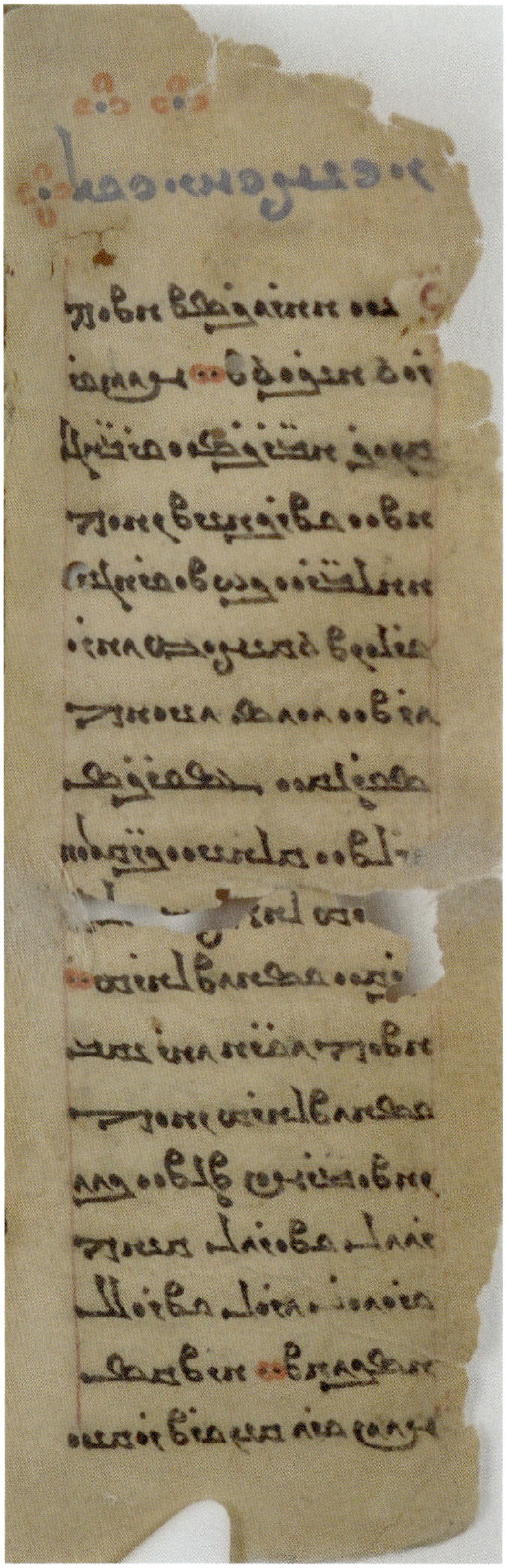

M801a (III 53) fol. C/v

P. 36 (BBB 566–583)

hdl. 36[–?]/ {*blue*} dyncyhryft | [cxš'pδ]
'[The commandment] Purity'

hdl. 36/ dyncyhryft

566 1/ wynyy[34] ''rwxsṭ 'ṭyh̲
567 2/ ryj 'nxyjṭ °° cww pr
568 3/ mzyx 'βrxsyy pr β'γt
569 4/ 'ṭyy pṭrk'ndṭ z'yh̲
570 5/ ''δβryy kšṭy pr'gn(d)[y]
571 6/ prδyzṭ jmncyq w'r
572 7/ wrṭyy wyws wndy'h̲
573 8/ sprγmyy ʿsprxs
574 9/ (w)rδṭyy mδ'ndyy xrmty'
575 10/ [ ](y)m δ'n c[ ](q)[ ].δ[y](h̲)
576 11/ [ṭ]xmyy[35] ps'wṭδ'rm °°
577 12/ 'ṭyh̲ wfr' w'r nmb
578 13/ ps'wṭδ'rm z'yh̲
579 14 / z'ṭyβrcy ṭγṭyy kww
580 15/ rwwδ pṭyrwδ mn'h̲
581 16/ prywyδ wryδ pṭryδδ
582 17/ 'skw'ṭ °° 'rṭms
583 18/ cww prw mnzprṭ rymnyy
{*at least one folio missing*}

may excite its lusts and desires. If, in great wantonness,[36] in gardens and smallholdings, planting (or) sowing the fertile[37] earth, (571) (giving) timely rainwater[38] to the orchards, on a spring morning I have touched the blossoms (and) buds of the trees, roses, medicinal herbs(?), dates(?),[39] ... grain ... (or) seeds; (577) and if I have touched snow, rain or dew, (so that) it entered the womb of the earth,[40] where (a plant) was growing (or) sprouting, (so that) I thereby incurred mixture and mingling; moreover, (583) if with impure, filthy [thoughts] ...[41]

{*at least one folio missing*}

---

[34] The first two letters, now hidden by a fold in the paper, can be seen in Weber 2000, Pl. 99.

[35] For the restoration *[ṭ]xmyy* 'seed' (Henning: *[r]xmyy*) see *DMT* III/2, 195a.

[36] *'βrxsyy*, lit. 'lust, lasciviousness', seems to be used as the converse of *dyncyhryft* 'purity', lit. 'religious behaviour'. Cf. above, p. 71 n. 32. The passage beginning here has a parallel in Text a below, where many of the same phrases occur, though in a different order.

[37] For *''δβryy* 'fertile' or 'cornfield', lit. 'grain-bearing' (not 'irgendwelche Frucht habend'), see Benveniste 1940, 223; Sims-Williams 1986, 414-15.

[38] Possibly *w'r* here is not the common word 'rain' but a verbal noun from *w'r* 'to rain, to water'.

[39] On *mδ'ndyy* 'medicinal herbs' and *xrmty'* 'dates', both quite uncertain, see *DMT* III/2, 111a and 216b.

[40] For the interpretation of this phrase see *GMS* §864 n. 1.

[41] What is meant here may be deduced from the continuation of Text a (cf. n. 36 above), which refers to 'male and female bodies'.

M801a (III 53) fol. L/r

P. 37 (BBB 584–588)

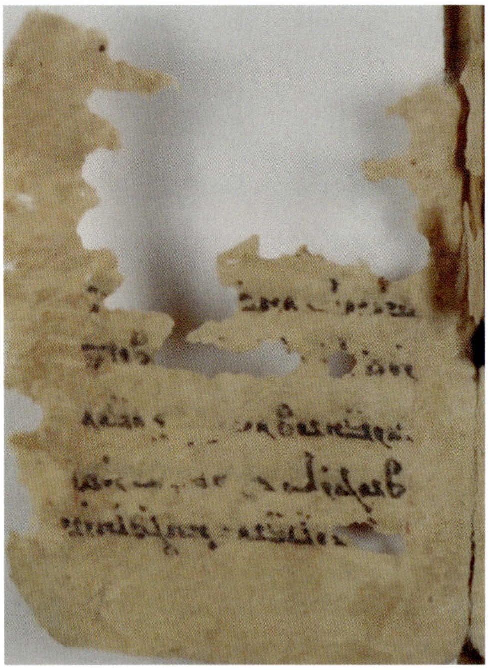

Photograph (III 53_13) reproduced by permission

M801a (III 53) fol. L/v

P. 38 (BBB 589–593)

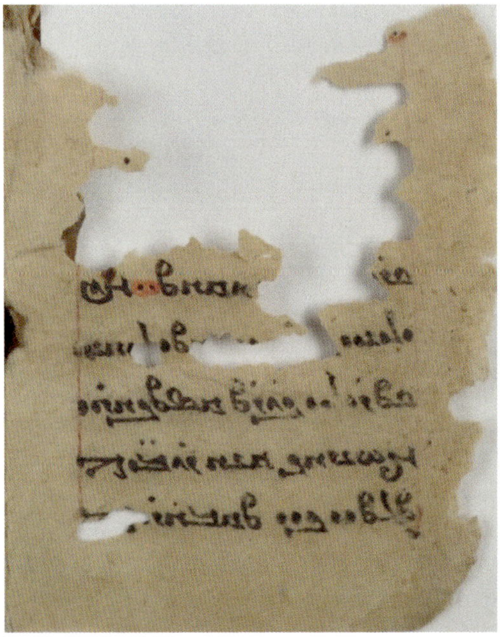

Photograph (III 53_15) reproduced by permission

M801a (III 53) fol. L/r

P. 37 (BBB 584–588)

{*headline and thirteen lines torn off*}	{*headline and thirteen lines torn off*}
584 14/ pr(yw)yδ w'f [znng'](n)	... though this so [manifold] desire ...
585 15/ ryj (δ....)[ ].ṭyẖ	the passions have brought both spiritual
586 16/ (n)yzβ'nyṭ w('x)[šy](k) wβyw	and physical diminution, impurity [and]
587 17/ ṭnygyrδ (qmb)[w](ny)r(y)m	harm(?) ...[43]
588 18/ ['](ṭ)[y](n)yδβn(wk[42])''γṭδ'rnd	

M801a (III 53) fol. L/v

P. 38 (BBB 589–593)

{*headline and thirteen lines torn off*}	{*headline and thirteen lines torn off*}
589 14/ pr.[ ]wm'ṭ °° cw	... was ... If ...[45] mixed food (or)
590 15/ yδynyy (k)[ ](')ṭy δw)'n(yy)[44]	intoxicating drinks have entered my mouth,[46] which the body ...
591 16/ pṭryδ(y)y xwrṭ msṭk'ryy	
592 17/ cšnd'k mn' rwβyẖ	
593 18/ ṭγṭyy kyy ṭmb'r(y)ẖ	
{*at least one folio missing*}	{*at least one folio missing*}

[42] As Henning points out, the word-division is unclear. Neither *nyδβnwk* nor *δβnwk* is attested elsewhere.

[43] A partial parallel to these lines is found in Text b below, lines 20–23.

[44] Assuming word-division before the *δ*, which is not certain, this seems the most likely reading. Henning suggested that the second letter should be *w*, *z* or *y*, and preferred to read the end of the word as °*'n(dy)* or °*'n(zy)*.

[45] As Henning suggests, *yδynyy* may be an adjective derived from the noun *yδ-* (in Text b, 36), but the meaning of this word is unknown; *(δw)'n(yy)*, however it is to be read, is also unknown.

[46] For *rwβ* 'mouth' (rather than 'stomach') see Benveniste 1940, 203.

M801a (III 53) fol. J/r

P. 39 (BBB 594–611)

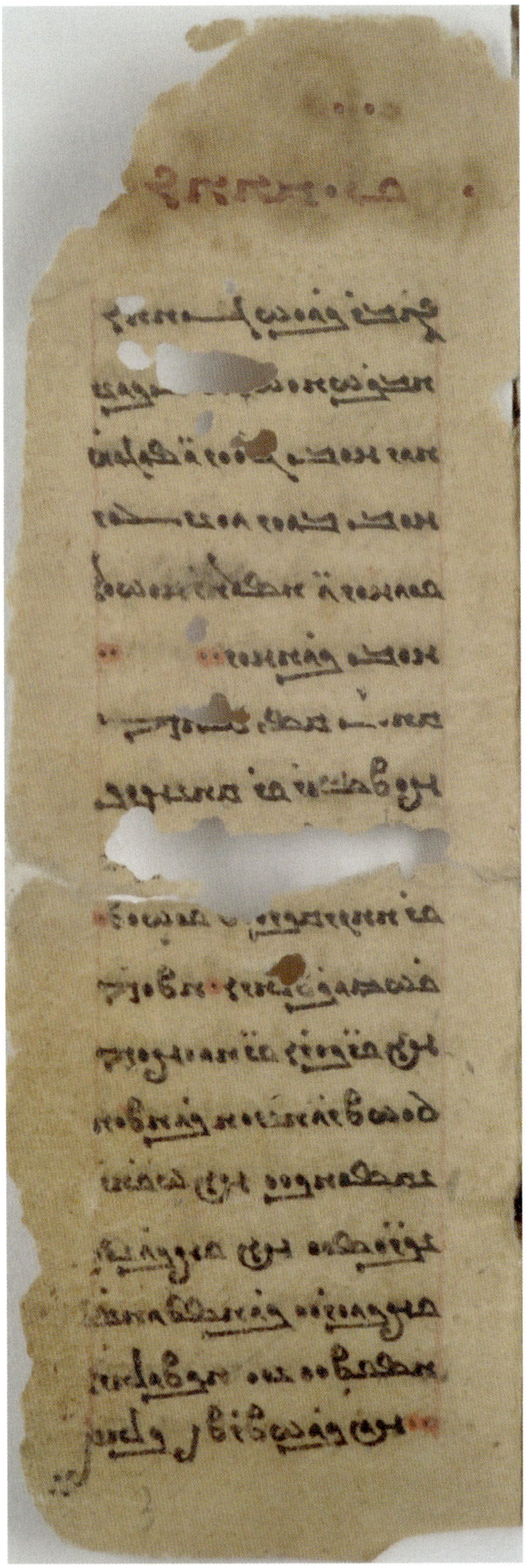

Photograph (III 53_17) reproduced by permission

M801a (III 53) fol. J/r

P. 39 (BBB 594–611)

hdl. [?–]39/ {*violet*} [...] |frm’’n
‘[...] command’

hdl. 39/ frm’’n

594 1/ {MP} ’br xwyš gy’’n
595 2/ ’bxš’y(šn h)[y](b) kwnd
596 3/ ’wd hyb g(r)yyd ẅ swgw’r
597 4/ hyb bwyd wyndʿyd
598 5/ pywhyd ẅ ’st’r hyštn
599 6/ hyb xw’hyd ◦◦ ◦◦
600 7/ {Sogd.} m’yδ ms (mn)’ẖ
601 8/ cyṭs’r pr m’nc(y)k
602 9/ [ ]
603 10/ pr ’’z(r)mk(ryyṭ) pyšyṭ ◦
604 11/ fšqwxṭδ’(r)n ◦ ’ṭyẖ
605 12/ cn frkyrn fr’wycyẖ
606 13/ jyšṭrw’ndy’ xw’ṭy’
607 14/ nmsy’kyy cn šf’r
608 15/ nxrysyy cn pcxwny(y)
609 16/ pckwyryy xw’sṭw’n(fṭ)[47]
610 17/ ’spṭyy nyy ’kṭwδ’r(n)
611 18/ ◦◦ cw xwšṭrṭ I kδ’m

{MP} ‘... on his own soul shall he have pity and he shall weep and mourn, beg and pray and ask for the forgiveness of sins’. (600) {Sogd.} So too, within me in (my) mental ... [and] in (my) injurious limbs, (if) I should have stumbled[48] and (if), (605) from negligence, forgetfulness, malice, weakness (or) compliance,[49] (or) from shame (or) reproach, (or) from fear of censure, I should not have made confession in full; (611) if (my) superiors

---

[47] Abbreviated for *xw’sṭw’nyfṭ* because of lack of space at the end of the line. So too in Text c below, line 22.

[48] Although *fšqwxṭδ’rn* is formally a transitive preterite, it seems that the verb is probably used intransitively, like Christian Sogd. *fšqwx-* ‘to stumble’ (Sims-Williams 2016, 81).

[49] Many translations have been suggested for *nmsy’k* (*GMS* §828 n. 1; Morano 1982, 26; Yoshida 2000, 76). The advantage of ‘compliance’ is that it fits both passages where *nmsy’k* is treated as a virtue (Yoshida 2000, 75, col. iii, line 8) and those where it regarded as as a failing (as here).

M801a (III 53) fol. J/v

P. 40 (BBB 612–629)

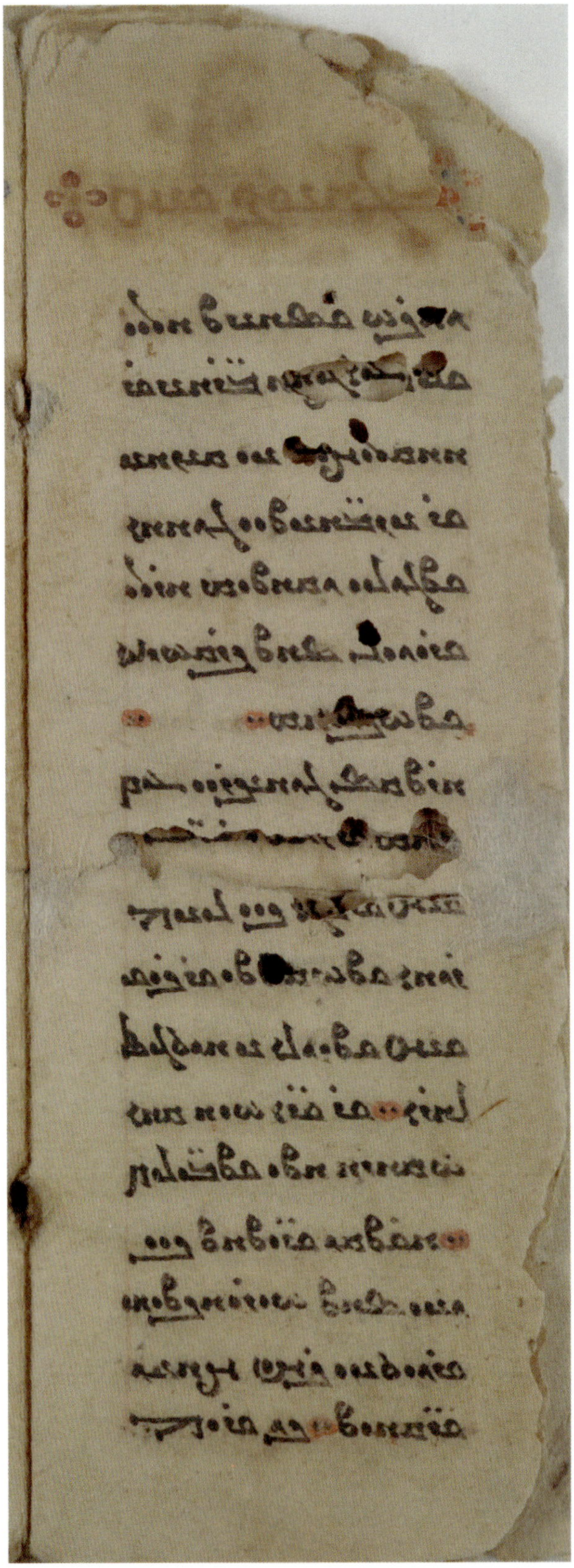

Photograph (III 53_32) reproduced by permission

M801a (III 53) fol. J/v

P. 40 (BBB 612–629)

hdl. 40–41/ {*green*} βγ’nyk pnc | prβγn
‘The five divine gifts’

hdl. 40/ βγ’nyk pnc

612 1/ w(’)xš ps’ndṭ ’tyy
613 2/ p(δyβ)[’](rc)[y]’[50] βr’nd pr
614 3/ ’’mtyc(y)[’] nyy mnz’nw
615 4/ pr nyzβ’nyṭyy γw’’n
616 5/ pṭγwδyy wm’ṭym ’rty
617 6/ prywyδ s’ṭ krmšwhn
618 7/ pṭšk[wy](’)m °° °°
619 8/ ’rṭms γw’nkryy ‘ym
620 9/ [ ]
621 10/ pnc p(rβ)γn kyy δynyẖ
622 11/ rw’n pṭšm[y](r)ṭy pr xyp[51]
623 12/ pnc pṭywδn ny ’wjγyst
624 13/ δ’rn °° pr frn šy’ m’n
625 14/ šm’(r)’ ’ṭy pṭβyδyẖ
626 15/ °° ’fṭmw fryṭ’ṭ kyy
627 16/ wnyy s’ṭ šyry’kṭy’y[52]
628 17/ prwyjnyy xcy c’nw
629 18/ frm’yṭ °° {MP} kw pryẖ

asked about any matter and made enquiries (and) I did not confess[53] truthfully, (but) was concealing (something) because of a sin of the passions: (617) for all that I ask absolution!

Moreover, I am a sinner [if ...] (621) I did not allow the five gifts,[54] which are considered the soul of the religion, to settle upon the five parts (of my soul), that is, upon ‘glory’, remembrance, mind, thought and perception. (625) Firstly love, which is the nurturer of all righteousness, as (Mani) teaches: {MP} ‘Where love

---

[50] Thus Henning 1946a, 732.

[51] Sic. Late form of *xypδ* (Sundermann 1997, 110 n. 51), used here to save space. Henning, who did not know this form, states that the word looks like *xypy*, but the apparent *y* is merely the regular thickening of the horizontal stroke at the end of a final *p*.

[52] To be read as a single word, see Sims-Williams 1985, 133 n. 117.

[53] The use of the negated imperfect form *nyy mnz’nw* ‘I did not confess’ is unusual if not incorrect, see Sims-Williams 1996, 179. Another example of the same irregularity is found in line 757: *nyy šym’rw* ‘I did not think’ (contrasting with the regular negated historic present *nyy ... pṭfr’wṭ kwn’m* ‘I was not able to remember’ in the immediately preceding lines).

[54] The ‘five gifts’ or cardinal virtues (see above, p. xii n. 23) are enumerated, and contrasted with the corresponding vices, in lines 631–8.

M801a (III 53) fol. F/r

P. 41 (BBB 630–647)

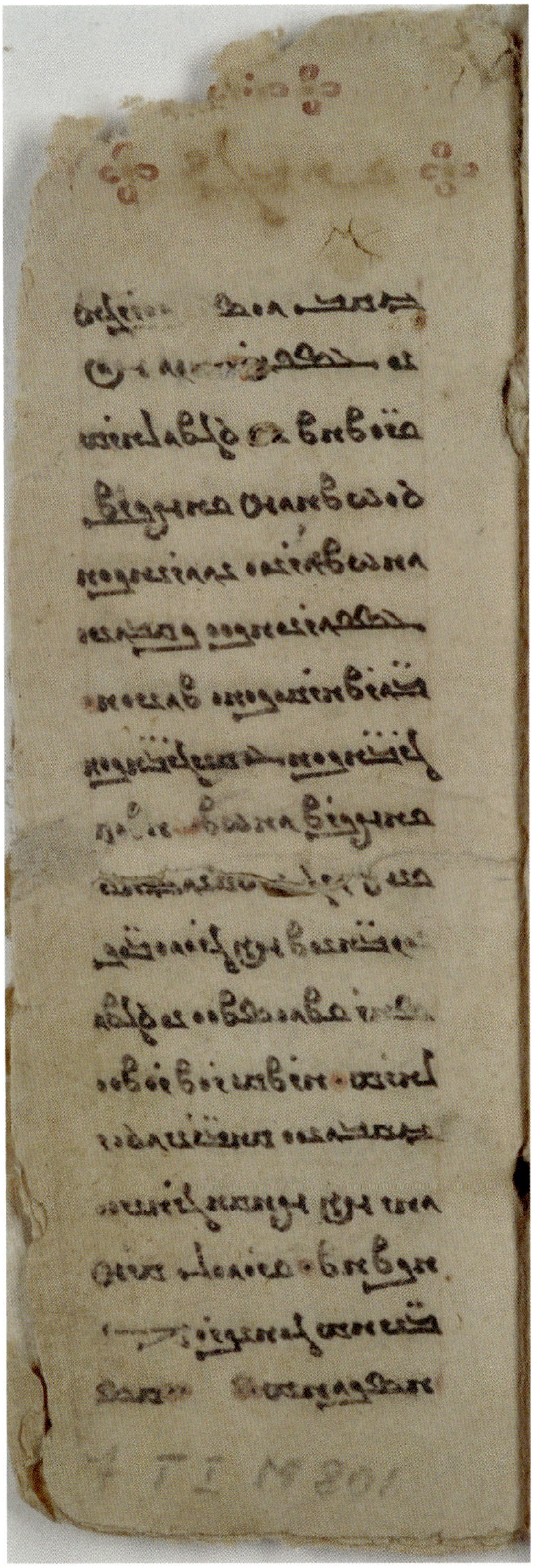

Photograph (III 53_23) reproduced by permission

M801a (III 53) fol. F/r

P. 41 (BBB 630–647)

hdl. 40–41/ {*green*} βγʾnyk pnc | prβγn
'The five divine gifts'

hdl. 41/ prβγn

630 1/ qmb wys[p](k)yrdgʾn
631 2/ ny ʿsp(wr) (°) {Sogd.} (ʾ)zw cw
632 3/ frytʾṭ (n)[y] jγṭwδʾrm
633 4/ jyšṭʾwc pʾckrṭ
634 5/ wʾšṭ wrnyy nwwrnʾkyʾ
635 6/ ʿspwrnyʾkyy kmbwnyy
636 7/ βwrṭʾrmykyʾy ṭwndyʾ °
637 8/ γrβʾky^{x}y mndγrβʾkyʾ
638 9/ pʾckrṭ wʾšṭ °° ʾṭyẖ
639 10/ pnc (z)ng[ʾ](n š)mnwqʾ(ny)
640 11/ nyzβʾnyṭ cn γrywy βyk
641 12/ sʾr pṭwysṭyy ny jγṭw
642 13/ δʾrm ° ʾrṭmy ryṭ ryṭyy
643 14/ qmbwnyy mʾβrnd wjyd
644 15/ wʾd cn cʾmʾ γrʾndyy
645 16/ ʾkṭʾṭ ° prywyδ mrc
646 17/ βndʾm γwʾnkryẖ
647 18/ ʾskwʾm °° °° ms

(630) is little, all deeds (are) imperfect'.[55] {Sogd.} If I have not had love, (if) hatred has stood in (its) place, unbelief (in place of) faith, (635) (spiritual) diminution (in place of) perfection, violence (in place of) patience, (if) unwisdom has stood in place of wisdom, and (639) (if) I have not kept the fivefold diabolical passions turned away from myself, and in many respects they have brought me (spiritual) diminution; (if) the Holy (644) Spirit should have become angry with me: for that I am a sinner under sentence[56] of death.

Moreover,

[55] Henning draws attention to the similarity between this quotation from a work of Mani's and Paul's First Letter to the Corinthians, chapter 13.

[56] On *βndʾm* 'penalty, sentence', a Bactrian loanword, see Sims-Williams 2007, 184b.

M801a (III 53) fol. F/v

P. 42 (BBB 648–665)

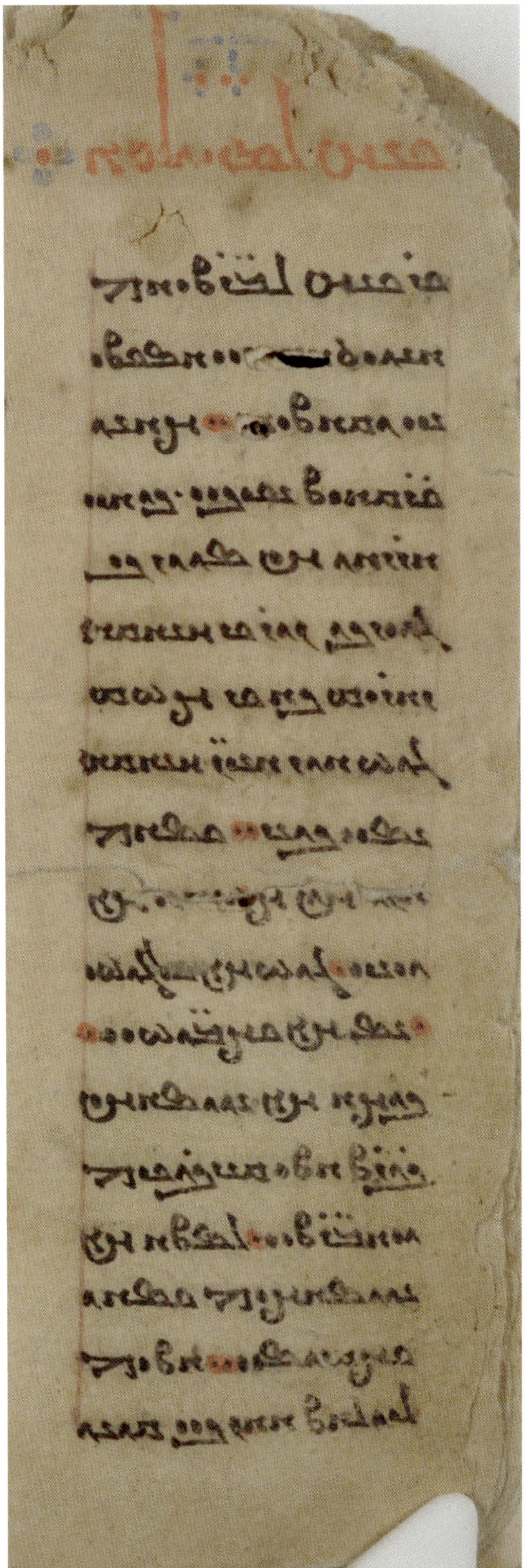

Photograph (III 53_25) reproduced by permission

M801a (III 53) fol. F/v

P. 42 (BBB 648–665)

hdl. 42–43/ {*red*} pnc δβrty’ | ’nwyj’mndy
‘The closing of the five gates’

hdl. 42/ pnc δβrty’

648 1/ pr pnc δβrṭy’ẖ
649 2/ ’njwyj(’)[mn](d)yy ’spṭy
650 3/ nyy wm’ṭy(m) °° c’nw
651 4/ frm’yṭ npykyy ° {MP} kw ’wy
652 5/ ’rd’w cy swwd ky
653 6/ gwyd kw zwr pd hn’m’n
654 7/ d’rym k’ pd cšm
655 8/ gwš ’wd ’nyž[57] hn’m’n
656 9/ nsyy kwnd °° {Sogd.} ps’ẖ
657 10/ (’zw) cw c(šmw)[58] cn
658 11/ wynyy ° γwš cn (p)tγwšy
659 12/ ° ns cn pcβwšyy °
660 13/ kwc’ cn nwws’cy
661 14/ xwrṭ ’ṭy mndxwpyẖ
662 15/ wy’βrṭyy ° δsṭ’ cn
663 16/ nwws’cyẖ ps’w
664 17/ pcm(r)wsyy °° ’ṭyẖ
665 18/ δywδ’ṭ ”z kyy mwnw

I have not been perfect in the closing of the five ‘gates’ (i.e. senses). As (Mani) (651) says in scripture: {MP} ‘Of what use is the righteous (man) who says: “I have strength in my limbs”, if he causes ruin through (his) eyes, ears and other organs?’. {Sogd.} So, (657) if I (should have kept open)[59] (my) eyes for seeing, (my) ears for hearing, (my) nose for smelling, (my) mouth for improper food and ugly (662) speech (and my) hands for improper touching and feeling, and (thus) demon-created Greed, who

[57] Pa. form in MP context.
[58] Or *c(šm)[y](y)*?
[59] The verbal phrase is finally reached in lines 676–7.

M801a (III 53) fol. E/r

P. 43 (BBB 666–683)

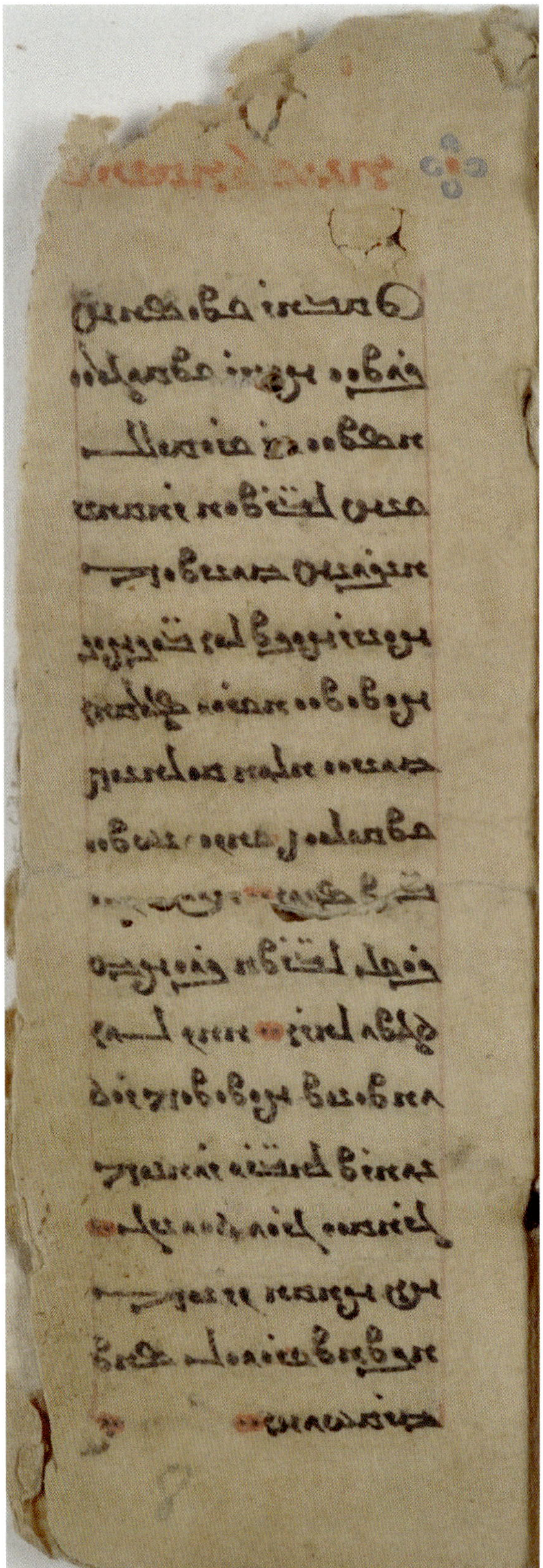

Photograph (III 53_25) reproduced by permission

M801a (III 53) fol. E/r

P. 43 (BBB 666–683)

hdl. 42–43/ {*red*} pnc δβrty’ | ’nwyj’mndy
‘The closing of the five gates’

hdl. 43/ ’nwyj’mndy

666 1/ ṭmb’r pṭys’c
667 2/ xwṭyy c(ynd)r pṭmwγtyy
668 3/ ’sṭyy (pr) prymyδδ
669 4/ pnc δβrṭy’ r’m’nd
670 5/ ’nxwnc qwndṭyẖ
671 6/ cyndrcykṭ δwn βykcyk
672 7/ cyṭyṭyy ’pryw sγtm’n
673 8/ qwndyy ’δw’ myδ’nyẖ
674 9/ pṭmyδyy I p’zyy nšṭyy
675 10/ β(w)ṭskwn ◦◦ cw(w) [’](zw)[60]
676 11/ xypδ δβrṭ’ xwycq
677 12/ jγṭw δ’rn ◦◦ ”z δwn
678 13/ w’ṭynyṭ cyṭyṭyẖ ryj
679 14/ nw’rṭ δ’βrw rw’nyẖ
680 15/ γr’myy gryw jywndg ◦◦
681 16/ cn c’m’ zrnyẖ
682 17/ ’kṭ’ṭ prywyδ s’ṭ
683 18/ qrmšwhn ◦◦ ◦◦

formed this body and is herself clothed in (it), constantly causes conflict by means of these five gates (671) (and) combines the internal (demons) with the external demons, (so that) between the two a ‘guest’[61] is destroyed every day—if I (676) should have kept my gates open, (so that) I gave Greed and the spiritual demons (their) desire (and) inclination,[62] (whereby) the treasure of the soul, the Living Self, (681) may have gone to waste through me: for all that (I ask) absolution!

---

[60] + line-filler?

[61] On *’yw-p’zy* or *I-p’zy* ‘guest’ (rather than ‘a little bit’) and the use of this term ‘as a metaphor for the light particles temporarily residing in the bodies of the Elect’ see *DMT* III/2, 48a.

[62] On the phrase *ryj nw’rṭ* ‘desire (and) inclination’ see Sims-Williams 1991, 327 n. 16.

M801a (III 53) fol. E/v

P. 44 (BBB 684–701)

Photograph (III 53_26) reproduced by permission
© Staatliche Museen zu Berlin, Museum für Asiatische Kunst / Lina Wällstedt

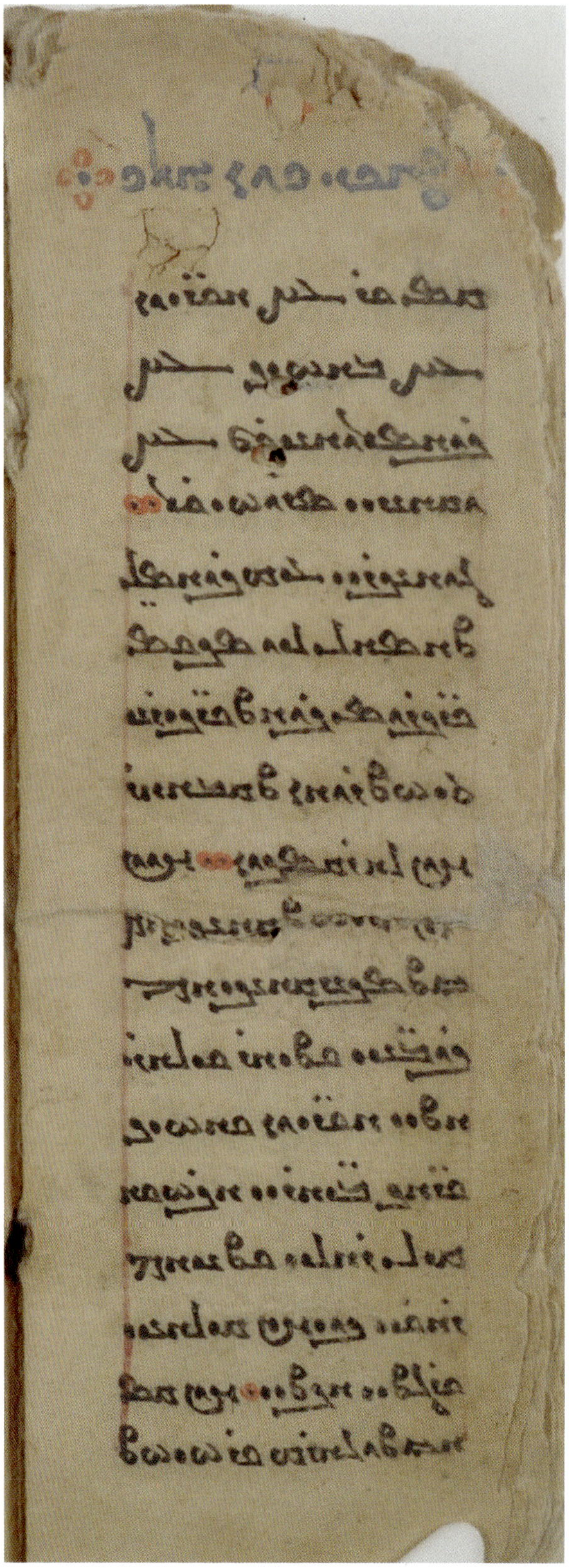

M801a (III 53) fol. E/v

P. 44 (BBB 684–701)

hdl. 44[–?]/ {*blue*} ’frwn ’ty | [b’šyk](?)
‘Prayers and [hymns](?)’

hdl. 44/ ’frywn ’ty

684 1/ ms pr VII ’frywn
685 2/ VII b’šyk VII
686 3/ xw’stw’nyfṭ VII
687 4/ wm’ndyy srwšyft °°
688 5/ γw’nkryy ‘ym xw’s<’>δ
689 6/ ṭ’s’δ δyw sk(f)s
690 7/ fr(x)rws xw’ṭ frkyrny
691 8/ jyšṭrw’n ṭmb’’r
692 9/ cw δ’rmskwn °° cww
693 10/ (cn) (jyš)ṭm’nk(y’)ẖ
694 11/ qṭskndm’nky’ẖ
695 12/ xwβnyy pṭy’r pyδ’r
696 13/ ’ṭyy ’frywn p’šyk
697 14/ fr’k βy’ryy ’xšp’
698 15/ myδ r’δyy pṭny’ẖ
699 16/ r’fyy (x)wycy myδ’nyy
700 17/ prγṭyy ’kṭyy ° cw ms
701 18/ ’qṭwδ’rm pr šyšṭ
{*one folio missing*}

Moreover, I am a sinner in respect of the seven prayers, the seven hymns, the seven confessions and the obligatory service of the seven (types of) alms.[63] (As for) the tired (and) weary, unreliable(?), obstinate(?), timid(?),[64] weak, neglectful, malicious body in which I am clad—if, (693) because of malice, destructive intention, falling asleep (or) misfortune, (it) has neglected the prayers and hymns,[65] morning or evening, night or day, on the road or in town, amidst sickness or pain; if, further, through inatt[ention][66] I have done ...

{*one folio missing*}

---

[63] On this passage see Sundermann 2005, 95–6, who interpreted *srwšyft* as the obligatory service of the hearers to the elect and referred to the ‘seven gifts’ (of the hearer to the church) mentioned in Turkish and Chinese texts. Henning took *wm’ndyy* as an adjective ‘grateful’, but *wmndṭyy* in M530, R2 (unpublished), must be a noun. The meaning ‘gift, alms’ seems to suit all contexts.

[64] A series of adjectives which occur only here. The translation is largely guesswork.

[65] Lit. ‘the prayers and hymns have been neglected (by it = by the body). As Henning suggests, it seems necessary to transpose the words *’ṭyy ’frywn p’šyk* in line 696: read **’frywn ’ṭyy p’šyk*.

[66] Hardly *šyšṭ* ‘30’ with Henning, for which Sogd. *šys* is now attested. Henning objected to restoring *šyšṭ[rw’ndṭy’]* (thus now *DMT* III/2, 189a) on the grounds that BBB uses the form *jyšṭrw’ndy’*, but the argument may be reversed: the occurrence of both forms in this MS suggests that *šyšṭrw’ndṭy’* ‘inattention’ is a different word from *jyšṭrw’ndy’* ‘malice’ (as proposed in *GMS* §451 n. 1).

M801a (III 53) fol. K/r

P. 45 (BBB 702–716)

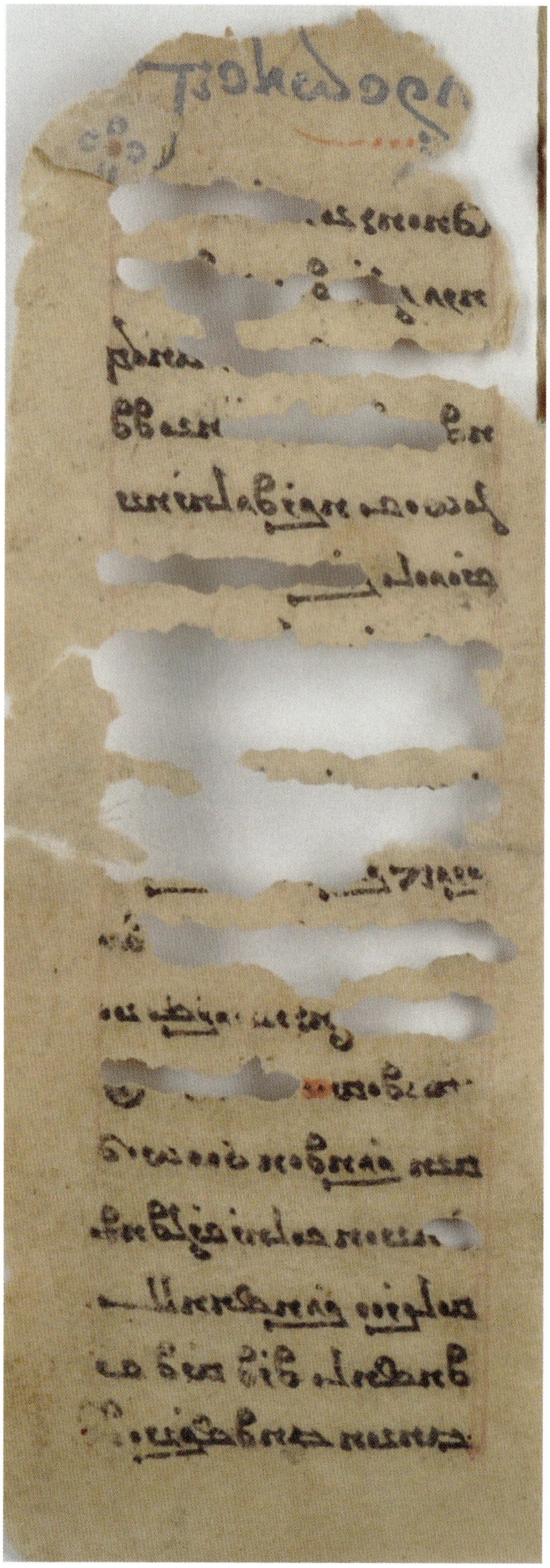

Photograph (III 53_15) reproduced by permission

M801a (III 53) fol. K/r

P. 45 (BBB 702–716)

hdl. [?–]45/ {*blue*} [...] | wzyštyh̲
'[...] zeal'

hdl. 45/ wzyštyh̲[67]

702 1/ {MP} ṭ'y'n ny .[ ]
703 2/ {Sogd.} 'zw wγ(r)[']ṭ[y](y)[ ]ṭ[ ]
704 3/ [ ](ṭ)[ny](wm)'tm[68]
705 4/ 'ṭ[y]ṭ[nyz](β)'nyṭṭ
706 5/ γyšyp 'krṭwδ'r'nd
707 6/ prywyδ (kr)[mšwhn]
{*three lines almost wholly destroyed*}
708 10/ xrwh̲x[w'n[69]](k)[ ]
709 11/ [ ]ṭ..
710 12/ [pw 'n]c'n[70] ('nd)wxsy nyy
711 13/ (w)m'ṭym °° [ ]c(n)
712 14/ mn' xw'ṭy' jyyšṭ
713 15/ (r)[w]'ndy' pyδ'r prγṭ 'ṭy
714 16/ myδkryy xw's''δδ
715 17/ ṭ's'δ ṭrṭ mrṭ pr
716 18/ q'ny' q'ṭsxndyṭ(ṭ)

{MP} ... thieves [do] not [...]. {Sogd.} (If) I was [not] awake ... (705) and(?) (thereby) the ... [pass]ions caused harm: for that [I ask] ab[solution]!

... preacher ... (if) (710) I was not striving cease[lessly; and if], because of my weakness (or) malice, (being) lax[71] and unjust,[72] tired, weary (and) confused[73] because of stupid talk[74] and pranks

---

[67] Part of the initial decoration not visible on the photo opposite can be seen on p. 104 below.— On *wzyštyh̲* 'zeal', a MP loanword, see above, p. 15 n. 26.

[68] Shortened for *wm'tym* due to lack of space at the end of the line (Henning).

[69] All three of the expected superscript points are omitted or lost in a lacuna. If rightly restored, this is a MP loanword, otherwise spelled *xrwhxw'n*. Henning read and restored two words, *xrwh̲ x[wndn]*, lit. 'to call out a call', and took them as part of a MP quotation, which is also possible.

[70] Thus restored in *DMT* III/2, 161b.

[71] *GMS* §1285 n. 1 (followed by *DMT* III/2, 118b) translates *prγṭ* as 'weary', on the basis that the comparative *prγṭr* occurs together with *nyz'wrsṭr* 'weaker' in M635i, R3–4 (cited in *GMS* §1243). Henning adopted a quite different interpretation, taking *prγṭ* as a verbal form: 'if because of my weakness or malice ... was left undone'.

[72] On *myδkryy* 'harmful, unjust' (rather than 'day') see *DMT* III/2, 118b.

[73] 'Confused, disordered', lit. 'hither-and-thither'.

[74] *q'ny'* is now attested in a Christian Sogd. text (E28/16, V7, in Sims-Williams 2017, 108) but the context does not fix the meaning precisely. In another Christian text (E27/126, V26, ed. Pirtea in Sims-Williams 2019a, 126), it is possible to restore *q'(n)[y'* as the translation of Syriac *lẅglg'* 'stammering, prattling (of children)'.

M801a (III 53) fol. K/v

P. 46 (BBB 717–731)

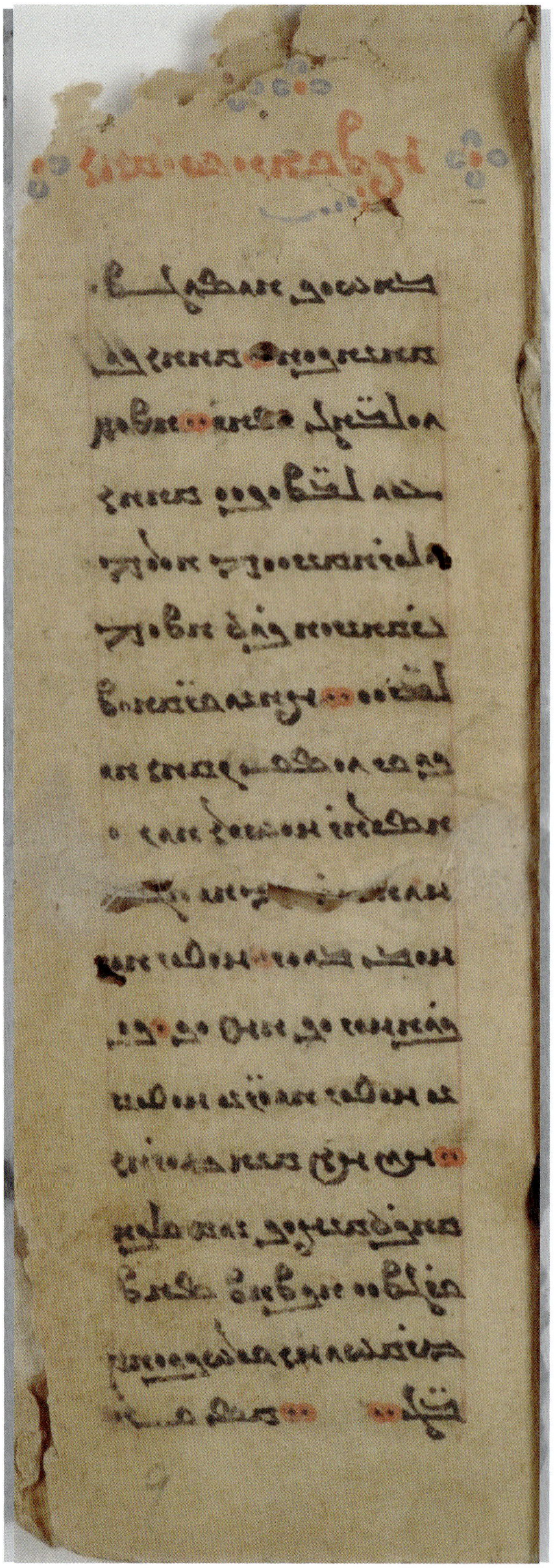

Photograph (III 53_17) reproduced by permission

M801a (III 53) fol. K/v

P. 46 (BBB 717–731)

hdl. 46–47/ {*red*} m’(x)j(m)ncyk | cṭf’r frm’n
‘The four Monday commands’

hdl. 46/ m’(x)j(m)ncyk

717 1/ [ ](β)[[75]]c[ ]ṭ(p)ww pṭpyy
718 2/ c[n](δ)[m’ny[76]](βyqp)”r[77]
719 3/ fš(m)ṭ[w]δ[’](r)[m[78]]
720 4/ gryw jy[wnd]g[p]ṭ[my]δ(y)y I
721 5/ p’zyy kyy ”p m’nwk
722 6/ (’..fr)[ ](ṭ)[[79]]c(n) ṭmp’ryy
{*three lines almost wholly destroyed*}
723 10/ ...[°°] °°
724 11/ ’ṭ[y m’xjmn]c(yk)
725 12/ pṭs’k IV [frm’n]
726 13/ IV (p)c(x)w’q pr
727 14/ kwjp(y)’k nyy jγṭ’ẖ
728 15/ kwn’m c’nw xw βγ(y)[y]
729 16/ frm’ṭyy xcy °° cww
730 17/ xw’sṭw’nyfṭ cn’wxy
731 18/ cnm’ny ’frywn ’ṭyẖ

[I] have sent [a brother](?) out of the h[ouse(?) at night](?) without a lamp, [so that] (720) every day the Liv[ing] Self, the ‘guest’ who ... like water, ... from the body ...

(724) And I am not able to keep the four [commands] and the four prohibitions of the [Monday] regulations with (proper) zeal, as God has commanded;[80] if (730) (I have omitted)[81] (saying) confession with mind and heart, (performing) the prayers and

---

[75] Or *](fr)[*? Only two superscript points survive.
[76] Quite uncertain.
[77] Less likely *(βyqs)’’r* with Henning.
[78] The letter *ṭ*, now lost, can be seen on an older photo.
[79] Henning’s tentative reconstruction *[nš](ṭ)[yy βw](ṭ)[* at the beginning of the line is impossible. The two superscript points (probably indicating *fr* or *β*) are clear.
[80] On the construction of this clause see Sims-Williams 2015, 91.
[81] The verbal phrase ‘may have been neglected’ is finally reached in line 747.

M801a (III 53) fol. D/r

P. 47 (BBB 732–748)

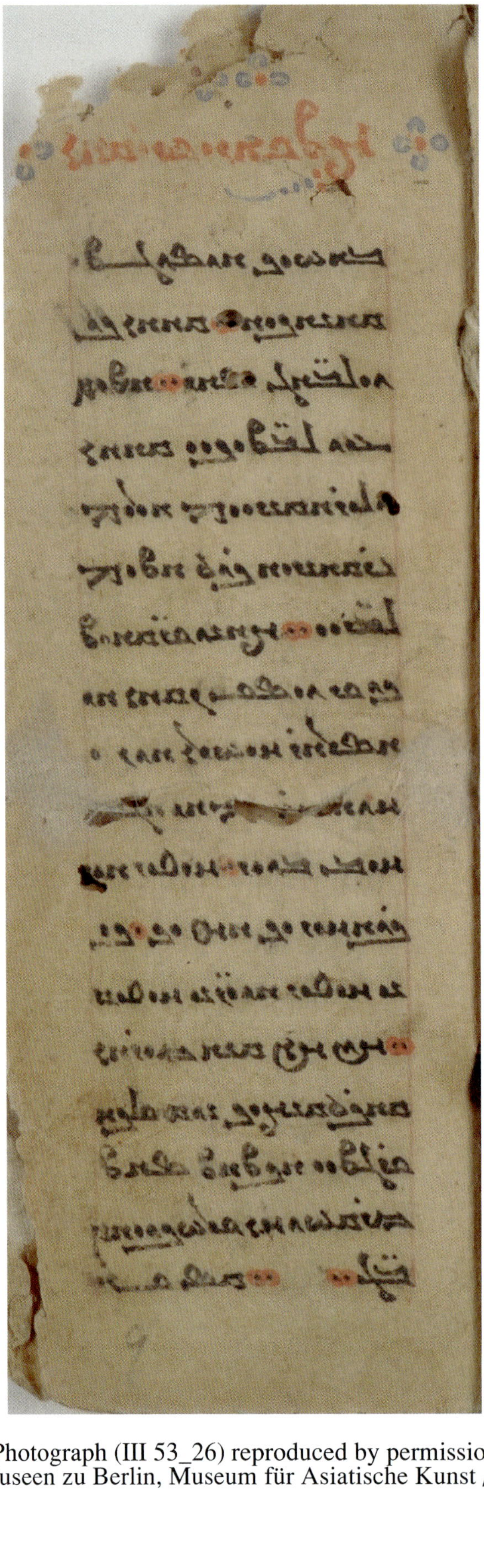

Photograph (III 53_26) reproduced by permission

M801a (III 53) fol. D/r

P. 47 (BBB 732–748)

hdl. 46–47/ {*red*} m’xj(m)ncyk | cṭf’r (fr)m’n
‘The four Monday commands’

hdl. 47/ cṭf’r (fr)m’n

732 1/ b’šyk ’wswγṭ °[82]
733 2/ m’n’ky’ °° m’’n kw
734 3/ wyδβ’γ (s)’r °° ’ṭyẖ
735 4/ ‘yw δβṭykyy m’’n
736 5/ (w)δyr’mndyyẖ ’tyẖ
737 6/ (p)rm’ndy’ xwj ’ṭyẖ
738 7/ δβryy °° c’nw frm’yṭ
739 8/ {MP} kw pd wysp zm’n ’w
740 9/ ’st’r hyštn ’wd
741 10/ hw’[m](wr)[zy](ẖ)[83] ’w
’g(ny)[n]
742 11/ hyb bwyd °° hylyd ’w(d)
743 12/ xw’hyd yk ’c yk ° ky
744 13/ ny hylyd ’wyž[84] ny hylynd
745 14/ °° {Sogd.} cw cn mn’ qyr’n
746 15/ m’xjmncyk nwm pδk’
747 16/ prγṭyy ’kṭ’ṭ s’ṭ
748 17/ qrmšwhn ptškwy’m
749 18/ βγ °° °° ms pr

hymns (in) purity of heart, (paying) attention to the sermon and (accepting) mutual changes of heart[85] and asking and granting forgiveness, as (Mani) says: (739) {MP} ‘At all times may you come together for remission of sins and forgiveness(?);[86] forgive and ask (pardon) of one another, (for) whoever does not forgive will not be forgiven’[87]—(745) {Sogd.} if on my part the Monday rule[88] may have been neglected: (for) all (this) I ask absolution, O God!

Moreover,

---

[82] The punctuation point is not circled in red ink (in this case perhaps because it is misplaced). See above, p. 53 n. 76.

[83] MP **hw’mwrzyẖ*, lit. ‘(act of) forgiving well’, does not seem to be attested, but such a word would fit both the traces and the context.

[84] Pa. form in MP context.

[85] Lit. ‘adjustment of the mind’.

[86] See n. 83 above.

[87] Lit. ‘him too they do not forgive’. Henning notes the parallel with biblical passages such as Matthew 6.15 and Ecclesiasticus 28.2.

[88] Lit. ‘law (and) rule’.

M801a (III 53) fol. D/v

P. 48 (BBB 750–767)

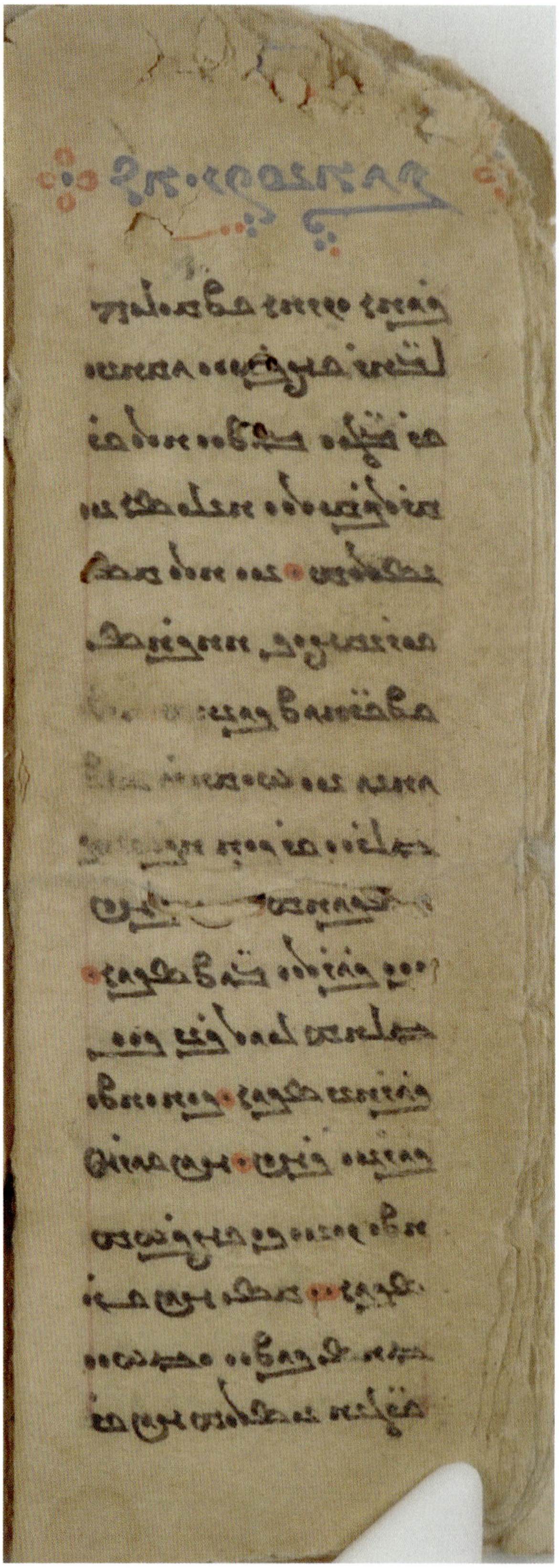

M801a (III 53) fol. D/v

P. 48 (BBB 750–767)

hdl. 48[–?]/ {*blue*} (x)w'nyzd'n | [...]
'The table of the gods ...'

hdl. 48/ (x)w'nyzd'n

750 1/ xw'n yzd'n pṭmyδyẖ
751 2/ δβ'r pcxšyy wm'ndy
752 3/ pr βγyy bwṭyy 'ty pr
753 4/ mrtxmytyy 'nδysn nyy
754 5/ nstym ° nyy 'ty ms
755 6/ pyrnmcyk ''x's
756 7/ pṭfr'wṭ kwn'(m ° 'ṭy)
757 8/ w'nw nyy šym'rw qṭ
758 9/ qδryy pr ky' 'xš(nyr)k
759 10/ ['](s)kw'm °[ ]c(w) (x)cy
760 11/ kyy xwrtyy βwṭskwn °
761 12/ qδ'm δywt xnd kyy
762 13/ xwr'ndskwn ° ky' y'ṭy
763 14/ (x)wrnyy xcy ° cw pwrc
764 15/ 'ṭy zynyy ky pcxšm
765 16/ skwn °° ms cw pr
766 17/ q's kwṭyy yqšyy
767 18/ frγn' nystym cw pr

I have not sat at the table of the gods to receive the daily gifts, the alms,[89] according to the example[90] of the God Buddha and of men. Nor (755) was I able to remember the primeval conflict; nor did I think:[91] 'In whose sign do I now dwell? What is it (760) which is being eaten? Which demons are they which one eats?[92] Whose flesh (and) blood is it? What (is) the loan (764) and deposit that I am receiving? Furthermore, why have I sat (at table) in the manner of a pig, dog (or) *yakṣa*?[93] What in ...?'.

---

[89] See p. 87 n. 63 above.
[90] On *'nδysn* 'example, model' (not 'thinking') see Benveniste 1959, 123–4.
[91] See p. 79 n. 53 above.
[92] Lit. 'they eat'.
[93] For a parallel passage regarding the right manner of receiving the gifts of food at the 'table of the gods' see the second folio of Text f below. For *nystym* 'I have sat (at table)', which Henning took as an otherwise unattested form meaning 'I am not', cf. *nstym* in line 754.

Part 3:

The manuscript M801a (III 53) as bound in antiquity

M801a (III 53) fol. a/r [BBB p. 27]

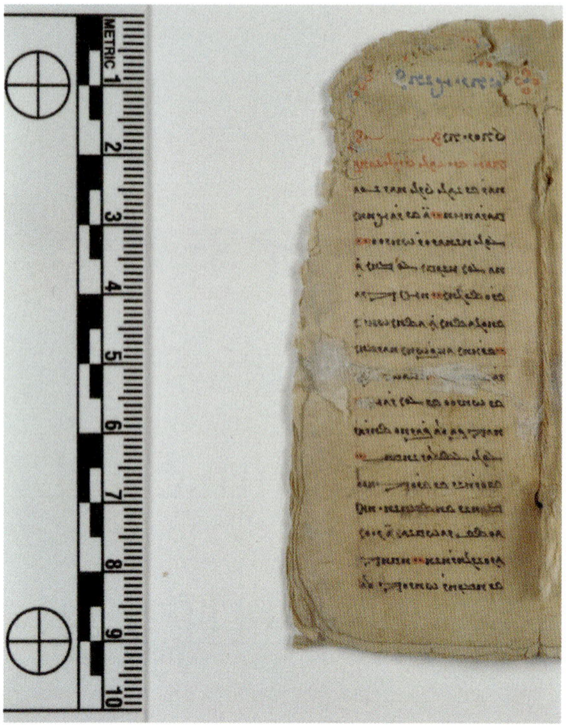

1. Photograph (III 53) reproduced by permission

M801a (III 53) fol. a/v – b/r [BBB pp. 28–29]

2. Photograph (III 53_2) reproduced by permission

M801a (III 53) fol. b/v – c/r [BBB pp. 30, 25]

3. Photograph (III 53_3) reproduced by permission

M801a (III 53) fol. c/v – d/r [BBB pp. 26, 13]

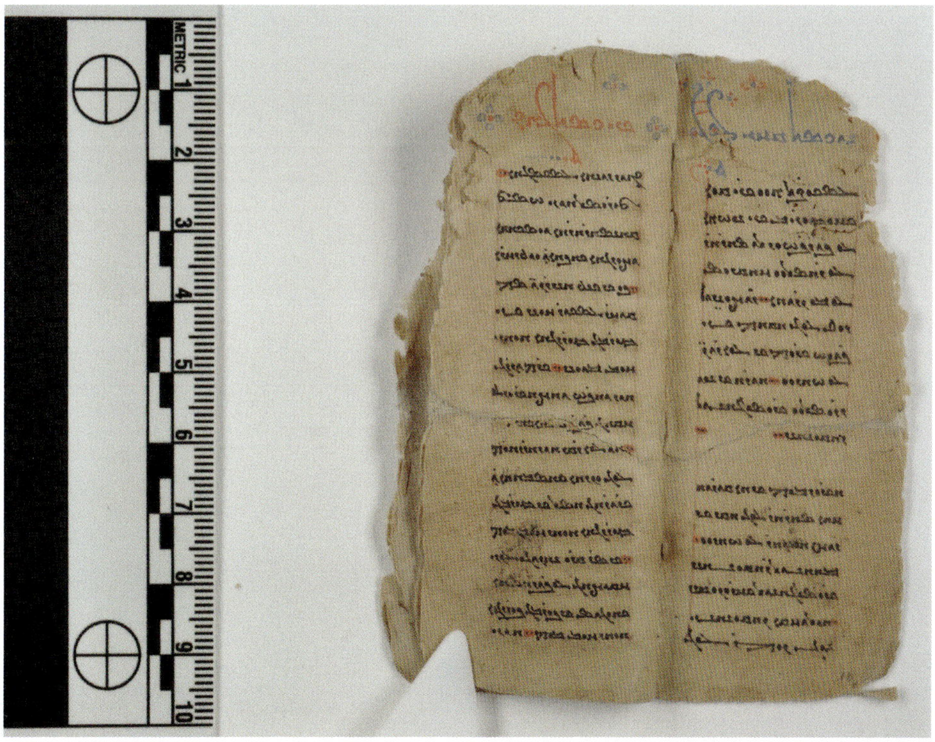

4. Photograph (III 53_4) reproduced by permission

M801a (III 53) fol. d/v – e/r [BBB pp. 14, 17]

5. Photograph (III 53_5) reproduced by permission

M801a (III 53) fol. e/v – f/r [BBB pp. 18–19]

6. Photograph (III 53_6) reproduced by permission

M801a (III 53) fol. f/v – g/r [BBB pp. 20, 7]

7. Photograph (III 53_7) reproduced by permission

M801a (III 53) fol. g/v – h/r [BBB pp. 8–9]

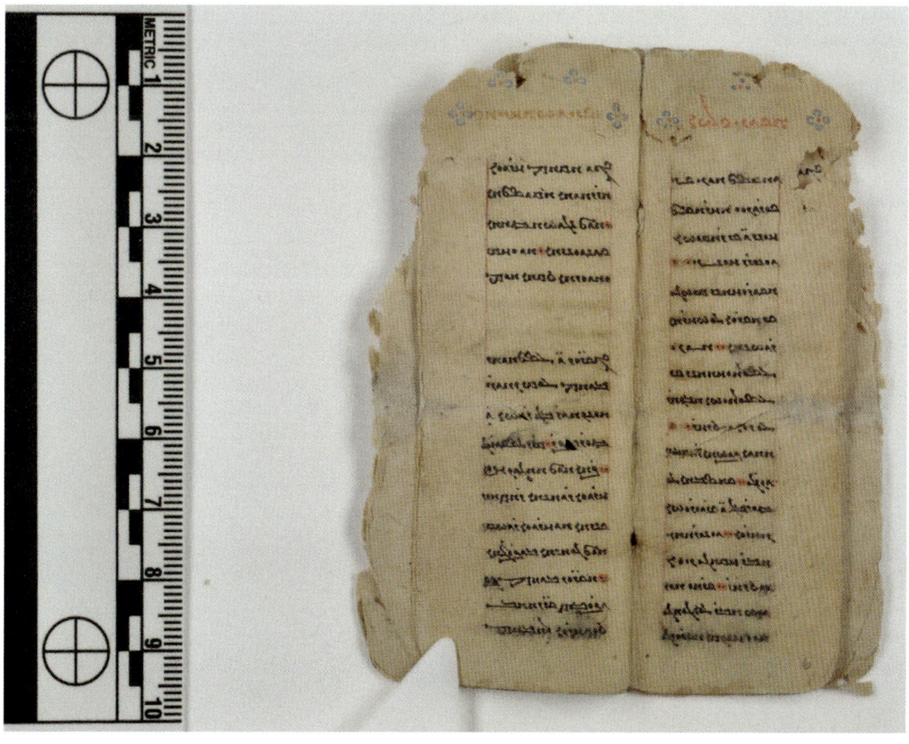

8. Photograph (III 53_8) reproduced by permission

M801a (III 53) fol. h/v – i/r [BBB pp. 10–11]

9. Photograph (III 53_9) reproduced by permission
© Staatliche Museen zu Berlin, Museum für Asiatische Kunst / Lina Wällstedt

M801a (III 53) fol. i/v – j/r [BBB pp. 12, 21]

10. Photograph (III 53_10) reproduced by permission
© Staatliche Museen zu Berlin, Museum für Asiatische Kunst / Lina Wällstedt

M801a (III 53) fol. j/v – k/r [BBB pp. 22, 15]

11. Photograph (III 53_11) reproduced by permission

M801a (III 53) fol. k/v – l/r [BBB pp. 16, 23]

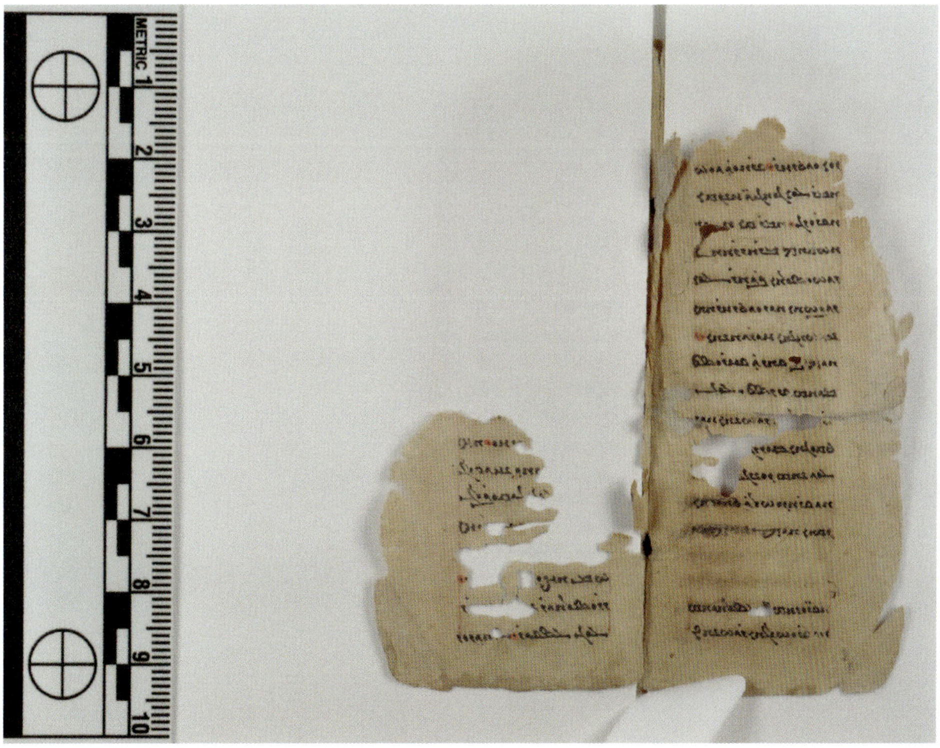

12. Photograph (III 53_12) reproduced by permission

M801a (III 53) fol. l/v – L/r [BBB pp. 24, 37]

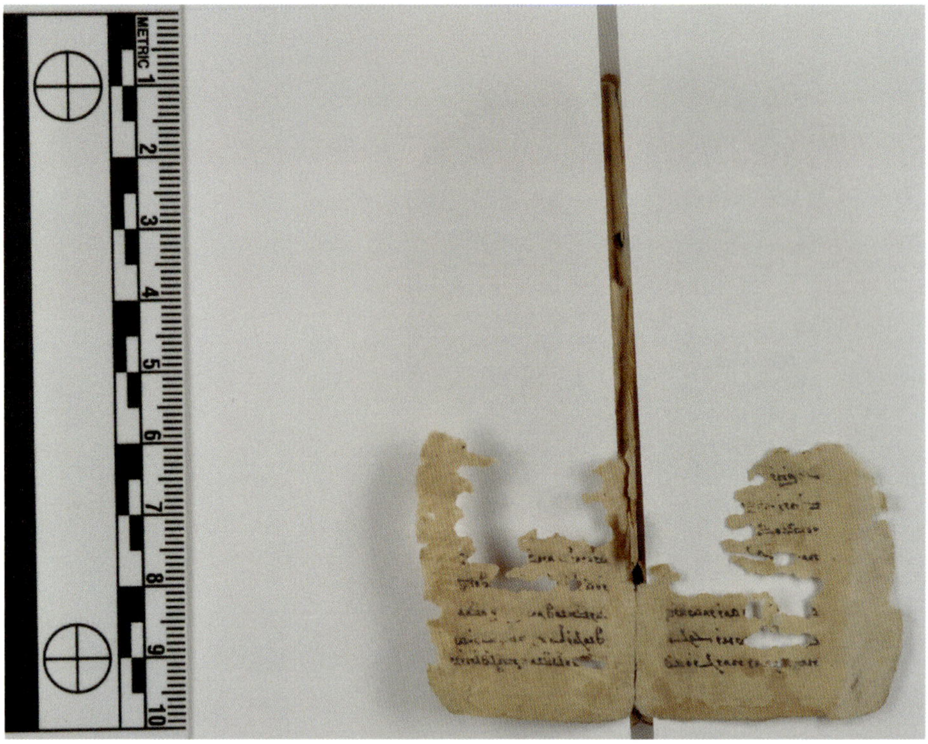

13. Photograph (III 53_13) reproduced by permission

M801a (III 53) fol. L/v – K/r [BBB pp. 38, 45]

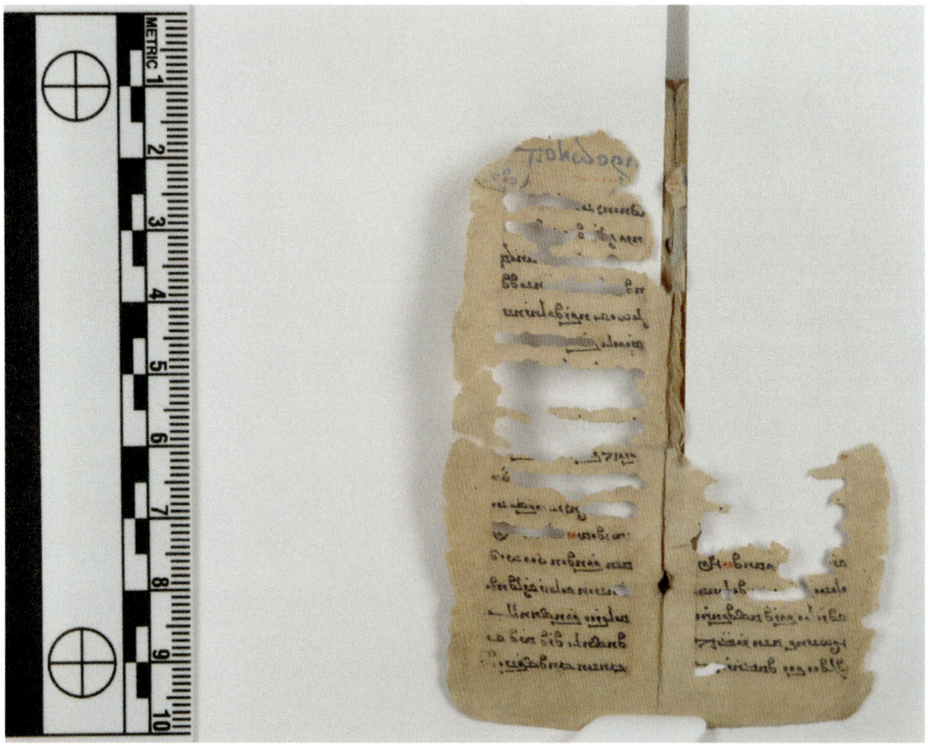

14. Photograph (III 53_15) reproduced by permission

M801a (III 53) fol. K/v – J/r [BBB pp. 46, 39]

15. Photograph (III 53_17) reproduced by permission

M801a (III 53) fol. J/v – I/r [BBB pp. 40, 1]

16. Photograph (III 53_20) reproduced by permission

M801a (III 53) fol. I/v – H/r [BBB pp. 2–3]

17. Photograph (III 53_21) reproduced by permission

M801a (III 53) fol. H/v – G/r [BBB pp. 4–5]

18. Photograph (III 53_22) reproduced by permission

M801a (III 53) fol. G/v – F/r [BBB pp. 6, 41]

19. Photograph (III 53_23) reproduced by permission

M801a (III 53) fol. F/v – E/r [BBB pp. 42–43]

20. Photograph (III 53_25) reproduced by permission

M801a (III 53) fol. E/v – D/r [BBB pp. 44, 47]

21. Photograph (III 53_26) reproduced by permission

M801a (III 53) fol. D/v – C/r [BBB pp. 48, 35]

22. Photograph (III 53_27) reproduced by permission

M801a (III 53) fol. C/v – B/r [BBB pp. 36, 31]

23. Photograph (III 53_28) reproduced by permission
© Staatliche Museen zu Berlin, Museum für Asiatische Kunst / Lina Wällstedt

M801a (III 53) fol. B/v – A/r [BBB pp. 32–33]

24. Photograph (III 53_31) reproduced by permission
© Staatliche Museen zu Berlin, Museum für Asiatische Kunst / Lina Wällstedt

M801a (III 53) fol. A/v [BBB p. 34]

25. Photograph (III 53) reproduced by permission

M801a (III 53) fol. A/v and a/r [BBB pp. 34, 27]

26. Photograph (III 53) reproduced by permission

Part 4:

Codicology

Codicology of an Iranian Manichaean Bema Service Book from Uygur Kocho

Zsuzsanna Gulácsi

As a physical object, M801a (III 53) is remarkable for a variety of reasons. Not only does it constitute the most complete fragment of a Manichaean codex from Central Asia known to date, but also it survives in a relatively good condition with rich codicological data. In fact, this manuscript is the only Manichaean fragment from Turfan for which much of the original codicological context either survives intact or is preserved in a fully reconstructible form. For all other codex fragments, this context must be inferred, risking possible mistaken extrapolations from isolated folia. Therefore, the understanding afforded through this manuscript of quire structure, intracolumnar organization, headers, as well as facing pages as coherent units of design in Iranian Manichaean codices is essential for interpreting the rest of the Turfan remains. Without this manuscript, we would not know that Manichaeans in Central Asia created multi-quire codices or that the use of paper by at least the middle of the 8th century (and most likely significantly earlier) permitted them to form quires consisting of as much as sixteen bifolios, that is, 32 folios (64 pages) each.

M801a (III 53) is one of the smallest Manichaean codices known and *the* smallest known made of paper. Yet, it exhibits a standard page design, a precise Manichaean script calligraphy, and an elegant program of scribal decoration in four ink colors in addition to black, all of which are exemplary of Manichaean book production that began in southern Mesopotamia with Mani's mission (240–277 CE), continued across the Iranian cultural region during the Sasanian empire (224–651 CE), and culminated at the end of the Uygur phase of Manichaean history (762–1024 CE). Moreover, the content of this manuscript belongs to the earliest Manichaean literature and includes an excerpt of Mani's *Seal Letter* in Middle Persian, numerous hymns in Parthian and Middle Persian, and a set of formulaic confessions of the elect in Sogdian. Through these texts, this fragmentary book preserves the words recited during the most important liturgy of the Manichaean Church—the annual Bema Ceremony—that commemorated Mani's death and expressed hope for the ultimate salvation of his followers.

The formal characteristics of M801a (III 53) hide an invaluable body of evidence about the life story of a Manichaean service book that was issued on paper during early medieval times in an Iranian speaking community in Central Asia. Its four stages of provenance include: (1) *the original production and use*, when an already existing liturgical content was copied into a paper codex at an unknown location and date (somewhere in West or East Central Asia, sometime between the 7th/8th and 9th/10th centuries) and the codex began to function as a service book; (2) *the decay and historical preservation*, when the book suffered an unknown damage, lost most of its bifolios, and what remained was saved and reassembled in an unusable order as one quire at an unknown location and date; (3) *the historical abandonment*, which arguably began in what originally was a Manichaean version of a *genizah* (that is, a storage area of worn-out books) in a *manistan* in Uygur Kocho likely sometime during the early 11th century, where this manuscript stayed under the ruins of that place until its discovery during the first German Turfan Expedition (1902–1904); and finally (4) *the modern archival conservation, exhibition, and scholarly access* in what is today the Central Asia collection of the Asian Art Museum in Berlin.[1]

Due to its unique history, this manuscript is a complex object to study. What follows below is an illustrated exploration of its materiality. While referencing the above noted episodes of provenance, this study is organized as an assessment of visual qualities. It begins with an overview of (1) *size and measurements*, (2) *preservation and photographic record* as published in Part 3 of this volume, followed by the reconstructed (3) *original page sequence and quire structure*. It continues with an examination of the principles that govern this manuscript's (4) *intracolumnar organization* and (5) *headers*; and concludes with assessing the (6) *facing pages as units of design*. The illustrations supplementing this study consist of diagrams, which show the manuscript's historical preservation and its two reconstructed quires, and photographs of various page details and twelve full views of the original facing pages of the open codex, six of which are preserved in the manuscript as such, while another six are digitally restored.[2]

SIZE AND MEASUREMENTS

M801a (III 53) is among to the smallest codices known from Turfan. When opened to a pair of facing pages, it is approximately 9.2 cm in height and 7.2 cm (2 x 3.6 cm) in width (**Fig. 1**).[3] These measurements also indicate the approx-

[1] Ruin α of Kocho as the site of this manuscript's discovery is noted by Le Coq (1923, 39) in museum records, and in all subsequent publications. For how the findings of the First Expedition were sorted and labeled, see Boyce 1960, x–xiii. In addition to Arabic numbers (1-12) enumerating all bifolios (see discussion below), the signature T I M 801 was written in the bottom margin of folio F/recto [BBB p. 41] (see photograph (III 53_23) on page 107/top in Part 3, above).

[2] The photographs of the manuscript M801a (III 53) illustrating this study were taken by Lina Wällstedt, supplied by the Staatliche Museen zu Berlin, Museum für Asiatische Kunst, and published here with permission. Their presentation was designed by the author. The associated digital imaging work was prepared by Ryan Belnap. Quotations of the BBB are from the English translation of Nicholas Sims-Williams published in Parts 1 and 2 of this volume.

[3] Previous publications give slightly different measurements ranging between 9.1 cm and 9.5 cm for the height, and between 7.2 cm and 7.5 cm for the width (Le Coq 1923, 39; Härtel–Yaldiz 1982, 175; and Gulácsi 2005, 39).

imate size of the sheets of paper that form the bifolios of this manuscript. Each bifolio has two binding holes along its vertical middle crease, pierced about 2.4 cm from the top and about 2.2 cm from the bottom and about 4.6 cm apart from one another. The paper is of high quality and evenly fine in texture throughout the manuscript.[4]

The various page elements—the four margins, the single column, and the half of the header with its decoration—are uniformly proportioned and mirrored between the two pages of the open book. These facing pages function in pairs as one symmetrical unit of design and share the one line of a header written across their upper margins.

The sizes of the four margins follow a standard pattern in two ways. Firstly, when looking at the open book, the symmetrical pairs of margins on the facing pages decrease in size in relation to one another based on their locations, that is, counterclockwise on the recto and clockwise on the verso pages (see Fig. 1a). The upper margins are the largest (H: ca. 1.7 cm), followed by the outer margins (W: max. 1.5 cm), the bottom margins (H: ca. 0.8 cm), and lastly the inner margins, which are the narrowest (W: ca. 0.5 cm). Secondly, since the quires in the original codex consisted of at least sixteen bifolios, the width of the outer margins on each bifolio varied slightly based on the bifolios' location within the original quire. Once the bifolios were nested, folded, and trimmed along their outer edges opposite from the binding, the margins became a few millimeters narrower on the interior bifolios of the quire.[5] This effect of trimming on the folded and closed quire seems to have survived at least partially on some pages.[6]

The single columns on all pages are ruled only vertically and in violet ink. They measure between 6.4 cm and 6.6 cm in height, and between 1.8 cm and 2.2 cm in width. Each column consists of 18 lines. Although there is no sign of horizontal ruling, the lines are spaced evenly, approximately 4 mm apart and with a 3 mm gap from one another (see Fig. 1b).[7] The height of the lines is around 1 mm. Their black-ink writing was done with a fine point dip pen, the thickest stokes of which measure about 0.3 mm in width. The high quality of penmanship main-

[4] The 12 surviving bifolios of this manuscript constitute 37.6% of what was, at minimum, a two-quire codex with a total of 32 bifolios, that is, 64 folios (128 pages). Based on the approximate thickness of what survives, the estimated total thickness of the 64 folios in the closed codex would have been just over 1 cm. Although the exact measurements are not available currently, the way this manuscript is framed, including the two sheets of glass, totals 5.0 mm. The estimated thickness of the glass (2 x 1.5 mm) leaves a 2 mm thickness for the opened codex displayed within, which if closed would be 4 mm. This number (as 37.6% of the total) brings the original thickness of the two quires to approximately 1.06 cm, without any covers.

[5] An analogous effect of trimming on the outer margins of single quire papyrus codices, when consisting of considerable number of folded sheets, is noted by both Turner (1977, 58–60) and Szirmai (1999, 12).

[6] The reconstructed original page sequence of Quire 2 (see Fig. 3) confirms this phenomenon at least partially. Even though all margins are damaged, the outer margins tend to survive with greater widths on folios that belonged to the exterior of Quire 2, as seen for example on the facing pages of BBB pp. 14–15 (see Fig. 12), where the margins are about 1.2 cm. In contrast, the outer margins are narrower on folios that were close to the middle of Quire 2, as on the facing pages of BBB pp. 28–29 (see Fig. 17), where they measure about 0.9 cm.

[7] Le Coq 1923, 39.

tained in both the Middle Persian and Sogdian parts of this manuscript is a testament to the skill of its one scribe (see Figs. 5–7).

The headers are written with a thicker dip pen and in larger script across the middle of the upper margins (see Fig. 1b). The width of their pen measures about 0.5 mm. The height of the writing is about 2 mm. Isolated from the columns below them, their texts are located approximately 6 mm above the columns and 9 mm below the upper edge of the page. Calligraphic letters increase their overall footprint to 5 mm below and 6 mm above the writing. The floral motifs, seen next to and occasionally above the half headers on all pages, measure about 4 mm in diameter.

In relation to the vast size range of Manichaean codices attested from the Uygur era, M801a (III 53) belongs to a size group that has been labeled "extra small," where the smallest example is a parchment bifolio, M8110 (III 103), that measures 5.7 cm in height and 3.4 cm in width. Its single columns have 13 lines per page and contain Middle Persian hymns.[8] "Extra large" codices reached over 50 cm in height and 30 cm in width. These extremes, however, are the exceptions in this corpus. Most fragments fall in one of three groups: "small" (H: 15–22 cm, W: 7–12 cm), "medium" (H: 23–30 cm, W: 13–18 cm) and "large" (H: 31–50 cm, W: 19–30 cm). The script size and line distance of M801a (III 53) are not uncommon in the small and medium groups. Examples of dated fragments include the bifolio M1 (III 203) from a hymn book that began to be written in 762 CE; and the bifolio illustrated with a sermon scene, III 8259, carbon dated to 889–1015 CE.[9]

Manichaean codices from Egypt also attest a wide range of sizes and include an extra small book. The *Cologne Mani Codex*, the smallest ancient codex known to date, is the size of a matchbox (4.5 x 3.8 cm). Its surviving 96 parchment folios (192 pages) contain the Greek translation of Mani's biography inscribed in a miniscule hand in single columns of 23 lines per page.[10] In contrast, the *Kephalaia,* which contains a Coptic translation of Mani's teachings with quotations from him, is among the most voluminous papyrus codices. Each of its two volumes has more than 260 folios (520 pages) with 28–32 lines in single columns per page (31.5 x 18 cm) and belongs to a corpus of seven Manichaean codices from Medinet Madi, carbon dated to the late 4th and early 5th centuries.[11]

[8] For a color illustration of both sides of this bifolio and a catalogue entry that includes the English translation of folio 1 by Durkin-Meisterernst (2006, 157) and Jason BeDuhn, see Gulácsi 2022, 354–55.

[9] See Gulácsi 2005, 41, 76–83 and Figs. 3/6, 3/9, 3/11.

[10] Sundermann 1992, 43–6.

[11] The first volume (*The Kephalaia of the Teacher)* is preserved in the Staatsbibliothek in Berlin and contains 261 folios (522 pages), with the last surviving chapter numbered 201. The second volume (*The Kephalaia of the Wisdom of My Lord of My Mani*), housed in the Chester Beatty in Dublin, contains 254 folios (508 pages), with the first surviving chapter numbered 220; see Gardner 2018; and Gardner–BeDuhn–Dilley 2018, 3.

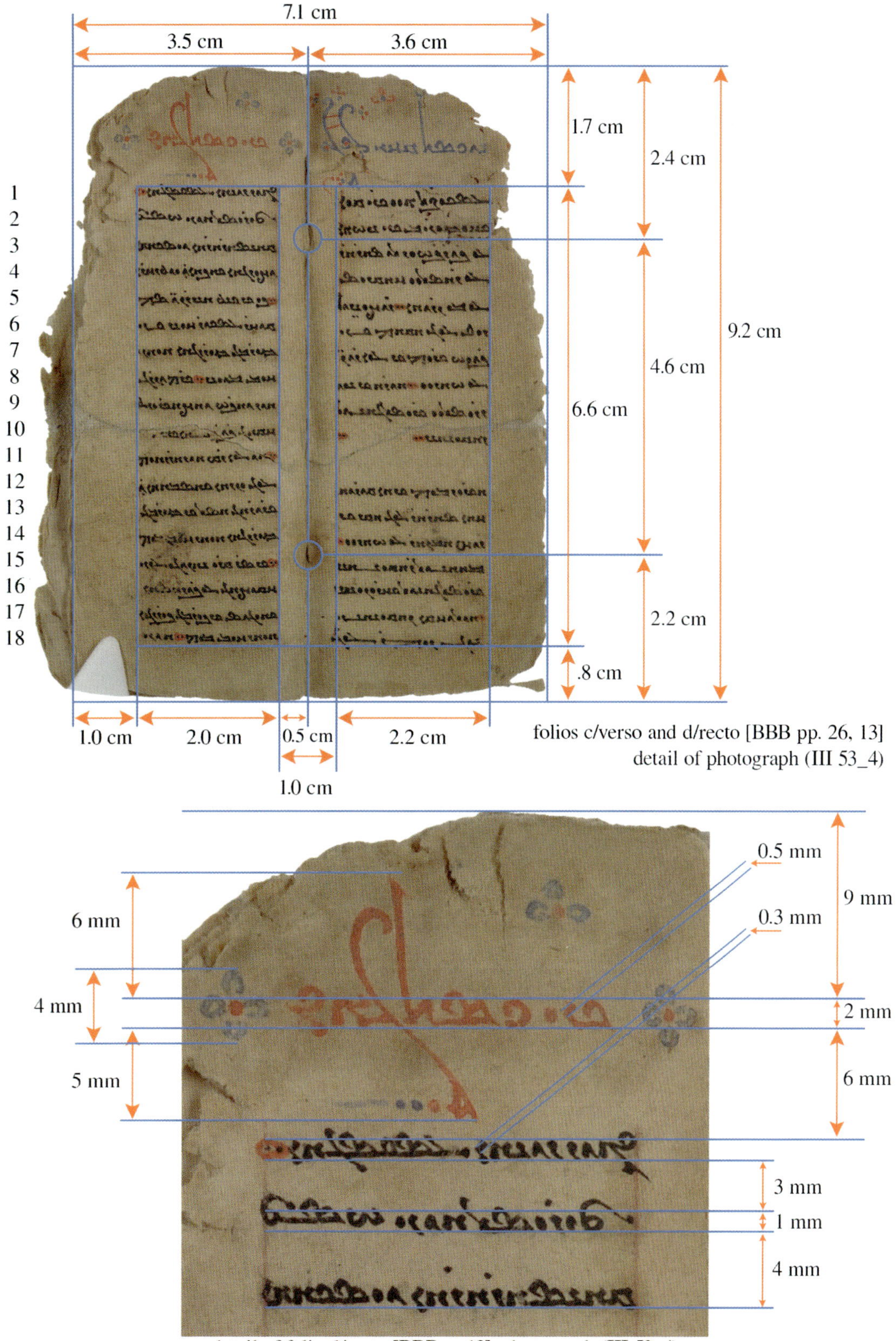

folios c/verso and d/recto [BBB pp. 26, 13]
detail of photograph (III 53_4)

detail of folio d/recto [BBB p. 13], photograph (III 53_4)

Fig. 1: Approximate measurements of manuscript M801a (III 53)

PRESERVATION AND PHOTOGRAPHIC RECORD

The condition of M801a (III 53) tells a tantalizing story about a historical effort to keep what is left from a book together even after it had suffered some sort of dam-age. This manuscript was discovered as a single quire of twelve nested bifolios. Its surviving bifolios were found tied together with a cord threaded through their original binding holes and secured with a sizable crude knot in the inner part of the quire. Folded in the middle, this stack of bifolios formed 24 folios (48 pages) of one solitary codex quire.[12] Being stored this way for about one thousand years, this quire naturally decayed. The tensile strength of its paper weakened, resulting in horizontal rips across the middle of all folios. Small worms or insects burrowed through its exterior, leaving holes of varying sizes with round edges across the text areas on the three outer bifolios. Much of what is today the outermost bifolio was lost this way. Only the lower margins and a few lines of text at the bottom of the columns are left from it.[13] These worm marks decrease towards the inner part of the quire. While they are significantly less on the second outermost bifolio and minimal on the third, the subsequent bifolios are unimpaired.[14] This unique state of preservation indicates that these bifolios were deliberately saved—assembled as one quire, folded, and stored as a booklet—prior to their decay, likely some-time during the late 10th and early 11th century.

With its ripped folios reinforced, this manuscript had been kept framed since the middle of the 20th century, initially, between a sheet of glass on top and a white cardboard on the bottom, and recently between two sheets of glass. In this frame, the quire is no longer folded. It is opened to a pair of facing pages. This is how it has been stored in Berlin, exhibited in the Metropolitan Museum of Art in New York in 1982, and published.[15] This is also how M801a (III 53) has been made available for research supplemented with a set of black and white photographs on paper, which appeared in print for the first time in 2000.[16]

In an initial documentation of this manuscript during the 1930s, Walter Bruno Henning assigned a letter of the alphabet (A/a – L/l) to each of the twelve bifolios as they lay stacked atop one another with the codex open, starting at the *innermost* bifolio, with the knotted cord at its central fold (**Fig. 2**).[17] This was

[12] A codex quire consists of a nested stack of bifolios that were secured to one another by the cord threaded through their binding holes and folded in the middle. Each bifolio consists of two folios with two pages: a recto (a page to be read first) and a verso (a page to be read subsequently).

[13] It is possible that more bifolios had been lost to worms or insects from the exterior of the BBB.

[14] For a diagram that shows the location of bifolio 1 (= folios L and l) in the historically bound quire, see Fig. 2, below. For illustrations of its two sides, see photographs (III 53_12), (III 53_13), and (III 53_15) on pages 103/bottom, 104/top, and 104/bottom in Part 3, above.

[15] Le Coq (1923, 39–40 and Plate 4d) illustrated the manuscript opened to folios c/verso – d/recto [BBB pp. 26, 13], see photograph (III 53_4) on page 99/bottom; while Härtel–Yaldiz (1982, 175), Gulácsi (2005, 39), and Morano (2018, 12) showed folios J/v – I/r [BBB pp. 40, 1], see photograph (III 53_20) on page 105/bottom, above. For the location of these pages in the historically preserved quire, see Fig. 2, below.

[16] Weber 2000, 27–8.

[17] Henning 1937, 3–4.

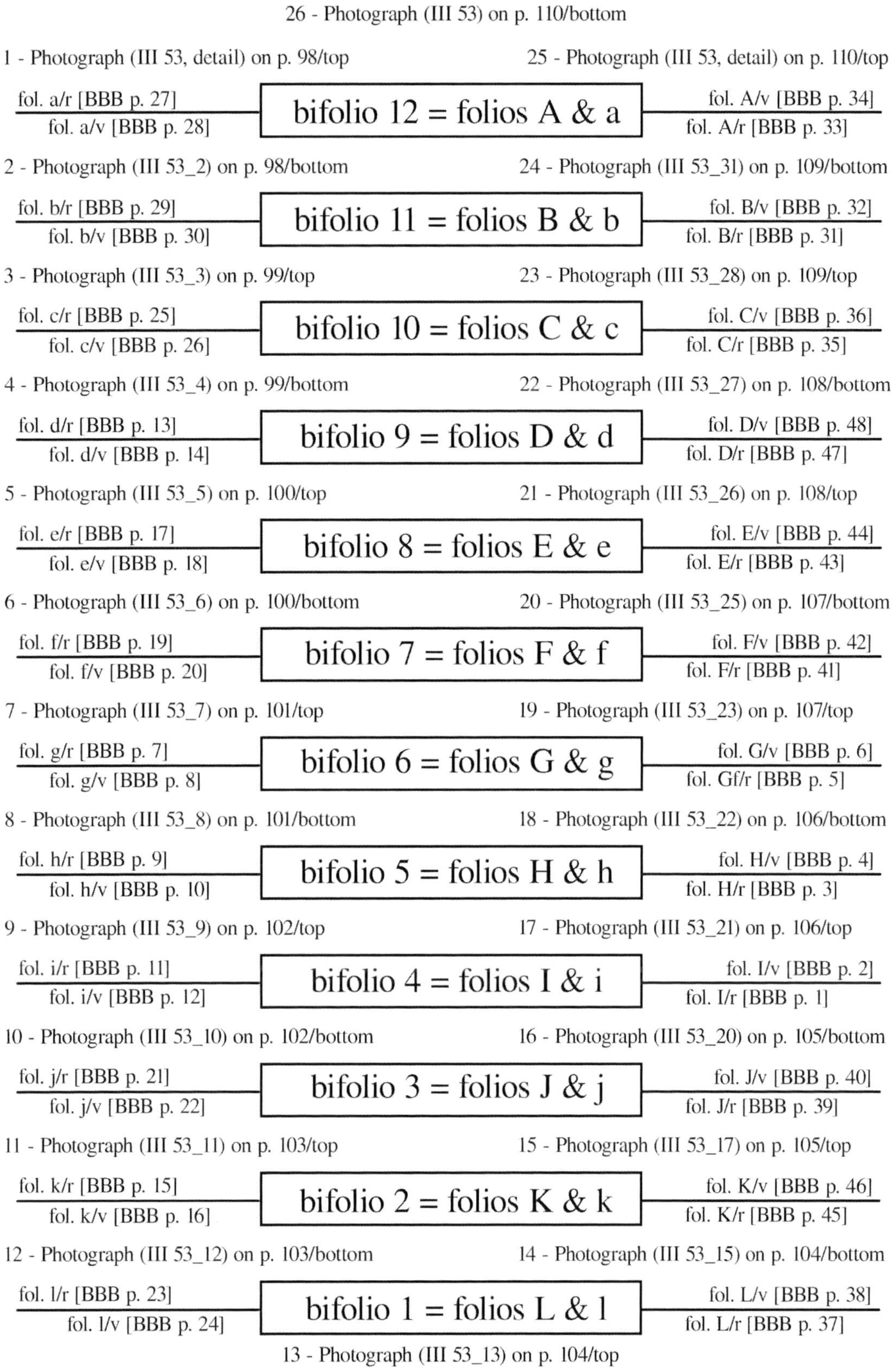

Fig. 2: Diagram of manuscript M801a (III 53)
bound historically as one quire

simply a device by which Henning kept track of the relationship among the folios as he investigated evidence that they were preserved in the manuscript out of their original order. His designations were not written on the folios themselves. Later, an unknown conservator added Arabic numerals in pencil to each bifolio, starting with the *outermost* bifolio, as appropriate for paginating a codex quire. This meant that the manuscript was flipped over relative to the way Henning had approached it, and Arabic numerals (1–12) were written in pencil in the two lower corners on the outer side of each bifolio. The inner sides of the bifolios were left unmarked. These two independent documentations of the manuscript have produced, therefore, two different systems of designating the folios that count them oppositely, with Henning's bifolio A/a equivalent to bifolio 12, and his bifolio L/l equivalent to bifolio 1. A key to correlating these two systems of pagination is readily comprehensible through a diagram.

The current volume of the Corpus Fontium Manichaeorum features high-resolution digital images that were taken to fully document this manuscript in color for the first time in a publication (**Part 3, pp. 97–110, above**). These photographs illustrate pairs of facing pages as the folios are turned, following Henning's approach of starting from the best preserved innermost bifolio of the manuscript. The diagram records each photo in relation to the location of the facing pages of the open manuscript they show (see Fig. 2). Starting at the upper left of the diagram and proceeding counterclockwise, the first photograph (III 53, p. 98/top) shows only the left page (a/recto) from the inner side of bifolio 12. The second photo (III 53_2, p. 98/bottom) shows the pair of facing pages when the prior page is turned: the right page (a/verso) from the outer side of bifolio 12 with the Arabic number "12" in its lower right corner, and the left page (b/recto) from the inner side of the bifolio 11. Analogously, the third photo (III 53_3, p. 99/top) shows the right page (c/recto) from the outer side of the bifolio with the Arabic number "11" in its lower right corner, and the left page (b/verso) from the inner side of the bifolio 10. And so on, all the way to the thirteenth photo (III 53_13, p. 104/top) that shows the full view of the outer side of bifolio 1, as it looks on the exterior of the flattened quire. On this most damaged bifolio, the Arabic number "1" can be seen faintly in the lower outer corners on both pages. Continuing to leaf through the manuscript, the rest of the photos illustrate the subsequent facing pages with the Arabic numbers now in the lower left corner of the *left page*, all the way to the twenty-fourth photo (III 53_31, p. 109/bottom), where the last Arabic number "12" can be seen in the lower left corner of the outer side of this bifolio. Turning this last page takes the viewer back to the inner side of bifolio 12. This twenty-fifth photo (III 53, p. 110/top) shows only the right page (A/verso) on the inner side of bifolio 12 and completes the visual documentation of the pages. The twenty-sixth photo (III 53, p. 110/bottom) shows the full view of the inner side of bifolio 12, where the binding cord and the historically tied knot are visible at the core of the quire.

The historical preservation of this manuscript in itself is rich in data. The way these pages were found and are kept today—as a stack of twelve paper bifolios nested on top of one another, tied together with a cord, and folded in the middle to form one single quire—is indicative of how sheets of bifolios (at first using parchment, and later using paper) were assembled in the individual quires of codices by the Manichaeans in East Central Asia already before the Uygur era of their history. To create a codex, such folded quires would have been laid on top of one another (with their binding on the right), attached to one another by stitching their binding cords together, and secured to a book cover.[18]

However, what appears to be a neatly preserved portion of a codex, in reality, is in disarray. This fact about M801a (III 53) was revealed in 1937 when its textual content was studied and translated into German by Henning. He discovered that in most cases the *original* order of the texts on these pages did not correspond with the *historical* order of the surviving bifolios, and numerous bifolios were missing from what survived. The intent to preserve the historical rebinding eliminated the possibility of physically restoring the original order by rearranging and rebinding the twelve bifolios based on their textual content. Therefore, the folios continue to be referred to by the designations they have received based upon their current (disordered) place in the preserved manuscript, even though now sequenced according to their original order, as in the edition and translation in Parts 1 and 2 of the present volume.

Accordingly, the diagram also notes the reconstructed original order of the surviving pages (see Fig. 2). Since Henning called to the manuscript "Bet- und Beichtbuch," the abbreviation "BBB" is the prefix of the reconstructed page by page numerical sequence of the surviving texts. For example, the diagram shows that Henning found the *first two surviving pages* of the BBB on the two sides of *folio I* (on folio I/recto [BBB p. 1] and folio I/verso [BBB p. 2]), that is, on the right half of what later was numbered as bifolio 4; and the *last two surviving pages* on the two sides of *folio D* (on folio D/recto [BBB p. 47] and folio D/verso [BBB p. 48]), that is, on the right half of bifolio 9. The English translation and the matching photographs in Parts 1–3 are labeled with Henning's letters, with the translation itself following his reconstructed original sequence of the text.

RECONSTRUCTED PAGE SEQUENCE AND QUIRE STRUCTURE

In the course of his philological study of M801a (III 53), Henning also conducted pioneering work on Iranian Manichaean codicology. While reconstructing the original page sequence, he recovered evidence about the quire structure of an early paper codex from Central Asia. As in any codex, in this manuscript fragment, too, *each folio* preserves a two-page long section of a continuous text between its recto and verso sides; and *each bifolio* preserves the same length of continuous content on its two folios located symmetrically between the two halves of the original quire. When a missing folio breaks the continuity of a passage in the first half of a quire, the same length of text is missing on the other, missing half of the bifolio in the second half of the quire.

---

[18] No full quires survive among the Manichaean fragments discovered at Kocho. For decorated book covers and the depictions of bound codices, see Gulácsi 2005, 83–8, and Plates 6b and 6d.

Based on these principles, Henning discovered that M801a (III 53) preserves parts of two quires (**Figs. 3 and 4**). They contain three genres of texts clustered in three groups:

1. Epistle	folios I/recto–I/verso [BBB pp. 1–2]	Quire 1
2. Hymns	folios I/verso–b/verso [BBB pp. 2–30]	Quires 1–2
3. Confessions	folios B/recto–D/verso [BBB pp. 31–48]	Quire 2

The first group has only one text. It survives intact in the form of a one-page-and-four-line excerpt from the holiest text of the Bema liturgy, called the *Seal Letter* in the header. It quotes the starting formula from the last epistle of Mani,[19] which likely was read out in full during the annual festivities of the Bema. The next group features various sets of Bema hymns surviving on twenty-nine pages. The texts in these two genres are written in Middle Persian and Parthian. Some of their captions are in Sogdian. The last surviving group consists of formulaic confess-ions of the elect on seventeen pages in Sogdian. Numerous pages are lost from the hymns and the confessions. Also lost are additional texts in unknown genres from the beginning of the first quire and the end of the second quire.

Nine of the twelve bifolios belonged to the second quire ("Quire 2") of what survives from the original codex (see Fig. 3). Based on the textual content of the pages in relation to one another, Henning deduced their sequence and noted the location of missing bifolios. The right half, that is, the first half of this quire contained hymns. The left half, that is, its second half contained the confessions. In the interior of the quire, the transition between these two parts occupied at min-imum one lost bifolio, that is, four pages of two missing folios. Important clues for reconstruction included evidence about the known order of the texts in both genres, since the numbers of the hymns were given in a caption at the end of each hymn group and the main confession texts followed the sequence of the elect's five commandments: (1) Truth-speaking, (2) Non-injury, (3) Sexual Purity, (4) Dietary Purity, and (5) Poverty. In addition, a few intact cases of these texts provide further clues for estimating the number of missing bifolios. The main points of Henning's assessment of Quire 2 may be best summarized starting with the confessions:[20]

---

[19] Mani wrote this letter before he died in prison at Gondeshapur (Syro-Aram Bēth Lāpāṭ) in the year 274 or 277 CE. Various small fragments of its later copies that survive in Middle Persian and Sogdian translation (Reck 2009, 228–39) allowed Sims-Williams to reconstruct the phrase "Mani, the apostle of Jesus *Aryaman*" lost from the start of the letter on the missing folio that preceded BBB p. 1 (see Part 1, p. 3 n. 5 above). This phrase is the Middle Persian equivalent (found also in fragments of the Middle Persian translation of Mani's *Living Gospel*; see Morano 2014, 86 and 90) for "Mani, apostle of Jesus *Christ* (lit. 'messiah')." Mani opened all of his epistles with this phrase and identified himself with it in Syriac language and Manichaean script on his rock crystal seal-stone, housed in the Bibliothèque nationale de France (INT. 1384 BIS, see Gulácsi 2013 and 2022, 354). The Parthian version of the phrase follows the Syriac in its word choice (as seen, e.g., in a preamble later added to a hymn written by Mani, where the Parthian and the Middle Persian versions are used together; see Durkin-Meisterernst–Morano 2010, 117).

[20] Henning 1937, 6–7.

(1) The entire confession of the first commandment (Truth-speaking) is lost from the interior of the quire. Based on the evidence detailed below, its text likely took up three pages from the four pages that were lost with *bifolio XVI*. After an intracolumnar blank space that amounted to ten (or twelve) lines, its text must have begun either on the lower part of the recto or the upper part of the verso of the *missing folio* on the right half of *bifolio XVI* and concluded somewhere close to the end of the verso of the *missing folio* on the left half of *bifolio XVI*.

(2) The confession of the second commandment (Non-injury) is the best preserved among the five texts. Even with its first few lines lost, its prose takes up four pages and six lines, including both sides of *folio B*, both sides of *folio A*, and six lines on the recto of *folio C*.

(3) The confession of the third commandment (Sexual Purity) is the second best preserved of these five texts. Its start is signaled by a pair of spaciously spaced double punctuation marks in red ink, in line six on *folio C* recto. From here, it continues across the full length of *folio C* verso, the two pages of the subsequent *missing folio*, and possibly the recto of *folio L* since the lines at the bottom of the latter page are still about Sexual Purity. Therefore, its end was somewhere before the lower third of *folio L* verso, which is claimed by the next confession. If so, the length of this confession was greater than 4 pages and 12 lines.

(4) The most damaged part of this quire contained the confession texts of the fourth commandment (Dietary Purity) and the fifth commandment (Poverty) on what most likely were at minimum seven pages. The confession about Dietary Purity began on the torn upper two-thirds of *folio L* verso, since five lines survive from the beginning of its prose at the bottom of that page. The rest of the fourth and the entire text of the fifth commandment are lost on six subsequent pages of *three missing folios*, which were located before *folio J*. If so, each text was around three-and-a-half pages long.

(5) Also missing is the start of an additional set of shorter confessional statements of the elect that occupied at least eleven pages. The first of these began on the verso of the above discussed *missing folio* and continued on the surviving six pages of *folio J*, *folio F*, and *folio E*, followed by two pages on a subsequent *missing folio* and the surviving four pages of *folio K* and *folio D*. The last confession does not end on *folio D* verso, indicating that more lost pages followed. The end of the last confessional statement, plus the rest of the content of this codex, were either part of the next quire, or could have been on the lost folio(s) at the end of this quire. If so, at minimum, one folio is lost from the exterior of Quire 2.

Henning's reconstruction of the confessions in the second (left) half of Quire 2 defines the order of the surviving folios and the number of missing folios in the first (right) half of Quire 2 (see Fig. 3). This part of the quire contains three sets

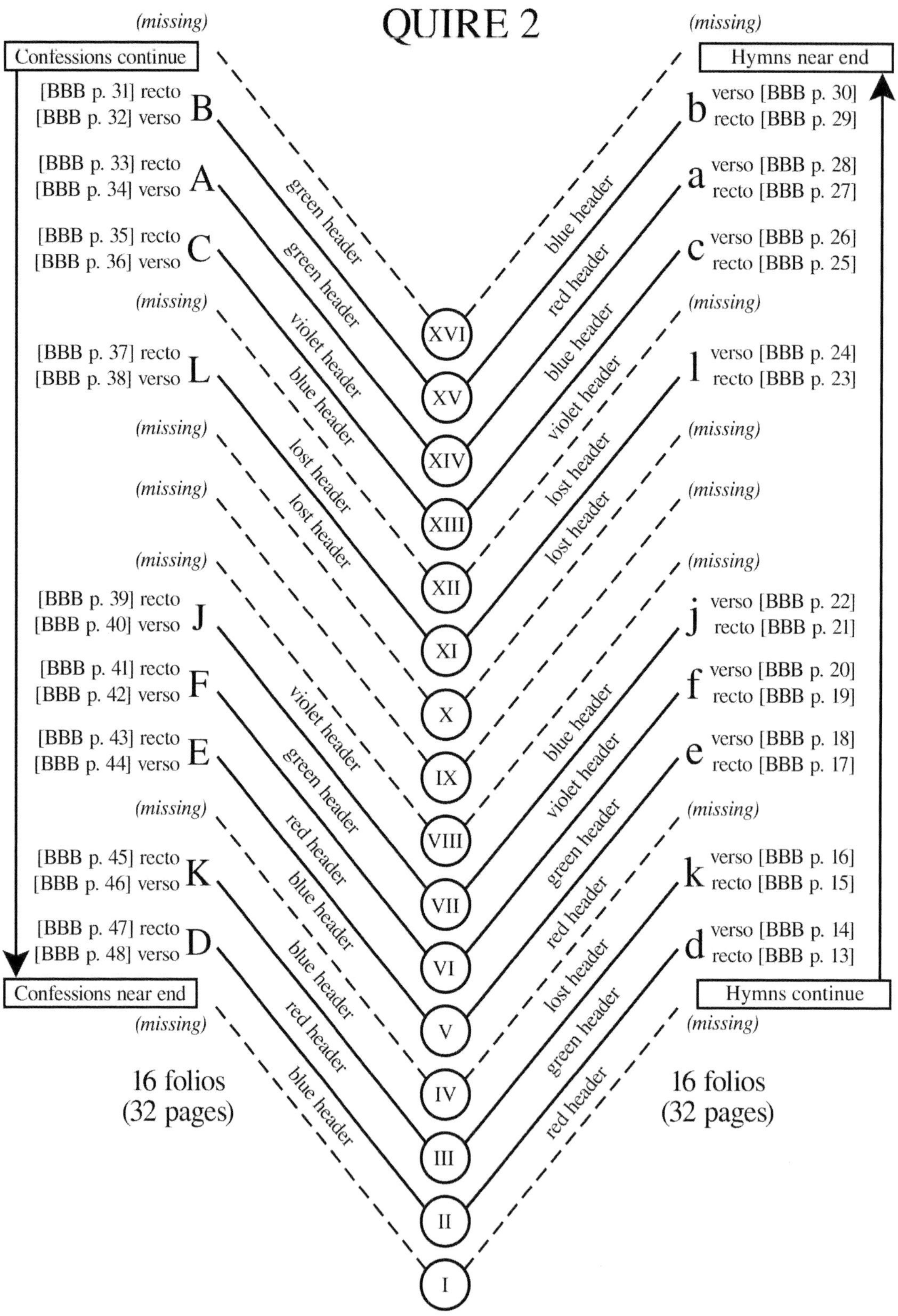

Fig. 3: Diagram of Quire 2 preserved in manuscript M801a (III 53)

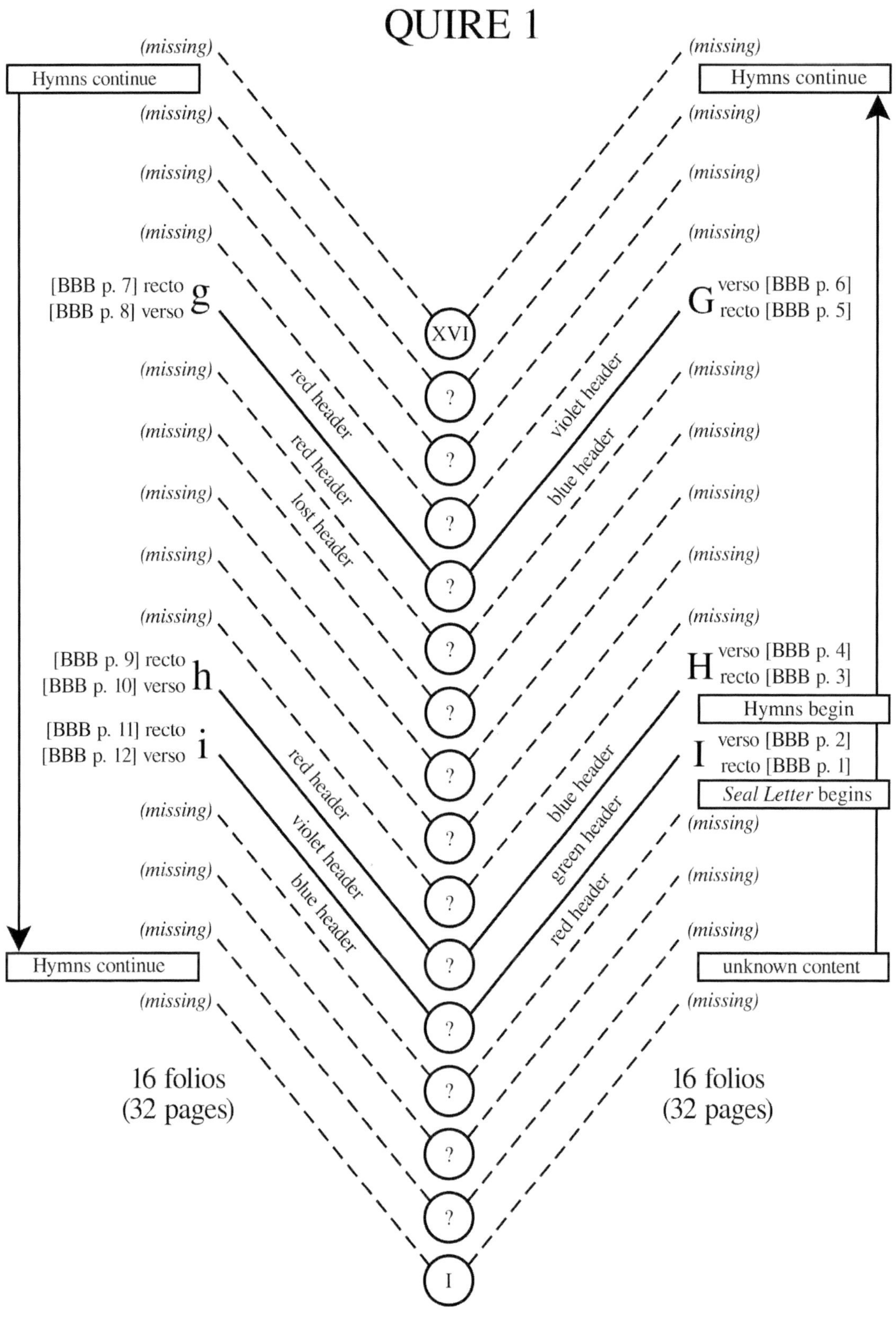

Fig. 4: Diagram of Quire 1 preserved in manuscript M801a (III 53)

of hymns, each of which consists of a certain number of hymns specified in a caption at the end of their group, as follows:[21]

(1) The first half of Quire 2 began with two "hymns of praise to the messengers" on what most likely amounted to eleven pages. These hymns could have started in the previous quire, or possibly on the first lost folio(s) of this quire. Either way, they continued on the surviving *folio d*, *folio k*, the *missing folio*, and *folio e*. They concluded on *folio f* recto in a red caption (lines 3–4) that states "here end the hymns of praise to the messengers, two in number."

(2) The next set of hymns contained three hymns on the most damaged part of this quire. They start on *folio f* recto, where a red caption (BBB p. 19 lines 15–16) announces "here begin the hymns of praise to the Bema," and end on *folio c* recto (BBB p. 25 lines 5–6) in a red caption, stating "here end the hymns of praise to the Bema of Light, three in total." Between them numerous folios are missing; the question is how many. Based on the first of these hymns being more than 3 pages, it would take at least seven or eight pages to complete two additional hymns of similar length. The length of the confessions on the left side of this quire, however, indicates the need for an additional missing folio (2 pages) beyond the minimum number arrived at by the calculation of the length of this set of hymns. This brings the number to thirteen full pages and two partial pages: *folio f* (1 partial page and 1 page), *folio j* (2 pages), three *missing folios* (6 pages), *folio l* (2 pages), the subsequent *missing folio* (2 pages) and *folio c* recto (1 partial page).

(3) The last set of hymns contained at least seven "hymns of joy" on minimum five pages. They started on *folio c* verso, continued on *folio a* and *folio c*, and possibly concluded on the first few lines on the recto of a *missing folio* that was lost with the right half of *bifolio XVI* in Quire 2. An additional lost bifolio at the interior of this quire would have provided room for four additional pages, which could have accommodated more hymns and a longer first confession, in addition to the blank lines of a gap between them. Since the number of hymns and the length of the first confession cannot be verified, no more than one lost bifolio can be confirmed.

While the above observations led Henning to the conclusion that Quire 2 had "more than fourteen bifolios," the details of his argument add up to a minimum of sixteen bifolios. A quire of this size contains 32 folios (64 pages), as confirmed by what survives from the confessions and the hymns in Quire 2.[22]

---

[21] Henning 1937, 6.

[22] The quire structure of a codex survives intact from Turfan only in the case of a Syriac Christian service book (III 45) from Bulayïq. Housed in the Asian Art Museum in Berlin, this manuscript preserves 61 paper folios (22.5 cm x 14 cm) in their original gatherings secured to one another by a historical binding cord. Its paper has been radiocarbon dated to 771–884 CE. Although numerous folios are lost today, what survives belonged to five quires, which were either *septoniones* or *octoniones*, that is, consisting of 7, 7, 7, 8, and 7 bifolios per quire ("14, 14, 14, 16, and 14 leaves"). Quire numbers added to them by a later hand indicate that 15 quires (with min. 210 folios) are lost from the beginning of the book (Hunter–Coakley 2017, 1–3 and 11–16).

From the preceding quire (Quire 1), three bifolios are preserved (see Fig. 4). Henning deciphered their order and noted what is missing in relation to them:[23]

(1) *Bifolio I/i* and *bifolio H/h* were next to one another, since their hymns and headers continue on what were originally two facing pages. In the first (right) half of Quire 1, *folio I* verso and *folio H* recto were connected by a green header that reads "Here begin the hymns of the Bema" (BBB pp. 2–3, see Fig. 10). In the second (left) half of this quire, *folio h* verso and *folio i* recto were connected by a violet header that reads "Here begin (the hymns of praise) to Jesus the life-giver" (BBB pp. 10–11, see Fig. 11).

(2) *Bifolio G/g*, which contains hymns, was closer to the interior of the quire than *bifolio H/h*, where the hymns begin in this quire. The number of missing bifolios between these two bifolios could be anywhere between 1 and 7. Five is indicated in the reconstruction diagram.

(3) Concerning the interior part of this quire, the continuity of the overall theme (Bema hymns) together with the lack of continuity between the texts on the verso of *folio G* and the recto of *folio g* confirm that, although their bifolio was closer to the interior of this quire, it could not have been the innermost bifolio. The number of missing bifolios lost from *bifolio G/g* up to (and including) the innermost bifolio could be anywhere between 1 and 7 in relation to the rest of the quire. Four is indicated in the reconstruction diagram.

(4) Additional bifolios are missing from the exterior part of this quire with unknown content prior to the excerpt of the *Seal Letter* (BBB p. 1) before the recto of *folio I* and the continuation of "Hymns of praise to [Jesus the life-giver]" (BBB p. 12) after the verso of *folio i*. Once again, the amount of lost bifolios must have been proportional to the rest of the quire; and so, their number could be anywhere between 1 and 7 bifolios. Four is indicated in the reconstruction diagram.

Based on the reconstruction of Quire 2, the bifolios in Quire 1 likely numbered sixteen, at minimum. If so, this quire also contained 32 folios (64 pages) in the original codex.

The surviving pages of Quire 1 exhibit codicological features that fully accord with what is attested on the pages of Quire 2. Their similarities positively confirm that all twelve bifolios surviving today in M801a (III 53) derived from the same codex. Moreover, together they document a program of book design that continued across, at minimum, the 64 folios (128 pages) of an Iranian Manichaean service book, gathered in two quires of a minimum of sixteen bifolios each.

---

[23] Henning 1937, 5–6.

INTRACOLUMNAR ORGANIZATION

M801a (III 53) exhibits a large repertoire of scribal techniques used for organizing content at the level of the columns. Throughout the pages, the monotony of the tightly spaced and fully aligned lines of neat, black-ink writing is interrupted by (1) spacing, (2) captions in red ink, and (3) punctuation in red ink; and sometimes enhanced by (4) calligraphic letters and occasional decorative motifs. These devices of intracolumnar organization are employed in combination with one another **(Figs. 5, 6, and 7).** They allow the one scribe of this manuscript to visually structure what (s)he writes by marking the start and end of the main sections of the book, groups of texts, and individual texts. While aesthetically pleasing, the application of these scribal tools is practical, assuring that the reader can navigate the pages with ease.

<u>Spacing</u>

Within the eighteen-line text area of the columns, spacing, that is, blank areas of various length, mark the start of something new—a new text, a new group of texts, or an entirely new section—in this book. They come in three sizes: a gaping ten-line area (*large spacing*), a couple of lines (*medium spacing*), and the length of a single word (*small spacing*). They are matched to the importance of what they signal, distinguishing categories of content between what was finished and what is to come. The same categories of content are separated by the same sizes of spacing. These blank areas of the columns faintly show the writing from the other side of the folio.[24]

Large spacing claims ten (and in one case even twelve) blank lines within the eighteen-line column to signal a new section in the book. Three examples survive on what is left from the original codex. The first separates the epistle from the hymns (BBB p. 2 lines 5–14, see Fig. 5a). It is centered in the column between four lines of text before and after it, and highlighted by one red-ink line before and after it. The second is employed in an analogous configuration after the last set of hymns to the gods and before the start of a new set of Bema hymns (BBB p. 19 lines 5–14, see Fig. 6a). The third example also separates two sets of hymns: the last hymn of praise from the first of the hymn of the joyful ones (BBB p. 25 lines 7–12) without being centered on the page. Instead, this gap follows six lines of writing and claims the rest of the column on this page. Thereby, it, too marks the start of a new section on the subsequent page.

Medium spacing is formed by either one, two, or three blank lines. The one- and two-line versions are used for separating individual hymns, while the three-line version signals the start of a multiple-page unit of shorter hymns. Eight examples survive in two sets. All are in Quire 2. Four cases of one-line examples can be seen between the individual "hymns of the joyful ones" (twice on BBB p. 28, see Fig. 5b; and once each on BBB p. 26 and p. 29). Three cases of two-line

[24] The intensity of how much the ink bleeds through varies slightly, depending on the nuances of manufacture and/or the sizing particular to the individual sheets of paper used in the making of this codex (e.g., BBB p. 2 vs. BBB p. 29). For more on the question of how inks of different color behave on the pages of M801a (III 53), see the discussion of green ink, below.

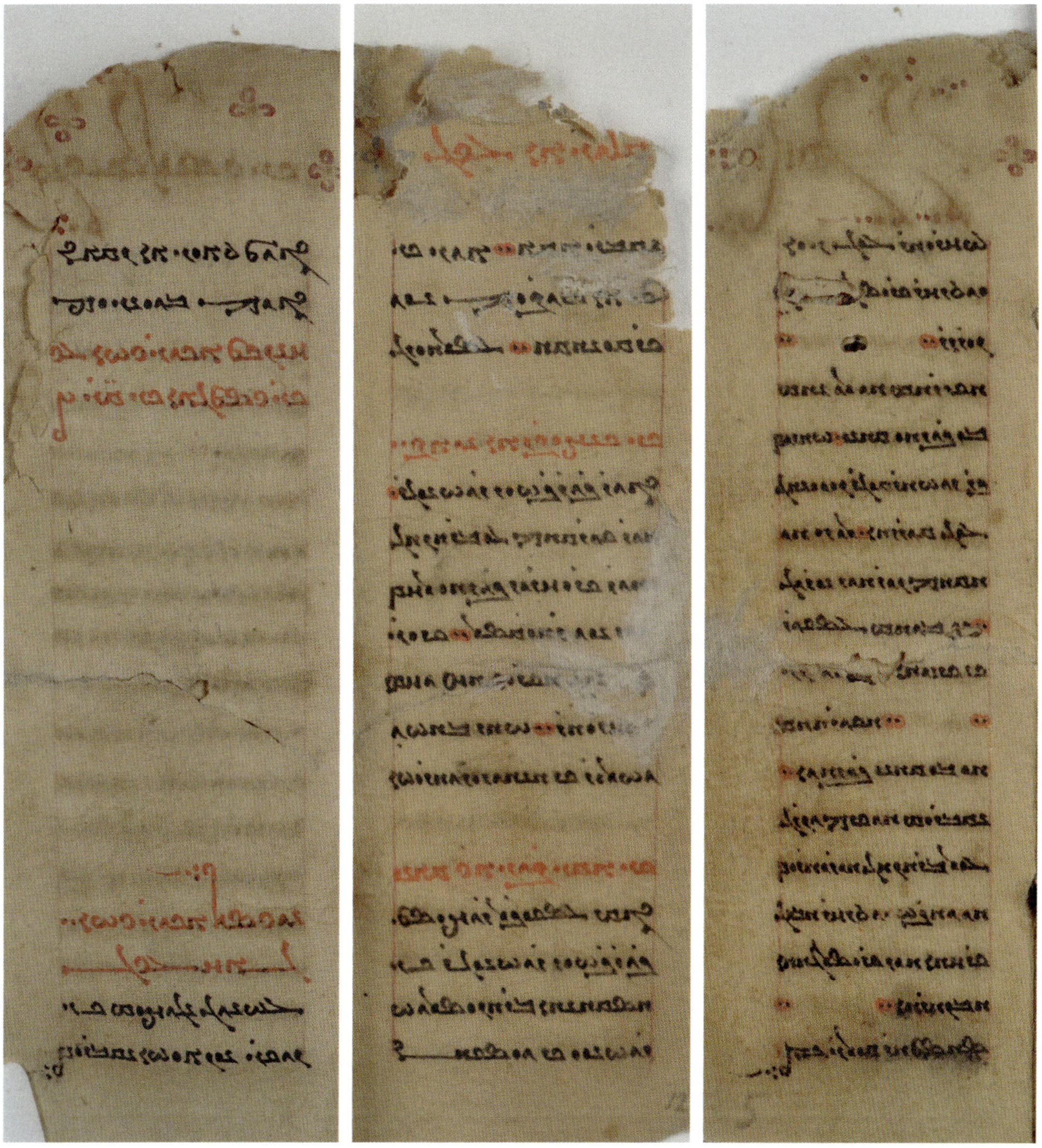

a: LARGE SPACING, RED INK CAPTIONS & PUNCTUATION folio f/recto [BBB p. 19], detail of photograph (III 53_6)

b: MEDIUM SPACING, RED INK CAPTIONS & PUNCTUATION folio a/verso [BBB p. 28], detail of photograph (III 53_2)

c: SMALL SPACING & RED INK PUNCTUATION folio H/recto [BBB p. 3], detail of photograph (III 53_21)

Fig. 5: Spacing and red ink in intracolumnar organization of manuscript M801a (III 53)

examples survive among what originally were the set of multiple hymns to Srōšahrāy (BBB p. 9, see Fig. 6b), Jesus the life-giver (BBB p. 12), and the messengers (BBB p. 16). Finally, the one case of a three-line example is between the set of multiple hymns to Srōšahrāy and the set of multiple hymns to Jesus the life-giver (BBB p. 10).

Small spacing is used for separating shorter texts by leaving a suitable amount of blank space in a line between a pair of decorative punctuations consist-

a: LARGE SPACING, RED INK CAPTIONS & PUNCTUATION
folio I/verso [BBB p. 2],
detail of photograph (III 53_21)

b: MEDIUM SPACING & RED INK PUNCTUATION
folio h/recto [BBB p. 9],
detail of photograph (III 53_8)

c: SMALL SPACING & RED INK PUNCTUATION
folio C/recto [BBB p. 35],
detail of photograph (III 53_27)

Fig. 6: Spacing and red ink in intracolumnar organization of manuscript M801a (III 53)

ing of double black dots encircled in red ink (°° °°). Such spacing may occur anywhere within a column at the start or the end of a line, depending on where the last word of a text ends. Although varying significantly, the length of such spacing is comparable to that of individual words. The longest versions can take up as much as two-thirds of a line (e.g.: BBB p. 5), while the shortest equal the length of just a few letters (e.g.: BBB p. 41).

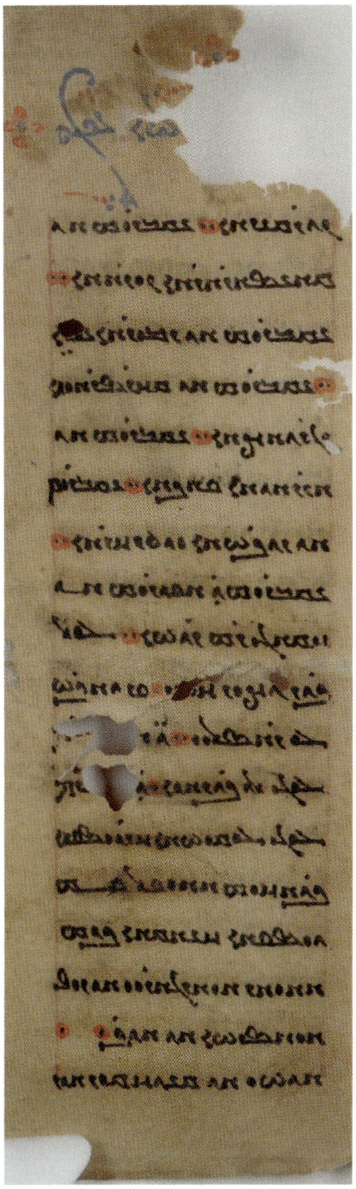

a: RED INK PUNCTUATION & SMALL SPACING
folio j/verso [BBB p. 22], detail of photograph (III 53_11)

b: RED INK PUNCTUATION & MOTIFS IN SMALL SPACING
folio g/recto [BBB p. 27] line 1, detail of photograph (III 53)

c: BLACK INK CALLIGRAPHY IN FIRST LINE
folio c/recto [BBB p. 39] line 1, detail of photograph (III 53_17)

d: RED INK PUNCTUATION & SMALL SPACING
folio h/verso [BBB p. 10] line 13, detail of photograph (III 53_9)

e: BLACK INK CALLIGRAPHY & MOTIFS IN LAST LINE
folio h/verso [BBB p. 10] line 18, detail of photograph (III 53_9)

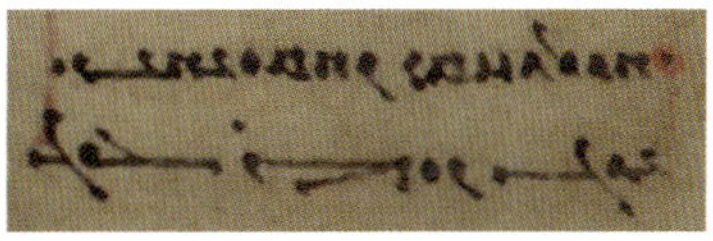

f: BLACK INK CALLIGRAPHY IN LAST TWO LINES
folio c/verso [BBB p. 26] lines 17-18, detail of photograph (III 53_4)

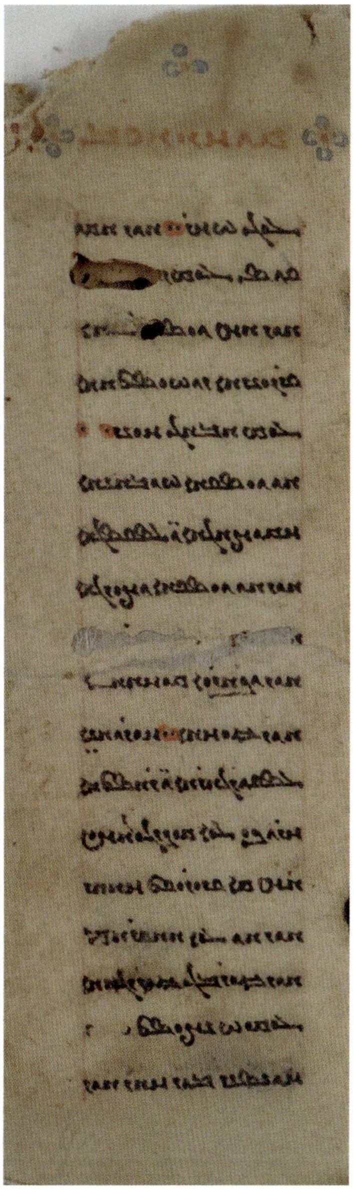

g: RED INK PUNCTUATION & SMALL SPACING
folio j/verso [BBB p. 1], detail of photograph (III 53_32)

Fig. 7: Punctuation and calligraphy in intracolumnar organization in manuscript M801a (III 53)

Examples of small spacing are attested in sets, including in twelve consecutive instances in one part of Quire 1 and in seven instances in two parts of Quire 2. In Quire 1, they are used three times per page among short hymns across the four pages of two folios, including Bema Hymns 2, 3, 4 (BBB p. 3, see Fig. 6c) and Bema Hymns 5, 6, 7 (BBB p. 4), followed by Bema Hymns 9, 10, 11 (BBB p. 5) and Bema Hymns 12, 13, 14 (BBB p. 6). In quire 2, they are used among the smaller confessions before resuming phrases such as: "Furthermore, …" (BBB p.

35, see Fig. 5c), "Moreover, ..." (BBB pp. 40, 41, 43, 47), and "And ..." (BBB p. 46). In one additional instance, this type of spacing is used within the confession text of the second commandment as it marks the start a subsection labeled as "The second part (of the commandment on Non-injury), concerning the Glory of the Religion ..." (BBB p. 34).

In three additional instances, small spacing is used as a filler within a line in connection with punctuation in red ink. All examples occur in Quire 1 among hymns that end short of filling out their last lines. Their execution varies. The first example is connected to the closing statement "Here end the Srōšahrāy (hymns). Six (hymns)" (BBB p. 10 line 13, see Fig. 7d and Fig. 11). It is added to the start of the line before the last word without the usual pair of double decorative punctu-ations. Most of the line here is simply left blank, as if the only word in that line was left-aligned. The second example is located after the end of the closing phrase "may the angels give you peace" and before the start of the subsequent blank lines (BBB p. 26 line 10, see Fig. 15). Here the small spacing is executed in the standard way. In a sense, what these two examples of small spacing separate is the last words of the hymns from the start of the blank lines of medium spacing. The third example is found at the end of the subsequent hymn, following the closing sentence "and may Wahman bring you new (and) eternal life" (BBB p. 27 line 1, see Fig. 7b). In this case, the scribe stretched the letters at the end of the column on the previous page (BBB p. 26 line 18, see Fig. 7f) to conclude the hymn on the next page. The resulting gap in the first line is filled out with a decorative version of small spacing that features red-ink floral motifs around a pair of red dots to mark the start and the end of the blank space at the end of the line. No blank lines follow.

Captions in Red Ink

Captions, that is, brief identifying statements are used for labeling the hymns either before (*pre-text captions*) or after their texts (*post-text captions*) within the columns of this Bema service book. These captions often occupy two lines, or parts of two lines. They may be written directly before and/or after the text in black or occasionally in red ink. When used in combination with spacing, red captions are especially striking.

Pre-text captions are attested in two roles. Some are seen announcing the start of a set of hymns as is the case with the following hymns: "Here begin the Bema (hymns)" (BBB p. 2 line 15, see Fig. 5a), "Here begin (the hymns of praise to) Jesus the life-giver" (BBB p. 10 line 17, see Fig. 11), and "Here begin the hymns of praise to the Bema" (BBB p. 19 lines 15–16, see Fig. 6a). Other examples may give a reference to a familiar tune of their melody in red ink and thus, indirectly announce the start of a single hymn, as seen in the case of hymn 3: "To the tune 'Come hither to new fortune' " (BBB p. 27 line 2, see Fig. 15); hymn 4: "To the tune *pncyxz'n*" (BBB p. 28 line 5, see Fig. 6b); hymn 5: "To (the tune) 'Lord Mani has come' " (BBB p. 28 line 14, see Fig. 6b); hymn 6: "This (one) to the tune 'You are the powerful god' " (BBB p. 29 lines 7–8, see Fig. 16); and hymn 7: "This (one) to the Sogdian melody" (BBB p. 30 lines 5–6).

Post-text captions also are attested in two roles. Some may directly announce the end of a section, which may consist of one important text, such as: “Here ends the *Seal Letter*” (BBB p. 2 line 4, see Fig. 6a); or sets of hymns, such as: “Here end the Srōšahrāy (hymns). Six (hymns)” (BBB p. 10 lines 12–13, see Fig. 11); “Here end the hymns of praise to the messengers, two in number” (BBB p. 19 lines 3–4, see Fig. 5a); and “Here end the hymns of praise of the Bema of Light, three in total” (BBB p. 25 lines 5–6). Other examples may indirectly announce the end of an individual hymn by adding a punctuation mark followed by the name of the hymn’s author. An undecorated version of this can be seen in the case of “Kirbakkarzādag” (BBB p. 12 line 2), when the punctuation is a black dot, and the name is also in black ink. A decorative version can be seen in the case of “Bay-Aryāmān” (BBB p. 30 line 4), when the punctuation and the name are both in red ink.

Punctuation in Red Ink

Punctuation marks provide a scribal tool for distinguishing content within an individual text. Their basic shape is that of a single dot (◦) or a pair of dots with a space between them (◦ ◦). They are placed at mid-level of the writing in relation to the height of the script behind a clause or a sentence, and occasionally also at the end of a small spacing that fills out the line following the punctuation at the end of a sentence. These dots are added by the scribe while writing and decorated subsequently. The decoration is a tight red line encircling the black dots. Each dot receives a red circle. Occasionally, double dots have a single circle around them. Other means of decorating punctuation marks involve the use of red dots supplemented with floral motifs. These, however, are attested seldomly and only in connection with *small spacing*, which are employed as fillers within a line at the end of text in this manuscript, as noted above.

Punctuation is most frequent in the texts of hymns in this service book. Even though composed as poetry (that is, in short rhythmic sections that may rhyme), they are written continuously, as in most examples of Iranian Manichaean poetic texts. One line of a hymn (marked by punctuation) might take up one-and-a-half lines in the column, as seen for example in a Middle Persian hymn of praise to the Apostle (BBB p. 22, see Fig. 7a):

> (1) [...] ◦ ◦ We revere the wise heads of (religious) houses. ◦ ◦ We revere the doughty scribes. ◦ ◦ We revere the melodious cantors. ◦ ◦ We revere the (6) pure elect. ◦ ◦ We revere the holy virgins. ◦ ◦ We revere and bless the whole flock of light, ◦ ◦ whom you yourself have chosen ◦ ◦ through the spirit (11) of truth. ◦ ◦ And [from] your majesty, O lord, ◦ and [from] the majesty of all these (afore mentioned), I beg (as) a boon for all my limbs that remembrance may come to my heart, (17) recollection to (my) mind, ◦ ◦ (18) awareness to (my) thinking, and ...

In this passage, there are eight pairs of black dots circled in red ink (◦ ◦), two cases of single black dots circled in red ink (◦), and one pair of black dots separated by *small spacing*, each circled in red ink (◦ ◦). The elect chanting or learning to chant this hymn from a text written in this way is guided as to the hymn's structure by this use of punctuation.

Calligraphic Letters and Decorative Motifs

Calligraphy is employed sparingly and always in combination with other means of organizing content within the column. Certain single letters in a line are written in their calligraphic forms. Their repertoire includes:

– initial " ʾ-"	at start of line, written with elongated lower stroke (e.g.: BBB p. 9 lines 1 and 8, see Fig. 6b; BBB p. 10 lines 1 and 18, see Fig. 11; BBB p. 19 lines 1 and 2, see Fig. 5a; BBB p. 20 line 1, see Fig. 14; and BBB p. 39 line 1, see Fig. 7c)
– final "-*b*"	at end of line, written in black ink elongated (e.g.: BBB p. 9 line 17, see Fig. 6b; and BBB p. 14 line 18, see Fig. 12)
– initial "*g*-"	at start of line, written elongated (e.g.: BBB p. 16 line 17; and BBB p. 19 line 16, see Fig. 5a)
– final "-*g*"	at end of line, written elongated (e.g.: BBB p. 19 line 16, see Fig. 5a; and BBB p. 26 line 18, see Fig. 7f)
– letter "*ẖ*"	in mid-line, written elongated (e.g.: BBB p. 9 line 1, see Fig. 6b; BBB p. 18 line 5, see Fig. 13; and BBB p. 26 line 18, see Fig. 7f)
– final "-*ẖ*"	at end of line, written with a curl (e.g.: BBB p. 9 line 17, see Fig. 6b)
– final "-*m*"	at end of line, written with elongated down stroke decorated with dots (e.g.: BBB p. 19 line 18, see Fig. 5a)
– final "-*n*"	at end of line, written enlarged (e.g.: BBB p. 16 line 18; and BBB p. 19 line 1, see Fig. 5a)
– final "-*t*"	in mid-line, written with elongated vertical stroke (e.g.: BBB p. 19 line 15, see Fig. 5a)
– letter "*y*"	in red caption, written as a circle (e.g.: BBB p. 19 lines 4 and 15, see Fig. 5a; and BBB p. 28 line 14, see Fig. 5b)

The shapes of these letters adhere to a standard design; and their distribution is not fully improvised either. Their occurrence follows a pattern and supports the work of the scribe in the columnar organization of content on pages already distinguished by large or medium spacing and red ink captions. A calligraphic letter may start the first word of a column or a new section below medium spacing within a column (see Figs. 5a-b and 6a-b). Similarly, the last letter of a word may also be written in a calligraphic form either in the first and/or last line of the page (see Figs. 5a-c and 7e) or at the conclusion of a section (see Fig. 5a).

Occasionally, simple motifs of scribal decoration are added to calligraphic letters in the columns. They consist of a few dots and sometimes a line in an arrangement that implies right-to-left direction, when added after the last word of the page. They occur when the text continues along the next page, as seen in the cases of a hymn to Maitreya (BBB p. 3 line 18, see Fig. 5c); as well as the first hymns among the many hymns of praise to Jesus the life-giver (BBB p. 10 line

18, see Fig. 7e) and to the Bema (BBB p. 19 line 18, see Fig. 5a). In one instance, a pair of such decorative motifs is drawn in mirror symmetry to start and conclude a small gap at the end of a hymn to the joyful ones (BBB p. 27 line 1, see Fig. 7b).

The Hand of the Anonymous Scribe

Arguably, M801a (III 53) was the work of one scribe, who wrote in three languages using the Manichaean script. The characteristic features of this scribe's handwriting can be observed throughout, as illustrated here by three pages that feature the three languages from the start, the middle, and the end of this service book (see Figs. 6a–c): The first example, BBB p. 2 from the first half of Quire 1, contains in Middle Persian the end of the *Seal Letter*, in Sogdian the two red-ink captions, and again in Middle Persian three lines of a hymn. The second example, BBB p. 9 from the second half of Quire 1, contains Parthian hymns. The third example, BBB p. 35 from the end of Quire 2, contains a passage from the confession of Non-injury in Sogdian.

The distinct shapes of certain letters specific to this scribe can be observed on these three pages and throughout the book. The initial form of the *aleph* (ʾ-) at the start of lines concludes in an elegantly stretched diagonal stroke in Middle Persian (see Fig. 6a lines 1 and 16), Parthian (see Fig. 6b lines 1 and 8), and Sogdian (see Fig. 7c). The loops of the letter "*s*" are uniquely angled in Middle Persian (Fig. 6a lines 2 and 3), Parthian (Fig. 6b line 2), and Sogdian (Fig. 6c lines 3, 6, and 8). While the shape of the letter "*ṭ*" is much improvised by this scribe, its initial form of at the start of lines characteristically concludes in a left-to-right curl in all three languages, as seen in a Middle Persian example (Fig. 5b line 2).[25] When the letter "*ṭ*" follows an "*s*," occasionally its upper loop morphs into a curve that concludes touching the second loop of the "*s*" in Middle Persian (see Fig. 5b line 15, Fig. 6b lines 2 and 8, and Fig. 7g line 17) and Sogdian (see Fig. 5b line 4).[26] Also distinct to this scribe is the motif of three dots ending in a curving line (see Fig. 5a lines 15 and 18, and Fig. 5c line 18). The headers and their decorative motifs likewise seem to indicate one hand (see Figs. 8 and 9).

HEADERS IN PRACTICAL AND DECORATIVE ROLES

The practice of identifying textual content beyond the level of the columns in Iranian Manichaean codices is thoroughly documented in M801a (III 53). In the form of "page headers" or "running headers"—written in one line across the upper margins on the pairs of facing pages of the open book—the scribe labels the main content of the texts two pages at a time. Accordingly, each pair of pages has one such "headline" or "header." Their presence is striking (**Figs. 8 and 9**). They are clearly separated from the body of the text area. In contrast with the

[25] Additional examples include in Middle Persian, BBB p. 7 line 8; in Parthian, BBB p. 5 line1 and BBB p. 6 line 7; and in Sogdian, BBB p. 43 line 1.

[26] For a unique, stretched version of a final "-*ṭ*" written with a straight diagonal line that terminates in a small counterclockwise curl (following an "-*š*-") in the last word on a Sogdian page, see BBB p. 32 line 18, Fig. 17.

monotony of the columns, the headers are highlighted and distinguished from the rest of the pages through their (1) isolated location, (2) vivid ink colors, (2) large script size, (4) select calligraphic letters, and (5) decoration. Thus, beyond their practical function, the headers adorn the manuscript. At the same time, their means of decoration firmly links them to the columns.

Location

The headers are isolated from the columns across the upper margins. They are slightly closer to the first lines of the text area than to the edge of the paper. Their distance from the top edge of the folio approximates the height of the bottom margins (see Fig. 1). Despite their precise alignment, there is no visible evidence for ruling.

In harmony with the symmetrical design of the two facing pages of the open codex, the start and the end of their lines are guided by the implied continuation of the vertical ruling of the two columns. Their texts are broken into two halves by the two inner margins. Depending on their length, the scribe may write a shorter phrase centered above the column, while concluding a longer phrase in the area of the outer margin as is the case with the violet header "Here begin (the hymns of praise) to Jesus the life-giver" (BBB pp. 10–11, see Fig. 11).

Ink Color

Black ink is never used in the headers in this manuscript. Instead, they are written in one of four colors: red, blue, violet, or green.[27] Among the thirty-two headers that survive (or are evidenced) in this manuscript, more frequent are headers written in red ink (11 examples) and blue ink (10 examples). Less frequent are headers in violet ink (6 examples) and green ink (5 examples), the latter surviving in much faded condition (see Figs. 3–4).

Facing page by facing page, the distribution of these four ink colors aids the navigation of the content. A mechanical sequence of their repetition would undermine this function. Instead, new content is always marked by a color different from that of the previous header, as indicated by this list of headers attested from the two quires of this Bema service book:

Quire 1

(missing folios)

(1) BBB, pp. ?–1 {*red*}: '[Here begins] the *Seal Letter*'
(2) BBB, pp. 2–3 {*green*}: 'Here begin the hymns of the Bema' (see Fig. 11)
(3) BBB, pp. 4–? {*blue*}: 'Hymns [for the Bema]'

(missing folios)

(4) BBB, pp. ?–5 {*blue*}: '[Hymns] for the Bema'
(5) BBB, pp. 6–? {*violet*}: 'Hymns [for the Bema]'

(missing folios at middle of quire)

[27] On the color wheel (based on the primary, secondary, and tertiary colors used in art history), the hue of the red ink is "red-orange," and the hue of the violet is "red-violet" in this manuscript (Gulácsi 2005, 97–8).

(6) BBB, pp. ?–7 {*red*}: '[Hymn of praise to] Narisah-yazad'
(7) BBB, pp. 8–? {*red*}: 'Hymn of praise [to Narisah-yazad]'
(missing folios)
(8) BBB, pp. ?– 9 {*red*}: '[Hymn of praise to] Srōšahrāy'
(9) BBB, pp. 10–11 {*violet*}: 'Here begin (the hymns of praise) to Jesus the life-giver' (see Fig. 12)
(10) BBB, pp. 12–? {*blue*}: 'Hymns of praise to [Jesus the life-giver]'
(missing folios)

Quire 2

(missing folio)
(11) BBB, pp. ?–13 {*red*}: '[Hymns of praise to] the messengers'
(12) BBB, pp. 14–15 {*green*}: '[Hymns of praise to the messengers]' (see Fig. 13)
(13) BBB, pp. 16–? {*?*}: '[Hymns of praise to the messengers]'
(missing folio)
(14) BBB, pp. ?–17 {*red*}: '[Hymns of praise to the messengers]'
(15) BBB, pp. 18–19 {*green*}: 'Here end (the hymns of praise) to the messengers' (see Fig. 14)
(16) BBB, pp. 20–21 {*violet*}: 'Hymns of praise to the Apostle' (see Fig. 15)
(17) BBB, pp. 22–? {*blue*}: 'Hymns of praise to [the Apostle]'
(missing folio)
(damaged folio BBB, pp. 23–24: header and ten lines torn off)
(missing folio)
(18) BBB, pp. ?–25 {*violet*}: '[Here end](?) the hymns of praise'
(19) BBB, pp. 26–27 {*blue*}: 'Here begin the hymns of the joyful ones' (see Fig. 16)
(20) BBB, pp. 28–29 {*red*}: 'Hymns of joy,' (see Fig. 17)
(21) BBB, pp. 30–? {*blue*}: 'The joyful ones [...]'
(missing folios at middle of quire)
(22) BBB, pp. ?–31 {*green*}: 'The commandment [Non-injury]'
(23) BBB, pp. 32–33 {*blue*}: 'The commandment Non-injury' (see Fig. 18)
(24) BBB, pp. 34–35 {*violet*}: 'The second part (of the commandment) Non-injury' (see Fig. 19)
(25) BBB, pp. 36–? {*blue*}: '[The commandment] Purity'
(missing folio)
(damaged folio BBB, pp. 37–38: header and thirteen lines torn off)
(missing folio)
(26) BBB, pp. ?–39 {*violet*}: '[...] command'
(27) BBB, pp. 40–41 {*green*}: 'The five divine gifts' (see Fig. 20)
(28) BBB, pp. 42–43 {*red*}: 'The closing of the five gates' (see Fig. 21)
(29) BBB, pp. 44–? {*blue*}: 'Prayers and [hymns](?)'
(missing folio)

a: '*Srōšahrāy*' in 2nd half of red header with blue motifs, folio h/recto [BBB p. 9], detail of photograph (III 53_8)

b: '*The messengers*' in 2nd half of red header with blue motifs, folio d/recto [BBB p. 13], detail of photograph (III 53_4)

c: '*For the Bema*' in 2nd half of blue header with red motifs, folio G/recto [BBB p. 5], detail of photograph (III 53_22)

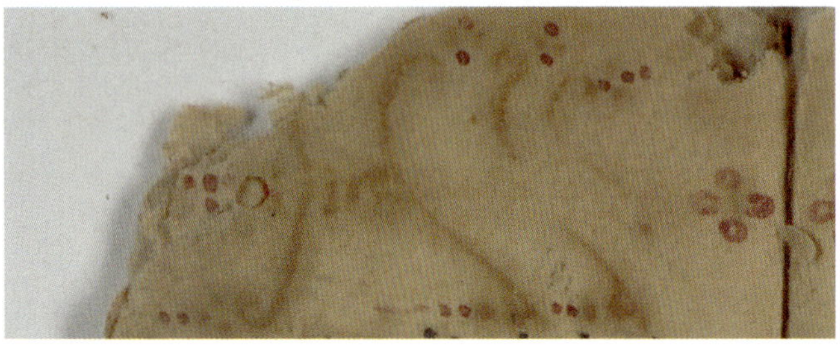

d: '*Of the Bema*' in 2nd half of faded green header with violet motifs, folio H/recto [BBB p. 3], detail of photograph (III 53_21)

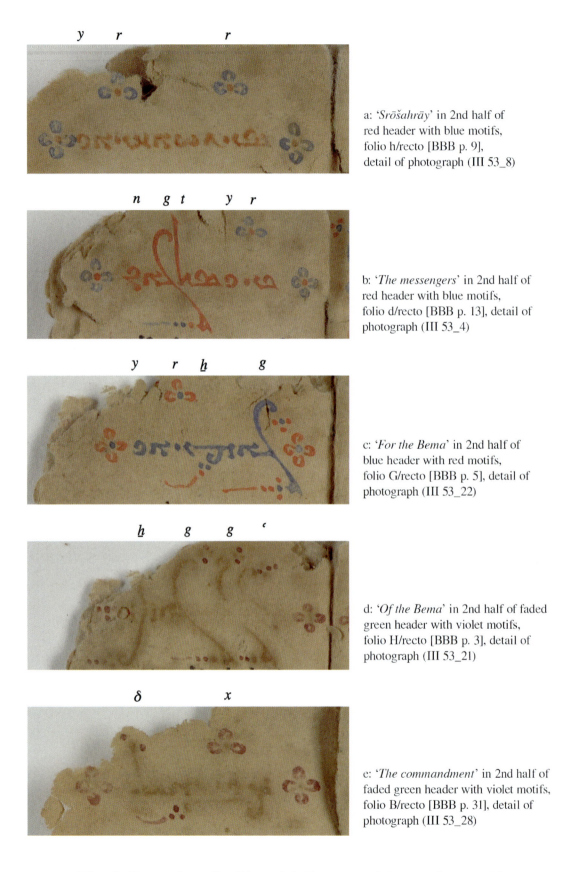

e: '*The commandment*' in 2nd half of faded green header with violet motifs, folio B/recto [BBB p. 31], detail of photograph (III 53_28)

Fig. 8: Examples of calligraphic letters and decorative motifs in half headers of manuscript M801a (III 53)

a: '*(Hymn of) praise*' in 1st half of red header with blue motifs, folio g/verso [BBB p. 8], detail of photograph (III 53_8)

b: '*Here begin the hymn[s]* of' in 1st half of blue header with red motifs, folio c/verso [BBB p. 26], detail of photograph (III 53_4)

c: '*Hymn[s] of*' in 1st half of blue header with red motifs, folio H/verso [BBB p. 4], detail of photograph (III 53_22)

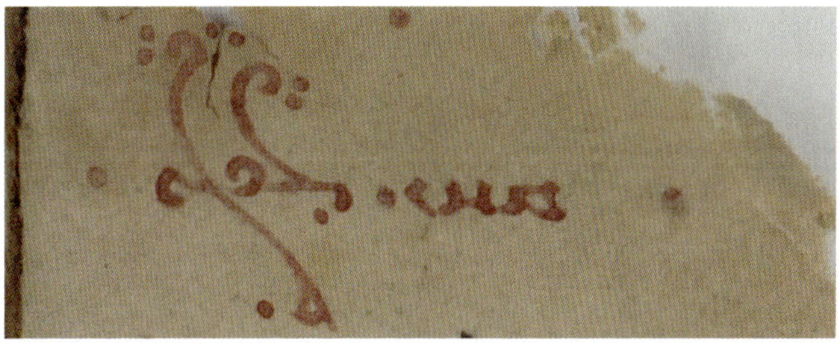

d: '*Hymn[s] of*' in 1st half of violet header with faded green motifs, folio G/verso [BBB p. 6], detail of photograph (III 53_23)

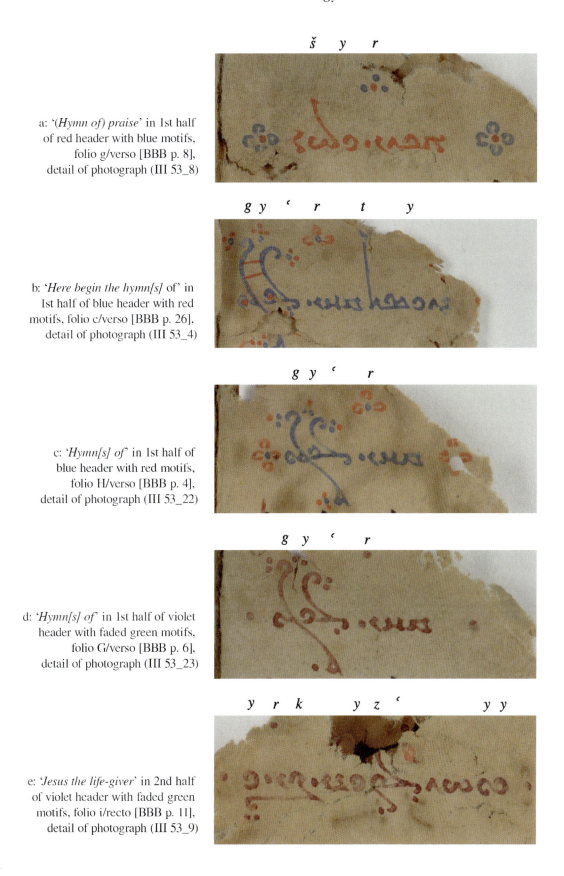

e: '*Jesus the life-giver*' in 2nd half of violet header with faded green motifs, folio i/recto [BBB p. 11], detail of photograph (III 53_9)

Fig. 9: Examples of calligraphic letters and decorative motifs in half headers of manuscript M801a (III 53)

(30) BBB, pp. ?–45 {*blue*}: '[...] zeal'
(31) BBB, pp. 46–47 {*red*}: 'The four Monday commands' (see Fig. 22)
(32) BBB, pp. 48–? {*blue*}: 'The table of the gods [...]'
(missing folio)

This list also demonstrates that when the same content continues over multiple pages, the scribe may choose to write the same header in the same color, as is the case with the red ink on two subsequent facing pages (BBB pp. ?–7 and 8–?). In all other instances of repeated headers, the ink colors are different: blue is followed by violet (BBB pp. ?–5 and 6–?), red is followed by green (BBB pp. ?–13 and 14–15), and violet is followed by blue (BBB pp. 21–22 and 23–?). The consecutive use of all four colors is attested only in two cases. In one of them, the order is red, green, violet, and blue (BBB pp. ?–17, 18–19, 20–21, and 22–?). In the other, the sequence is violet, green, red, and blue (BBB pp. ?–39, 40–41, 42–43, and 44–?). In the only additional surviving example of a four–header sequence, there is no green and one color is repeated: violet, blue, red, and blue (BBB pp. ?–25, 26–27, 28–29, and 30–?).

Although these ink colors are thoroughly documented in Manichaean codices from the Uygur era, their chemical composition, material source, and techniques of manufacture have not been studied. Their use seems to have a long history in Iranian Manichaean book culture, which started well before codices began to be made of paper among the Manichaeans by the middle of the 8th century.

In this regard, the case of the green ink is especially remarkable. Green is the only color that did not hold up on the paper of M801a (III 53). Its hue had faded beyond recognition. Its liquid had spread out around the letters and bled through the paper so that the mirror shapes of many letters are clearly recognizable on the other side of the folio. In contrast, red ink, blue ink, and violet ink leave no visible mark on the other side of the paper. Green ink had also faded in the calligraphic headers of all Manichaean codex fragments made of paper, including the paper bifolio M1 (III 203) that dates from 762 CE.[28] Green ink, however, does maintain its color and quality on parchment. When the writing surface is parchment, green ink is not impaired. This fact is evidenced on a page of the parchment bifolio M178 (III 4990) that preserves the first half of a green header in perfect condition.[29] It is therefore possible that green ink for writing the headers across the facing pages of codices was originally developed for parchment—at a time when, and a region where parchment was the material of Manichaean books—and its use did not carry over successfully to paper, which

[28] On M1 (III 203), the four half headers preserve their texts and floral decorations in the combination of two ink colors: red and faded green. On the historical repair of this bifolio, see Gulácsi 2005, 71–4.

[29] This large and exceptionally well-preserved Sogdian parchment bifolio, M178 (III 4990), retains four half headers: three have blue texts with blue motifs and one has green text with green motifs. Red ink is employed for writing the first two and the last line in each column, and for encircling the punctuation marks. Violet ink is not used in any form (Gulácsi 2005, 66, 100, Plate 1 and Fig. 3/17a; Morano 2018, 13–16, and 34–5).

became the preferred writing material of the Manichaeans during the Uygur era of their history.

Script Size

In this manuscript, the headers are further distinguished from the columns through the size of their writing. Their script size is considerably larger (see Fig. 1). They are written with a thicker dip pen (0.5 mm) and in a line height (2 mm) that is twice the height of the lines in the columns. In addition, select calligraphic letters further enlarge the footprint of the headers, occasionally reaching as much as 13 mm. Their upper extent reaches either the tip of the letter "*t*," the curving end of the letter "*g*," or the diacritical dot of the letter "*r*" (see Figs. 9b and 10b). Their lower extent is defined by the curving end of the lower half of the letter "*g*."

Calligraphic Letters

Certain letters that lend themselves to artfully modified forms in the headers are written in their calligraphic versions (see Figs. 8 and 9). The modifications are unique to each letter, but always increase the overall size of the header. The most frequent examples are:

- letter " ʿ " diagonal upper part of letter elongated, lower body concludes in a left curve in Middle Persian and Sogdian headers (see Figs. 8d–e)
- letter "*δ*" vertical part of letter elongated in Sogdian headers (see Fig. 9e)
- letter "*g*" diagonal part of letter elongated above and below the line (see Figs. 8b–d); final form concludes in a right-to-left circle left open at 5 o'clock in Middle Persian headers (see Figs. 9b–d)
- letter "*k*" horizontal part of letter below line elongated in Sogdian headers (see Fig. 8e)
- letter "*r*" diacritical mark above letter placed at exaggerated distance (and enclosed in three floral petals) in both Middle Persian and Sogdian headers (see Figs. 8a–c and 9a–d)
- letter "*t*" vertical part of letter elongated in Middle Persian headers (see Figs. 8b and 9b)
- letter "*x*" horizontal part of letter below line elongated, diacritical mark above letter placed at exaggerated distance and enclosed in three floral petals in Sogdian headers (see Fig. 9e)
- letter "*y*" written as circle left open at 7 o'clock (see Figs. 8a–c and 9a–e) in both Middle Persian and Sogdian headers; "*yy*" written as an infinity symbol ("∞") left open at 10 o'clock and 5 o'clock in a Sogdian header (see Fig. 9e)

Due to their varied textual content and combination of letters, the calligraphic program is unique to each header. Rarely, when a header or a phrase in a header is repeated, as in "Hymn[s] of" (BBB p. 4 and p. 6), the letters " ʿ," "*g*," "*r*," and "*y*" take the same form (see Figs. 10c and 10d).

Decorative Motifs

A harmonized program of decoration around the headers adds a further distinction to the upper margins in this manuscript. All headers are surrounded by *floral motifs*; and, occasionally, an arrangement of *dots and lines* accessorize certain letters. While these adornments frame each half of a header one page at a time, they also function together framing the full text of a header two pages at a time.

Floral motifs are standard parts of the headers. Their appearance and distribution follow a strict pattern. All flowers are drawn in the same abstract way, consisting of four petals around a dot (see Fig. 1b). The dot in the center is the same color as the ink of the header's text, while the petals are in one of the other three contrasting ink colors (as noted below). Such floral motifs flank each half header. Without exception, there is a pair of them on each page, one at the outer and another at the inner margin, that is, before and after the header's word(s) on that page. Thus, each full header is adorned with four flowers, at minimum. Additional flowers occur above a header when it contains the letter "*r*," whose diacritical mark is routinely turned into the core of a floral motif directly above the letter, at an exaggerated distance that fits the calligraphic size of other letters (see Figs. 9a–c, 10a–e). Flower motifs are not used below the header in this manuscript.

Dots and lines may be added as further decoration to certain calligraphic letters below and/or above the header. They tend to feature one or two larger dots, drawn in the same ink color as that of the writing, next to the tip of the longest part of the letter, in any direction suited for that location as in the case of the letters " ʿ " and "*g*" in the first half of a violet header on BBB p. 6 (see Fig. 10d). Additional smaller dots may be added in the ink color of the flowers, as seen for examples in the letters "*g*" and "*ẖ*" in the second half of a red header on BBB p. 5 (see Fig. 9c). The smaller dots may be followed by a relatively short line (3–5 mm) that can be straight or gently curving, as seen with letters "*g*," "*ẖ*," and "*x*" in many headers (see Figs. 9a–e).

The harmonized combination of colors between the motifs and the writing in relation to the columns below them adds a certain elegance to the headers' aesthetics. As if it was no effort at all, the scribe contrasts the decoration with the header's text in a set pattern. Red is always paired with blue, and violet is always paired with green. That is, the decorative motifs are red when the header's text is blue, blue when the text is red, violet when the text is green, and green when the text is violet. In this manuscript, there is no exception to these color pairings. This choice of color combination results in the headers always harmonizing with the rest of the facing pages, since all headers contain either red or violet and these two inks are also used in every column. Red is the color of intracolumnar captions and punctuation decoration; and violet is used for the columns' vertical ruling on all pages in this manuscript.

FACING PAGES AS UNITS OF BOOK DESIGN

The Bema service book preserved in M801a (III 53) is designed in two-page units. These units of book design are built on the practicalities of how a codex can transmit not only its written content, but also the structure of that content. What the reader accesses is a series of facing pages of the open book crowned by the one header written across them. While the two columns are separated from one another by the two inner margins, they are also united in their symmetrical placement under the header they share and within the continuous border created by the upper, outer, and bottom margins around them. All facing pages are framed in the formal symmetry of this layout. At the same time, the direction of the writing (shown enlarged in the header) and the sequence of the two columns imply a right-to-left movement among these units—fulfilled when the pages are turned.

Remarkably, twelve such pairs of facing pages survive from the original Bema service book in M801a (III 53); they are published here for the first time (**Figs. 10–21**). Six are retained intact in the historically preserved manuscript, including two that belonged to Quire 1 and four that belonged to Quire 2. The other six pairs are retained in two halves from Quire 2. In lieu of their physical restoration, the latter six can be restored digitally by virtually matching their pages in photographic reconstructions, as noted below:

Quire 1

(1) folios I/verso and H/recto [BBB pp. 2–3] with green header
'Here begin the hymns of the Bema' (see Fig. 10)
(2) folios h/verso and i/recto [BBB pp. 10–11] with violet header
'Here begin (the hymns of praise) to Jesus the life–giver' (see Fig. 11)

Quire 2

(3) folios d/verso and k/recto [BBB pp. 14–15] with green header
'[Hymns of praise to the messengers]' (digitally restored, see Fig. 12)
(4) folios e/verso and b/recto [BBB pp. 18–19] with green header
'Here end (the hymns of praise) to the Messengers' (see Fig. 13)
(5) folios f/verso and j/recto [BBB pp. 20–21] with violet header
'Hymns of praise to the Apostle' (digitally restored, see Fig. 14)
(6) folios c/verso and a/recto [BBB pp. 26–27] with blue header
'Here begin the hymns of the joyful ones' (digitally restored, see Fig. 15)
(7) folios a/verso and c/recto [BBB pp. 28–29] with red header
'Hymns of joy' (see Fig. 16)
(8) folios B/verso and A/recto [BBB pp. 32–33] with blue header
'The commandment Non–injury' (see Fig. 17)
(9) folios A/verso and C/recto [BBB pp. 34–35] with violet header
'The second part (of the commandment) Non–injury' (digitally restored, see Fig. 18)

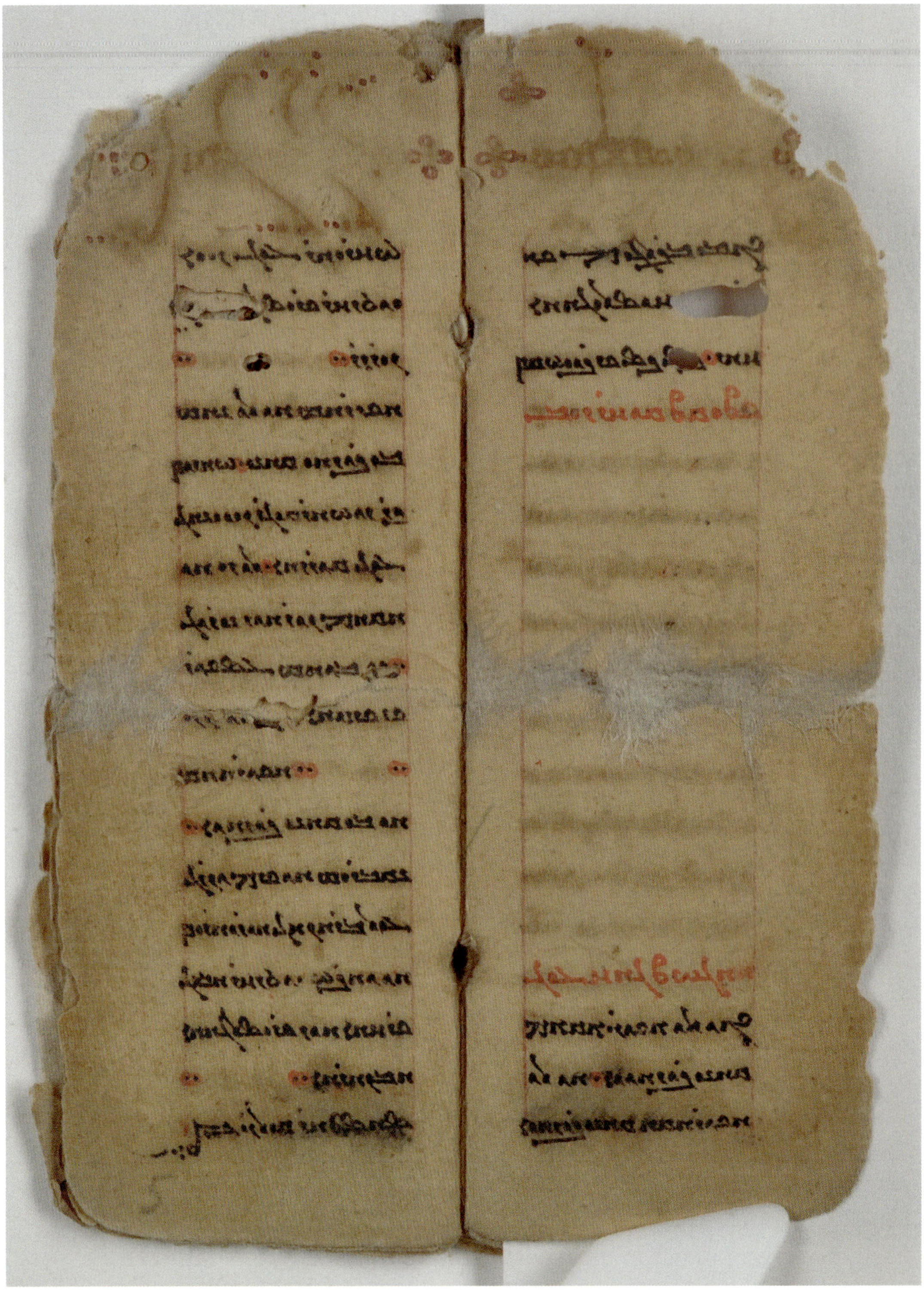

folios I/verso and H/recto [BBB pp. 2-3] preserved in manuscript M801a (III 53), detail of photograph III 53_21 (p. 106/top)

Fig. 10: First pair of facing pages surviving from Quire 1 with faded green header '*Here begin the hymns of the Bema*' and violet decoration

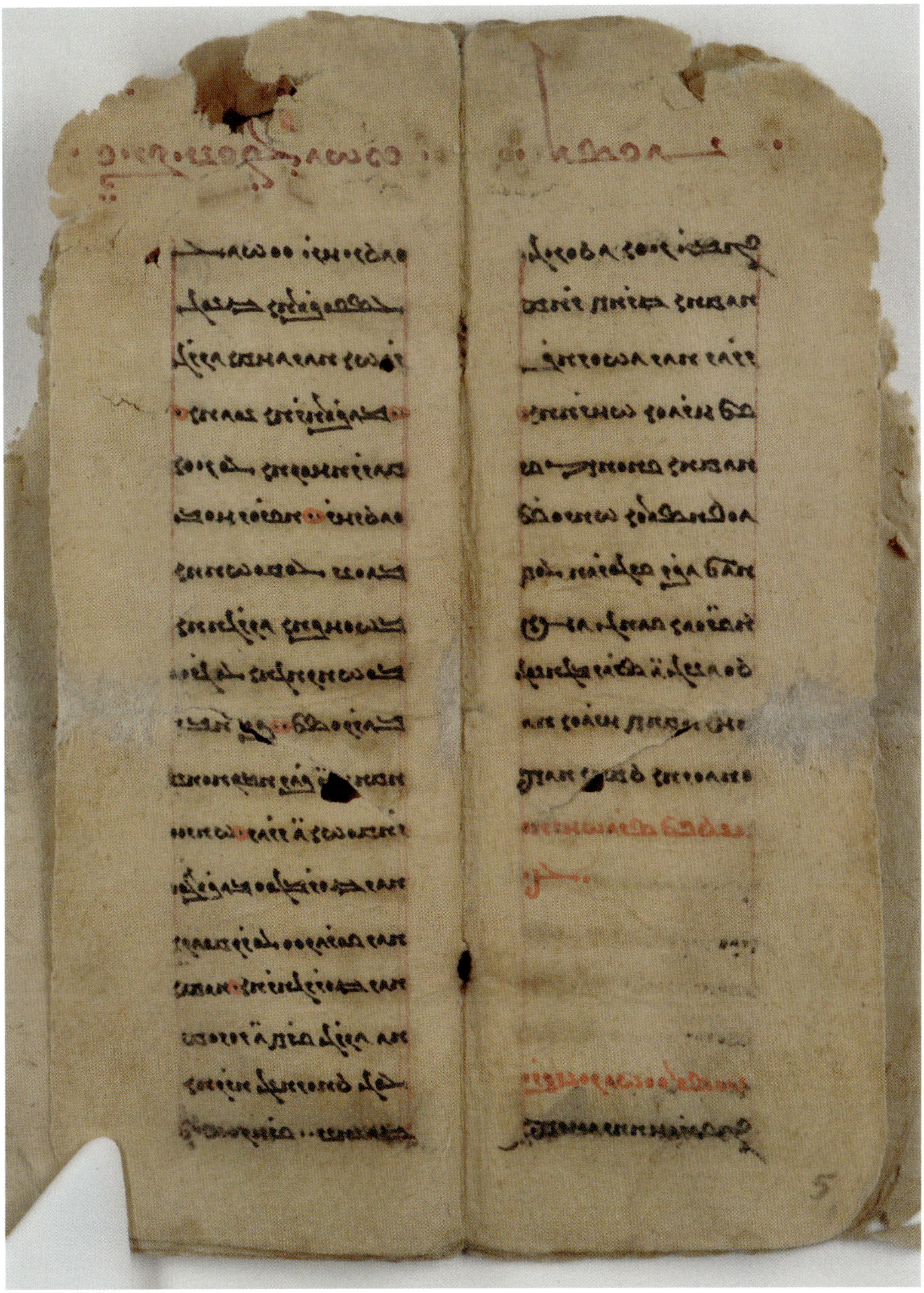

folios h/verso and i/recto [BBB pp. 10-11] preserved in manuscript M801a (III 53), detail of photograph III 53_9 (p. 102/top)

Fig. 11: Second pair of facing pages surviving from Quire 1 with violet header '*Here begin (the hymns of praise) to Jesus the life-giver*' and faded decoration

(10) folios J/verso and F/recto [BBB pp. 40–41] with green header 'The five divine gifts' (digitally restored, see Fig. 19)
(11) folios F/verso and E/recto [BBB pp. 42–43] with red header 'The closing of the five gates' (see Fig. 20)
(12) folios K/verso and D/recto [BBB pp. 46–47] with red header 'The four Monday commands' (digitally restored, see Fig. 21)

These twelve pairs of facing pages (24 pages) are 50% of the full surviving content (48 pages), and close to 19% of the total original content of the two quires with 16 bifolios each (128 pages). Also remarkable is that in four instances, two pairs of facing pages were preserved in an intact sequence from Quire 2: the first case is found on BBB pp. 18–19 and 20–21 (Figs. 13–14), the second on BBB pp. 26–27 and 28–29 (Figs. 15–16), the third on BBB pp. 32–33 and 34–35 (Figs. 17–18), and the fourth on BBB pp. 40–41 and 42–43 (Figs. 19–20).

Additionally, twenty-four cases of half pairs of facing pages are preserved in M801a (III 53). They include eight examples from Quire 1 and sixteen examples from Quire 2 of the original codex, such as BBB p. 13 (see Fig. 1a).[30]

Quire 1

(1) folio I/recto, BBB p. 1
(2) folio H/verso, BBB p. 4
(3) folio G/recto BBB p. 5
(4) folio G/verso, BBB p. 6
(5) folio g/recto, BBB p. 7
(6) folio g/verso, BBB p. 8
(7) folio h/recto, BBB p. 9
(8) folio i/verso, BBB p. 12

Quire 2

(9) folio d/recto, BBB p. 13
(10) folio k/verso, BBB p. 16
(11) folio e/recto, BBB p. 17
(12) folio j/verso, BBB p. 22
(13) folio l/recto, BBB p. 23
(14) folio l/verso, BBB p. 24
(15) folio c/recto, BBB p. 25
(16) folio b/verso, BBB p. 30
(17) folio B/recto, BBB p. 31
(18) folio C/verso, BBB p. 36
(19) folio L/recto, BBB p. 37
(20) folio L/verso, BBB p. 38
(21) folio J/recto, BBB p. 39
(22) folio F/verso, BBB p. 42
(23) folio E/recto, BBB p. 43
(24) folio D/verso, BBB p. 48

One page at a time, these twenty-four cases attest the same program of design, identical in layout and decoration to what is found on the twelve intact pairs.

Together the intact and half pairs of facing pages demonstrate that the original Bema service book preserved in M801a (III 53) was uniform in its design. The same principles of layout and decoration are followed on them throughout the codex, in both quires, and on all pages. Although it remains unknown how the first (recto) and last (verso) pages of the original codex looked, all pairs of facing

[30] In M801a (III 53), BBB p. 13 (folio d/recto) is preserved following BBB p. 26 (folio c/verso), see Fig. 1a, and Fig. 2/4-photograph (III 53_4) on p. 99/bottom. In the original Bema service book, these two pages did not belong together. While BBB p. 13 lost its original facing page, BBB p. 26 (folios c/verso) can be digitally matched with its own pair, BBB p. 27 (folio a/recto), as noted above; see Fig. 15.

pages in between them were structured uniformly. While these two groups constitute only 48 pages (24 + 24 pages), that is, 37.6% of the total original content of two quires (128 pages), their surviving parts from BBB p. 1 to BBB p. 48 exhibit the same program of design (see Figs. 3–4).[31]

Within this uniformity, however, each pair of facing pages is distinct. The program of decoration (color repertoire, calligraphy, motifs, and columnar organization) is improvised on each by the scribe. As (s)he writes, the scribe employs them as tools in making the codex user-friendly. Thus, what may appear to be pretty accessories to the text, on a cursory view, are much more than mere "decoration" in the eye of the reader. They aid the reader in comprehending structure and navigating the codex, while, at the same time, making this Bema service book aesthetically pleasing, special—a work of art.

The program of decoration is fitted to the content and the significance of that content. The starting and concluding pairs of pages get more scribal attention, as documented in the three surviving cases with such content. The phrase "*Here begins*" is used in a header when a new content appears on the right page, that is, on the verso of the previous folio, as seen on BBB pp. 2–3 (Fig. 10), BBB pp. 10–11 (Fig. 11), and BBB pp. 26-27 (Fig. 15). "*Here ends*" is used when more than a page is claimed by the previous content and the new content appears somewhere along the left, that is, on the recto of the next folio, as seen on BBB pp. 18–19 (Fig. 13). These examples include the two most decorated pairs of surviving facing pages (BBB pp. 2–3 and BBB pp. 18–19), accessorized by a combination of all available means suited to their columnar content. They all use (1) green headers (the rarest ink color), and their columns feature (2) large spacing, (3) multiple lines of red captions, as well as numerous (4) calligraphic letters, and (5) decorative motifs.

The three parts of the book (Epistle, Hymns, Confessions) are not evenly accessorized either, due to the differences of their genres. The Confessions are the least decorated. The long prose of the five main Confessions does not require the same level of intracolumnar organization as the shorter texts in the other two genres (see Figs. 17–21). The Hymns, in contrast, are the most decorative part of what survives from the original codex. Their shorter texts require the most spacing (medium and small), red captions, red punctuation, and calligraphy (see Figs. 10–16). Especially striking is the presentation of the *Hymns of Joy* under a blue header (BBB pp. 26–27, see Fig. 15) and red header (BBB pp. 28-29, see Fig. 16).

Although it is unknown how the full extent of what we understand to be the Epistle part of the codex was presented, based on the level of decoration in the only passage that does survive from it, this part of the book likely received special attention. The sole page under the half header "*Seal Letter*" (BBB p. 1, see Fig. 7g) contains the bulk of the Middle Persian excerpt of the letter. It is quoted below together with its restored reference to Mani in the opening formula,

[31] These two groups together contain 72 pages (24 + 48 pages), which equals to just over 56% of the total original content (128 pages). Nevertheless, their survival from BBB p. 1 to BBB p. 48 confirms a unified book design across both quires (see Figs. 3–4).

which is lost with the previous page,[32] and the end of the excerpt, which is preserved on the subsequent page (BBB pp. 2–3, see Fig. 10):

> {MP} [(From) Mani, the apostle of Jesus Aryaman, the persecuted, whose name is spurned by the rulers] (1) of the world, ◦ ◦ and (from) Ammo my [most beloved] son, and from all the most beloved children (5) who are with me. ◦ ◦ (6) To all pastors, teachers and bishops, and all the elect [and hearers, brothers] (10) and sisters, (11) old and young, ◦ ◦ the pious, the perfect and the righteous, all you who have received this gospel from me, (15) and have found contentment in these precepts and good works which I have taught, and are undivided in (20) (your) firm [belief]. ◦ To each one in his own name. (22) {Sogd.} Here ends the *Seal Letter*. {*ten lines left blank*}

This passage of twenty-one lines features five cases of red ink punctuation and one small spacing, before it concludes in a red caption in Sogdian, followed by a large spacing. Each punctuation is encircled in red ink: the one single black dot (◦) on BBB p. 2, the two pairs of black dots (◦ ◦), and the pair of black dots separated by small spacing (◦ ◦) on BBB p. 1. The red within the black writing in the column(s) is accentuated by the matching red ink in the large text of the header "[*Here begins*] *the Seal Letter*" (BBB pp. ? –1).

CONCLUSION

The remarkable survival of a paper edition of a Bema service book, preserved in manuscript M801a (III 53) in the Asian Art Museum in Berlin, documents how a Central Asia Manichaean codex was crafted to be an efficient, professional tool in the service of "the work of the religion." Beyond its superb craftsmanship, this book exhibits a nuanced and cohesive program of design. Through an expert application of color, calligraphy, motifs, and columnar organization (all of which avoid any mechanical repetition), an anonymous scribe made this codex an exemplary memento of Pre-Islamic Iranian book art.

M801a (III 53) preserves the most complete body of codicological evidence available today about Iranian Manichaean codices in Central Asia. Therefore, this manuscript is essential for understanding the codicology of the Turfan manuscript fragments known from the Uygur era of Manichaean history (755/762–1024 CE). The rest of the circa 5000 fragments of loose folios, full folios, parts of bifolios, and the occasional intact bifolios discovered at Kocho and other Uygur sites hold bits and pieces of the kind of data that survives here intact within a service book. This codex originally consisted of at least two quires with 16 paper bifolios, that is, 32 folios (64 pages) each. Its continuously written columnar content was organized into three main parts, which were subdivided into sections and subsections. All content was presented in two-page units of the open book under one large and decorated header. Short of creating an illuminated manuscript, the skillful application of a decorative (yet suitably limited) repertoire of scribal

[32] See note 19, above.

accessories attested on these facing pages allowed the scribe to visually distinguish the start of a new part and the many sections and subsections within this codex. Analogous principles of book design are attested on many of the Iranian and Turkic Manichaean fragments. Now, their fragmented codicology can be interpreted in light of the baseline provided by these two quires.

Beyond its Uygur context of use and preservation, M801a (III 53) is a window to a superb book culture that all but became erased from the archaeological record. From the start of their activities in the 240s CE in Sasanid Syro-Mesopotamia, the Manichaeans constituted one of the "Peoples of the Book." Their religion was anchored in books from the start. The extensive doctrine of their founder was safeguarded in the many volumes authored by Mani and subsequently the leading members of the early community. The book, as Mani explained, could preserve and accurately transmit his teachings in writing, and in one case even in painting (in a solely pictorial volume of the canon, the *Book of Pictures*). The codex format was the main vehicle for this. Manichaean codices could be made of paper instead of parchment in Central Asia likely well before the first confirmed paper codex among them in 762 CE. In the same year, the conversion of Bügü Khagan and many leading tribes of the Uygurs to this religion begins a golden age of Manichaeism across East Central Asia, where Mani's followers enjoyed protection and patronage for close to three centuries.

M801a (III 53) holds fertile potential for future research. A radiocarbon dating of its paper could narrow the currently understood ca. 400 years long period of its possible manufacture ($7^{th}/8^{th}$ to $9^{th}/10^{th}$ centuries) to 126 years. At the same time, this manuscript could be subjected to the latest advances in paper restoration in order to stop its noted decay and secure its long-term preservation. The material analysis of its five inks (black, red, blue, violet, and green), paper, and binding cord would yield critical evidence for contextualizing its production. The calligraphy of its headers and the organization of its columns would offer critical data for understanding scribal practices. Moreover, comparative analyses of its penmanship and calligraphy could explore how this extensive (48 pages long) record left behind by a single scribe relates to the rest of the Turfan fragments. Such studies combined with an already completed radiocarbon dating of the Parthian and Middle Persian bifolio fragment illustrated with a sermon scene (III 8259) may lead to discoveries in Iranian Manichaean paleography and lineage of scribes.[33] It is hoped that this codicological study of the BBB will serve as a starting point to many such projects.

[33] III 8259 was found in Ruin α of Kocho with its binding holes repaired (see Le Coq 1923, 46; and Gulácsi 2005, 67–71). Its radiocarbon dating (authorized by Marianne Yaldiz in 1996) introduced the benefit of scientific evidence to already existing chronologies in Turfan studies established based on names of historical figures and regional artistic styles. Moreover, it led to identifying the hand of an anonymous book painter on three fragments, who was active sometime between 889 and 1015 CE (95.6% probability) and possibly between either 897 and 908 or 959 and 998 CE (68.4% probability), illustrating Iranian Manichaean codices (Gulácsi 2003, 8–18; and 2005, 39–58).

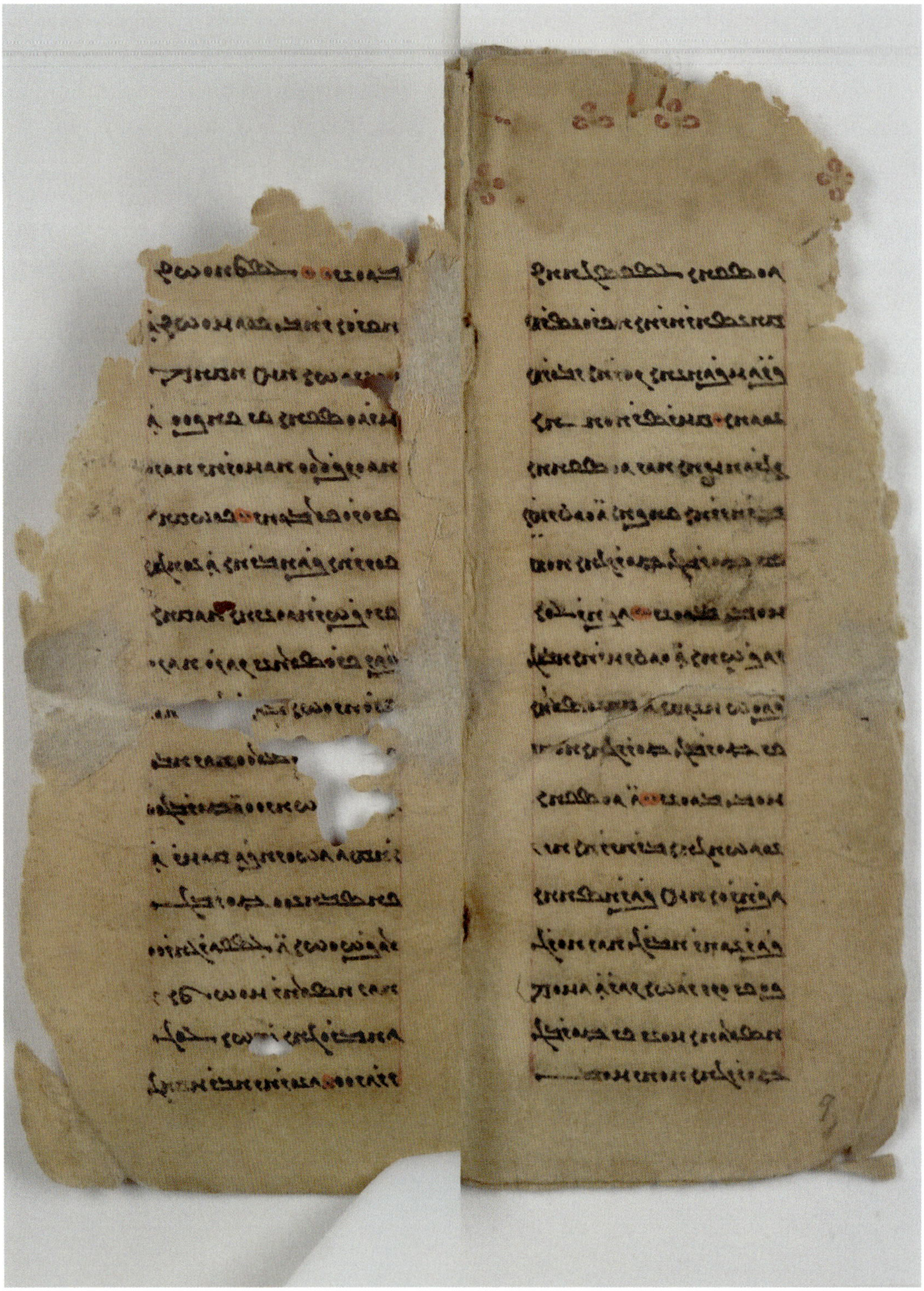

folios d/verso and k/recto [BBB pp. 14-15] preserved in manuscript M801a (III 53), digitally matched details of photographs III 53_5 (p. 100/top, right page) and III 53_11 (p. 103/top, left page)

Fig. 12: Third pair of facing pages surviving from Quire 2 with reconstructed faded green header '[*Hymns of praise to the messengers*]' and violet decoration

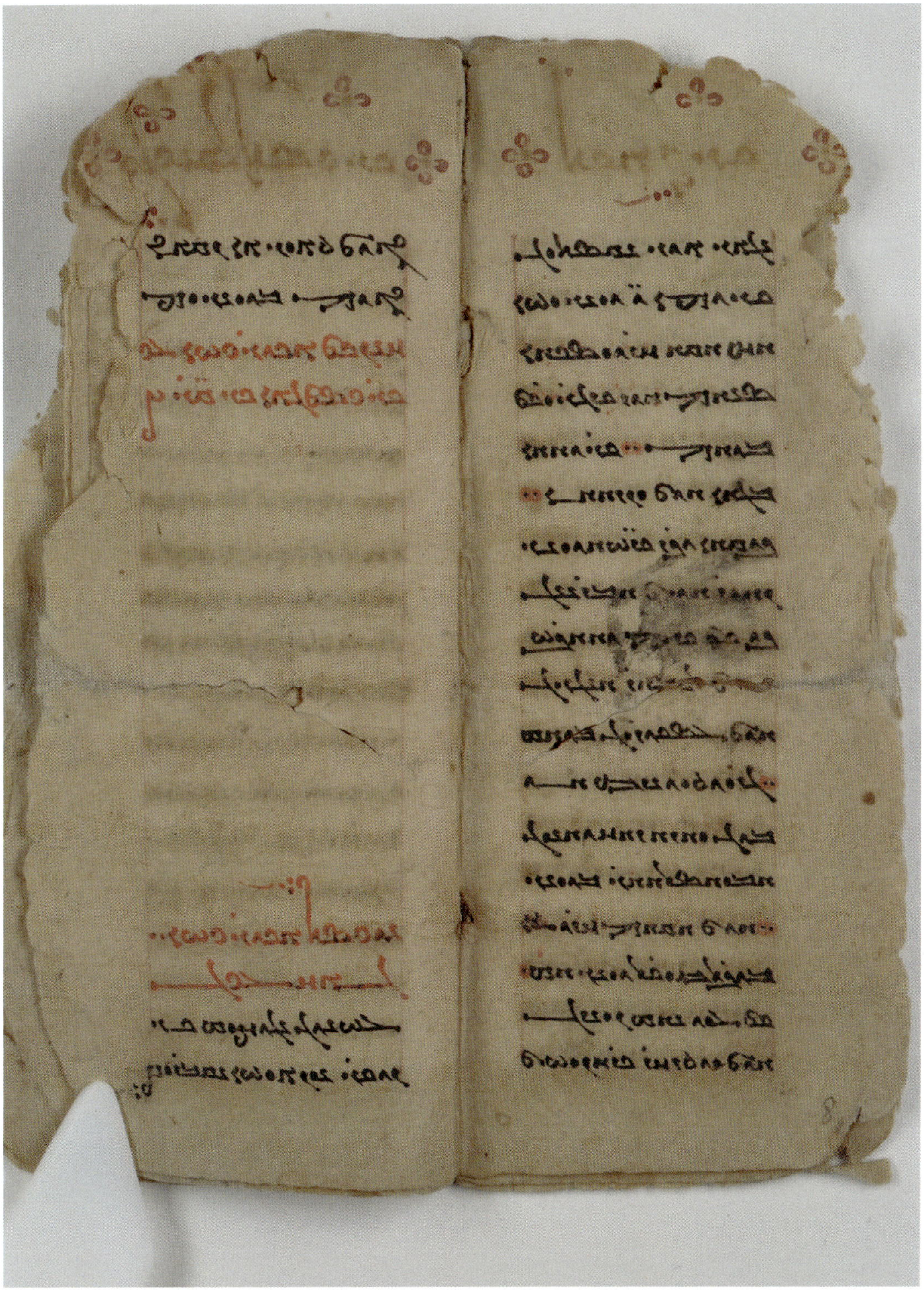

folios e/verso and b/recto [BBB pp. 18-19] preserved in manuscript M801a (III 53), detail of photograph III 53_6 (p. 100/bottom)

Fig. 13: Fourth pair of facing pages surviving from Quire 2 with faded green header *'Here end (the hymns of praise) to the messengers'* and violet decoration

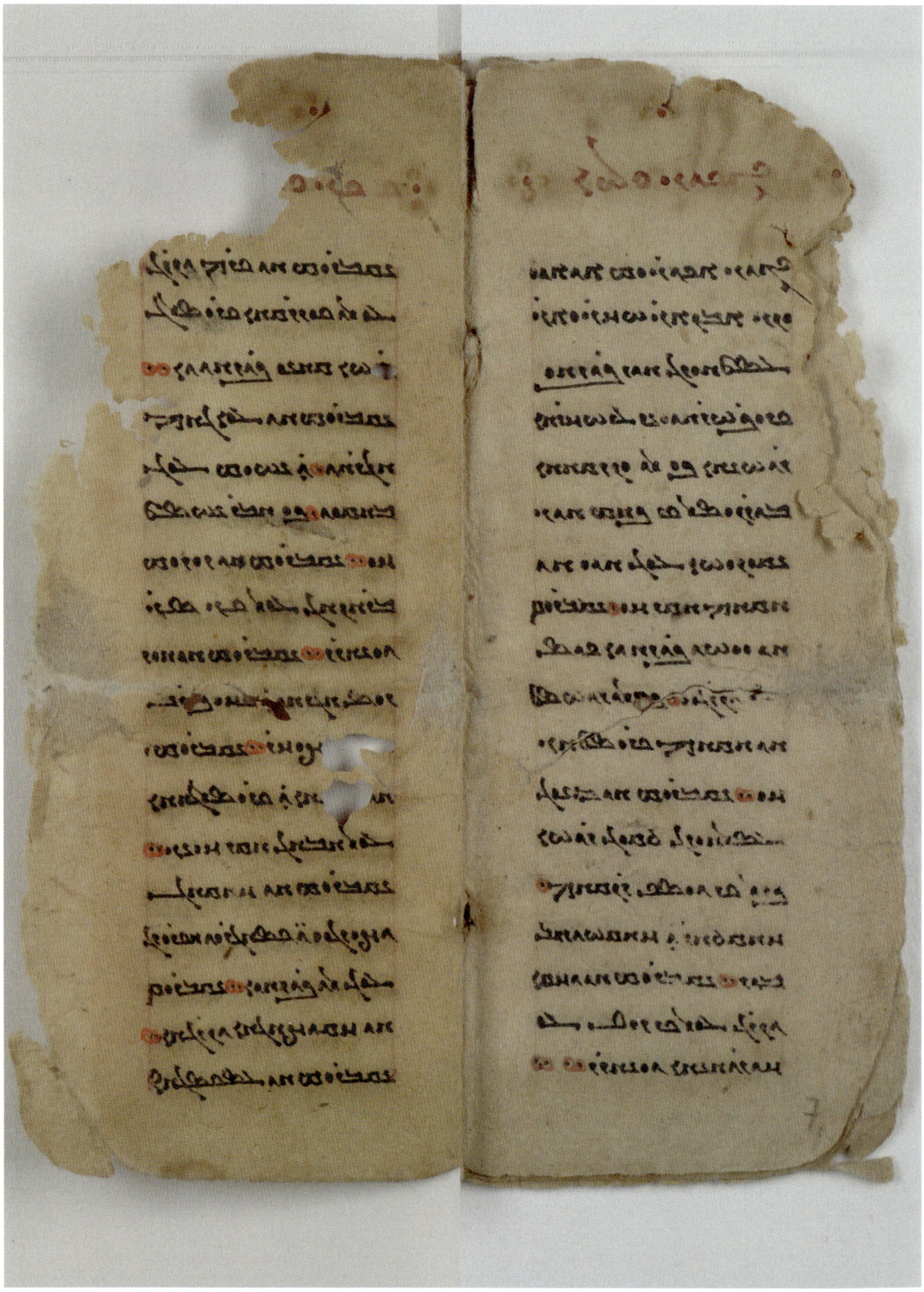

folios f/verso and j/recto [BBB pp. 20-21] preserved in manuscript M801a (III 53), digitally matched details of photographs III 53_7 (p. 101/top, right page) and III 53_10 (p. 102/bottom, left page)

Fig. 14: Fifth pair of facing pages surviving from Quire 2 with violet header *'Hymns of praise to the Apostle'* and faded green decoration

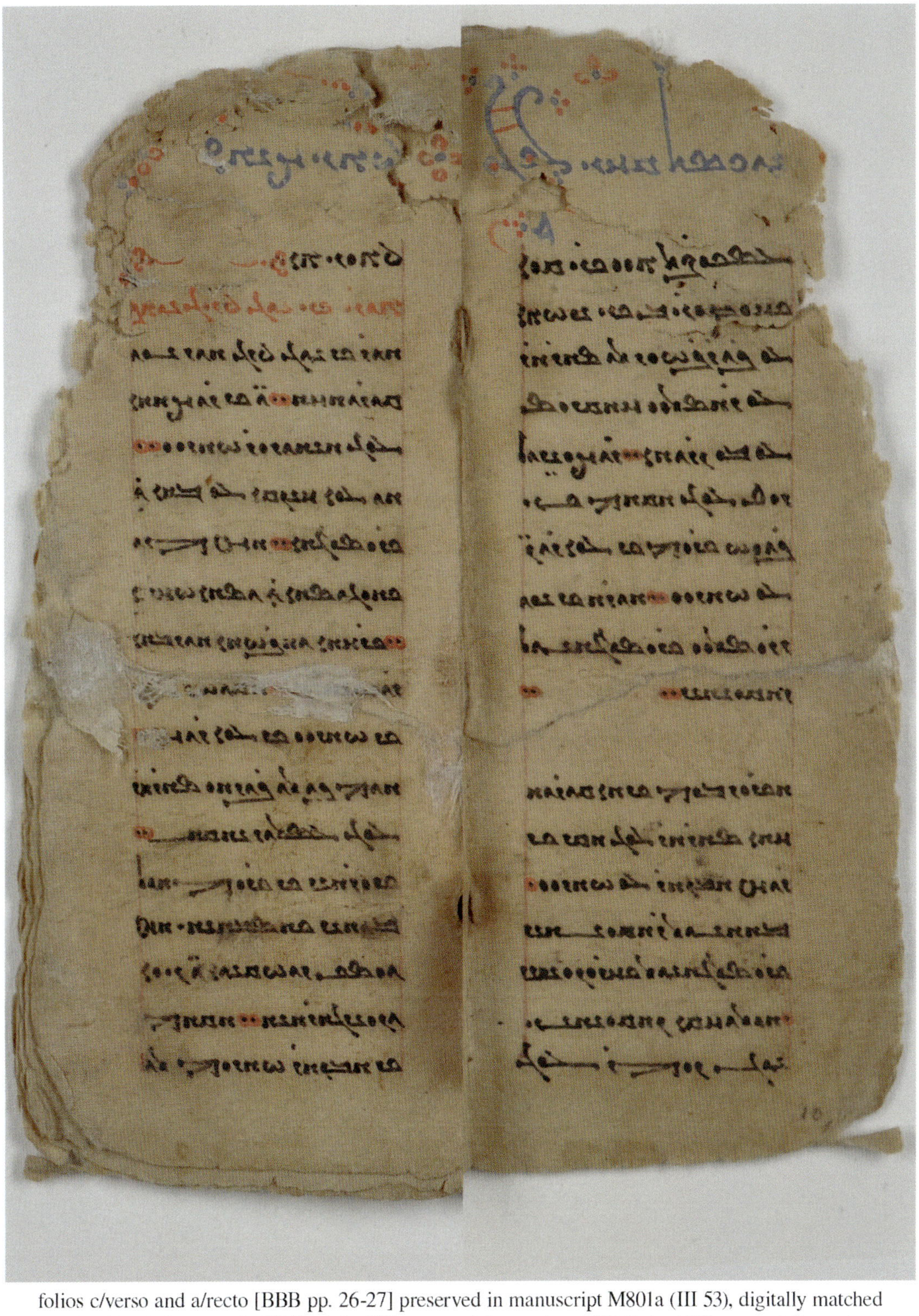

folios c/verso and a/recto [BBB pp. 26-27] preserved in manuscript M801a (III 53), digitally matched details of photographs III 53_4 (p. 99/bottom, right page) and III 53 (p. 110/bottom, left page)

Fig. 15: Sixth pair of facing pages surviving from Quire 2 with blue header *'Here begin the hymns of the joyful ones'* and red decoration

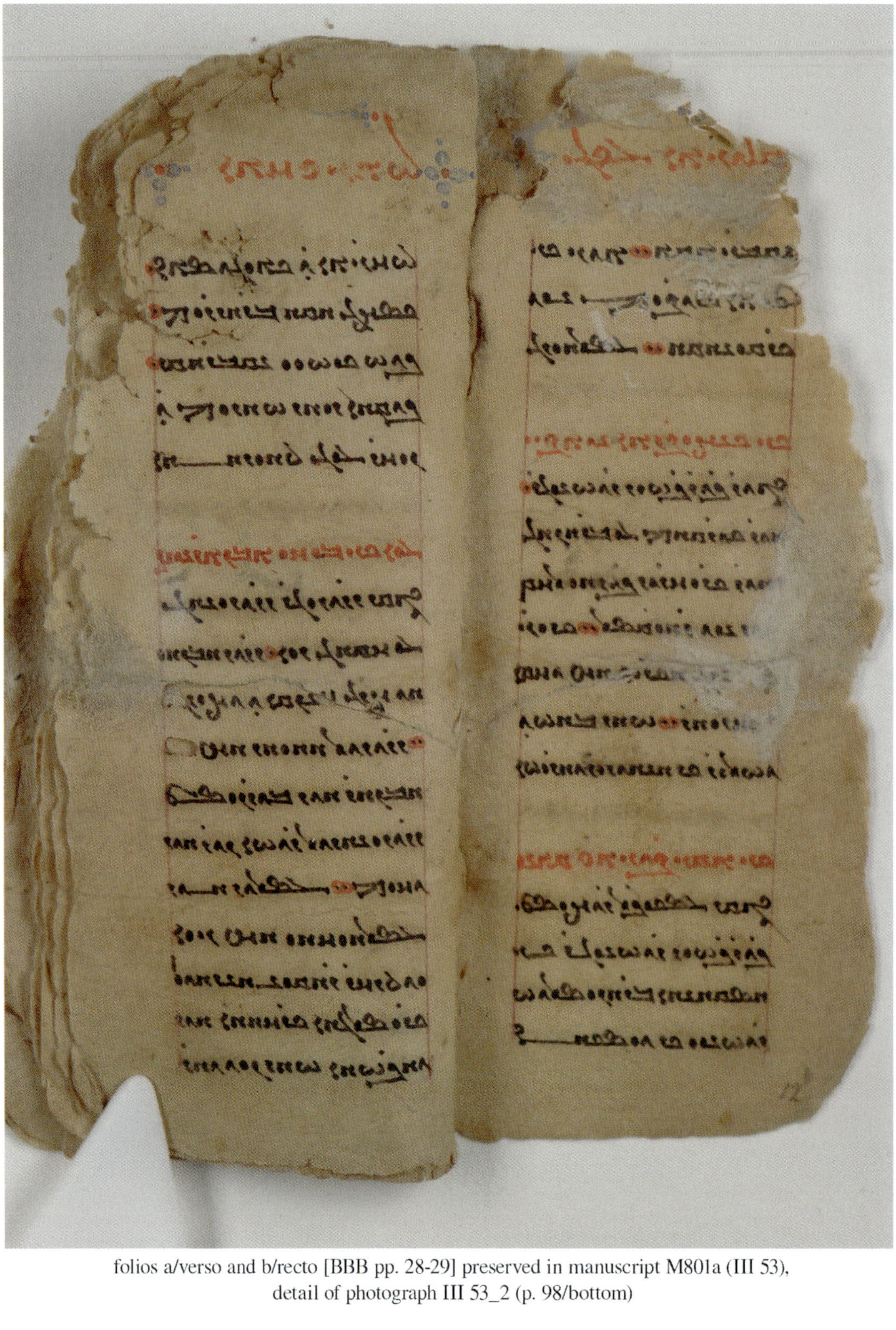

folios a/verso and b/recto [BBB pp. 28-29] preserved in manuscript M801a (III 53), detail of photograph III 53_2 (p. 98/bottom)

Fig. 16: Seventh pair of facing pages surviving from Quire 2 with red header *'Hymns of joy'* and blue decoration

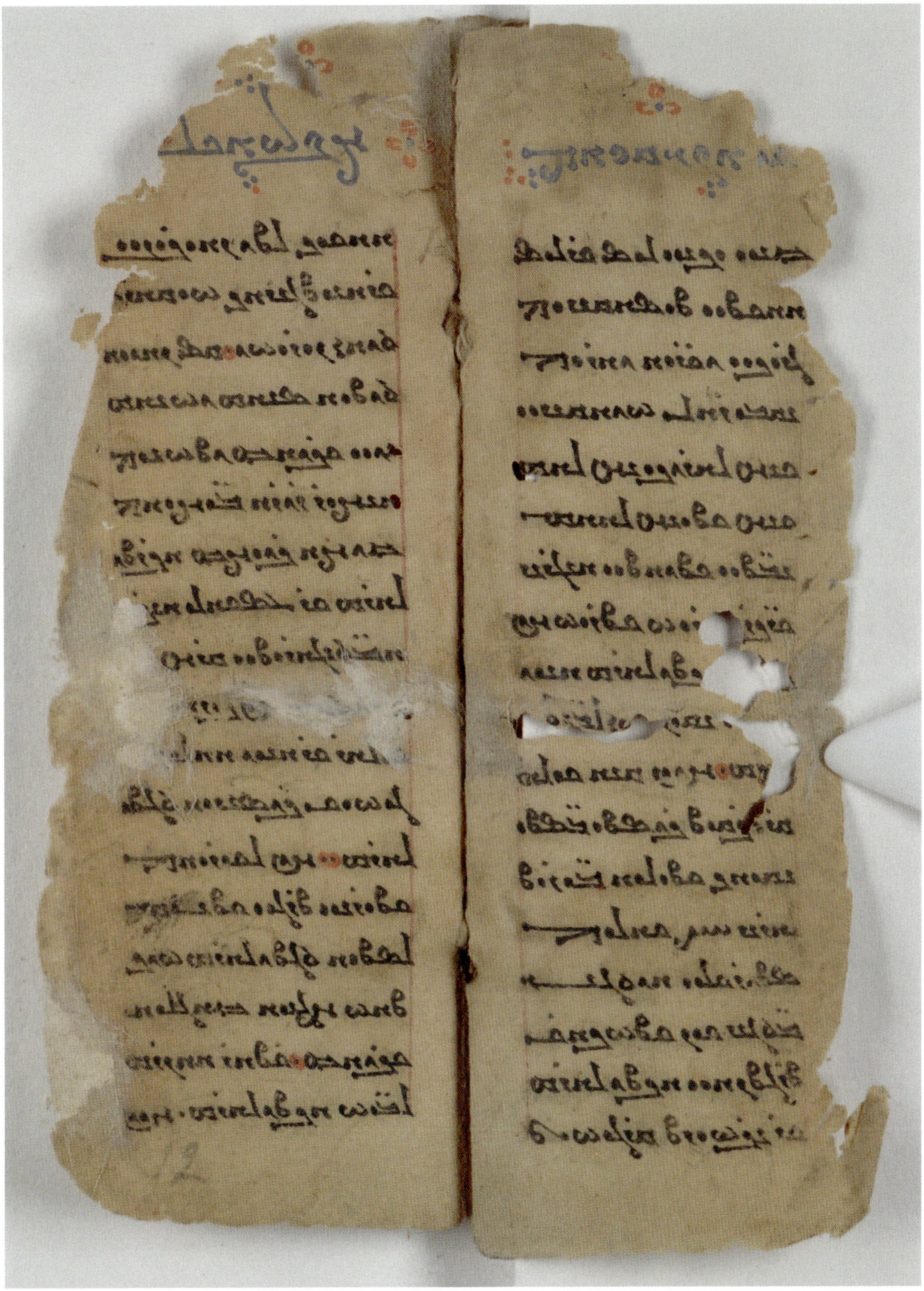

folios B/verso and A/recto [BBB pp. 32-33] preserved in manuscript M801a (III 53), detail of photograph III 53_31 (p. 109/bottom)

Fig. 17: Eighth pair of facing pages surviving from Quire 2 with blue header *'The commandment Non-injury'* and red decoration

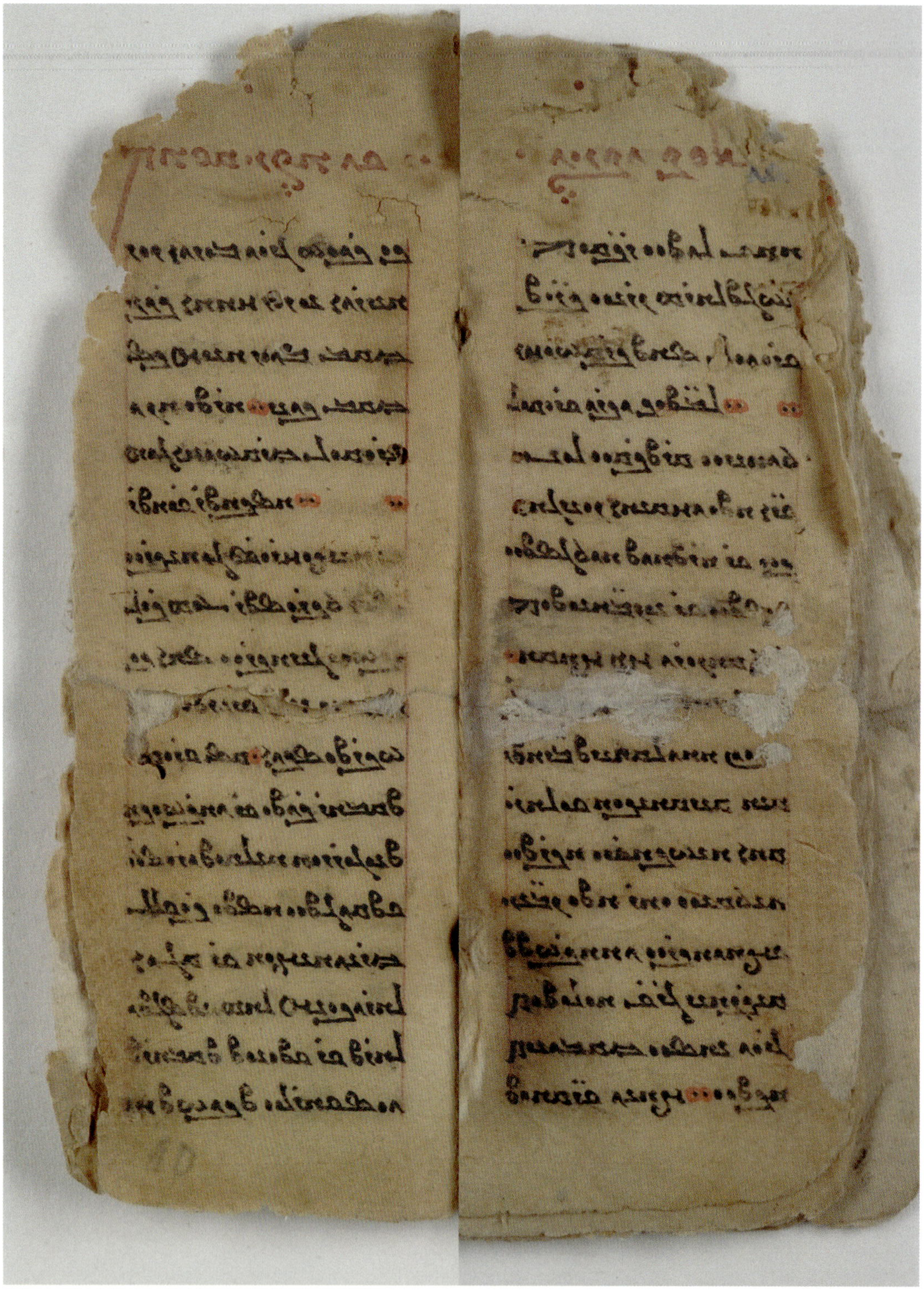

folios A/verso and C/recto [BBB pp. 34-35] preserved in manuscript M801a (III 53), digitally matched details of photographs III 53 (p. 110/bottom, right page) and III 53_27 (p. 108/bottom, left page)

Fig. 18: Ninth pair of facing pages surviving from Quire 2 with violet header *'The second part (of the commandment) Non-injury'* and faded green decoration

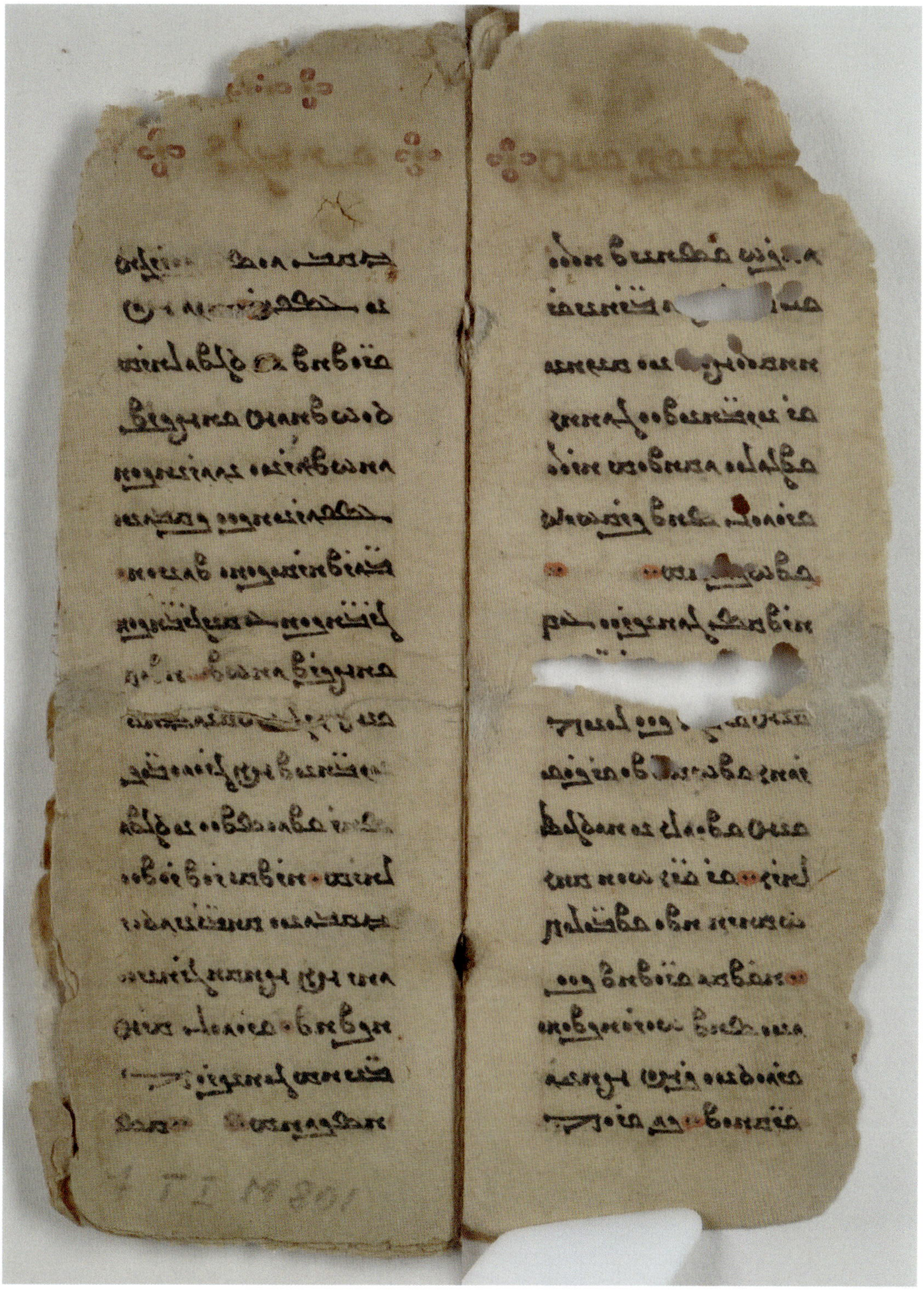

folios J/verso and F/recto [BBB pp. 40-41] preserved in manuscript M801a (III 53), digitally matched details of photographs III 53_20 (p. 105/bottom, right page) and III 53_23 (p. 107/top, left page)

Fig. 19: The tenth pair of facing pages surviving from Quire 2 with faded green header *'The five divine gifts'* and violet decoration

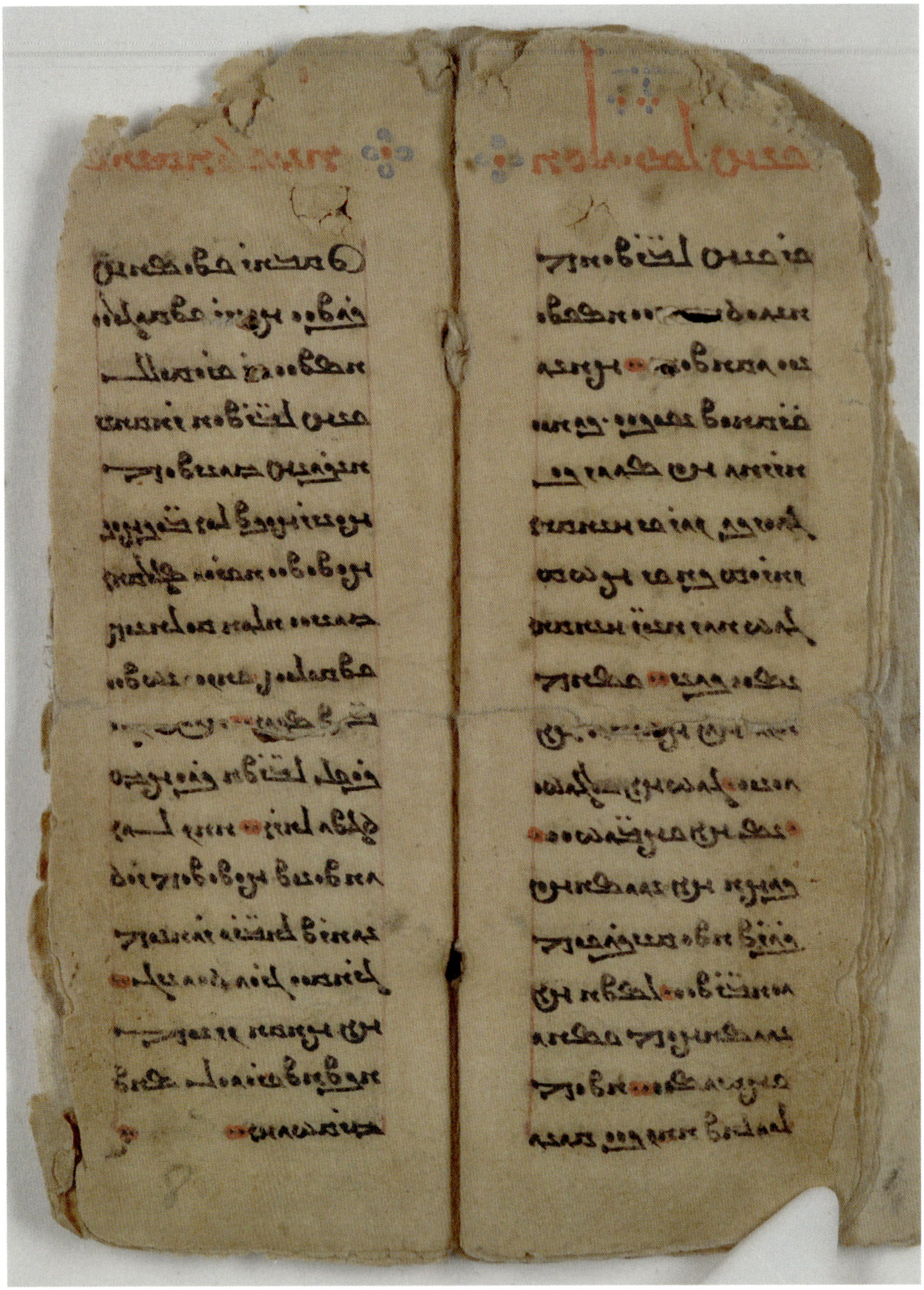

folios F/verso and E/recto [BBB pp. 42-43] preserved in manuscript M801a (III 53), detail of photograph III 53_25 (p.107/bottom)

Fig. 20: The eleventh pair of facing pages surviving from Quire 2 with red header *'The closing of the five gates'* and blue decoration

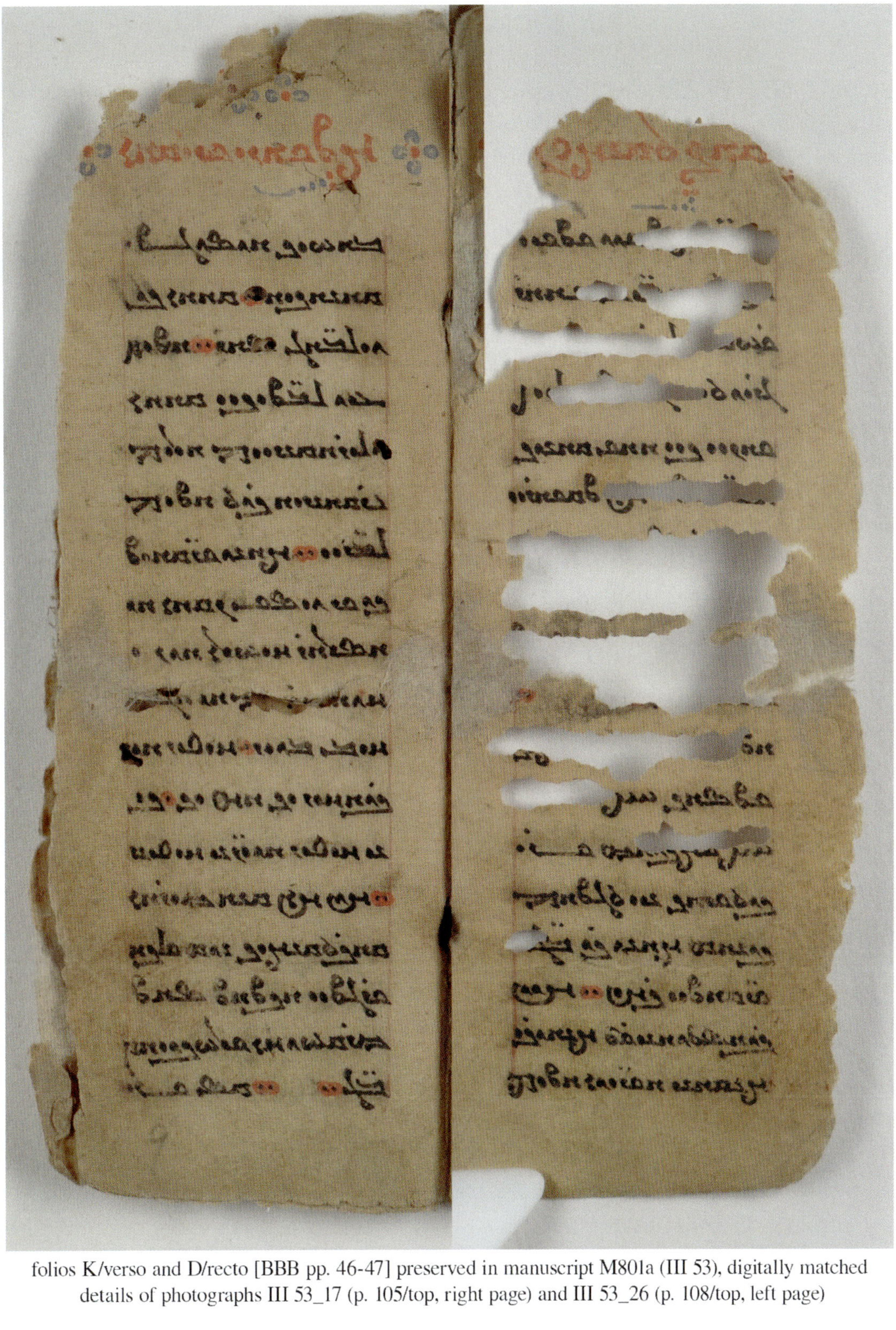

folios K/verso and D/recto [BBB pp. 46-47] preserved in manuscript M801a (III 53), digitally matched details of photographs III 53_17 (p. 105/top, right page) and III 53_26 (p. 108/top, left page)

Fig. 21: The twelfth pair of facing pages surviving from Quire 2 with red header '*The four Monday commands*' and blue decoration

BIBLIOGRAPHY TO PART 4

Boyce 1960 = M. Boyce, *A catalogue of the Iranian manuscripts in Manichean script in the German Turfan collection*, Berlin.

Durkin-Meisterernst 2006 = D. Durkin-Meisterernst, *Hymns to the Living Soul: Middle Persian and Parthian texts in the Turfan collection* (Berliner Turfantexte 24), Turnhout.

Durkin-Meisterernst–Morano 2010 = D. Durkin-Meisterernst & E. Morano, *Mani's Psalms: Middle Persian, Parthian and Sogdian Texts in the Turfan Collection* (Berliner Turfantexte 27), Turnhout.

Gardner 2018 = I. Gardner, "*Kephalaia*," *Encyclopædia Iranica*, online edition, available at http://www.iranicaonline.org/articles/kephalaia.

Gardner–BeDuhn–Dilley 2018 = I. Gardner, J. BeDuhn, & P. Dilley (eds.), *The Chapters of the Wisdom of My Lord Mani, Part III: Pages 343-442 [Chapters 321-347]*, Leiden.

Gulácsi 2003 = Zs. Gulácsi, "Dating the '*Persian*' and Chinese Style Remains of Uygur Manichaean Art: A New Radiocarbon Date and its Implications for Central Asian Art History," *Arts Asiatiques* 58, 5–33.

Gulácsi 2005 = Zs. Gulácsi, *Mediaeval Manichaean book art: A codicological study of Iranian and Turkic illuminated book fragments from 8th–11th century East Central Asia*, Leiden.

Gulácsi 2013 = Zs. Gulácsi, "The Crystal Seal of 'Mani, the Apostle of Jesus Christ' in the Bibliothèque Nationale de France," *Manichaean texts in Syriac* (Corpus Fontium Manichaeorum: Series Syrica 1, ed. N. A. Pedersen & J. M. Larsen), Turnhout, 245–67 and Plates 16–23.

Gulácsi 2022 = Zs. Gulácsi, "Manichaeism" essay and four catalogue entries, *Persia: Ancient Iran and the Classical World* (ed. J. Spier *et al.*), Los Angeles, 352–8.

Härtel–Yaldiz 1982 = H. Härtel & M. Yaldiz, *Along the ancient silk routes: Central Asian art from the West Berlin State Museums,* New York.

Henning 1937 = W. B. Henning, *Ein manichäisches Bet– und Beichtbuch* (APAW 1936, No. 10), Berlin. [Reprinted in Henning 1977, I, 417–557].

Henning 1977 = W. B. Henning, *Selected Papers*, I–II (Acta Iranica 14–15), Tehran–Liège.

Hunter–Coakley 2017 = E. C. D. Hunter and J. F. Coakley, *A Syriac service–book from Turfan: Museum für Asiatische Kunst, Berlin, MIK III 45* (Berliner Turfantexte 39), Turnhout.

Le Coq 1923 = A. von Le Coq, *Die manichäischen Miniaturen. Die buddhistische Spätantike in Mittelasien*, II, Berlin.

Morano 2014 = E. Morano, "Some Aspects of the Translation into Iranian Languages of the Works by Mani," *Vom Aramäischen zum Alttürkischen: Fragen zur Übersetzung von manichäischen Texten. Vorträge des Göttinger Symposiums vom 29./30. September 2011* (ed. J. P. Laut & K. Röhrborn), 85–91.

Morano 2018 = E. Morano, "Some codicological remarks on the corpus of the Berlin Turfan Manichaean Sogdian manuscripts in Manichaean script,"

Written Monuments of the Orient, *special edition 2* (ed. Ch. Barbati & O. Chunakova), 11–38.
Müller 1913 = F. W. K. Müller, *Ein Doppelblatt aus einem manichäischen Hymnenbuch (Maḥrnâmag)* (APAW 1912, No. 5), Berlin.
Reck 2009 = C. Reck, "A Sogdian version of Mani's *Letter of the Seal*," *New Light on Manichaeism. Papers from the Sixth International Congress on Manichaeism* (ed. J. BeDuhn), Leiden, 225–39.
Sundermann 1992 = W. Sundermann, "*Cologne Mani Codex*," *Encyclopaedia Iranica* 4/1, 43–6.
Szirmai 1999 = J. A. Szirmai, *The archaeology of medieval bookbinding*, Aldershot.
Turner 1977 = E. G. Turner, *The typology of the early codex*, Philadelphia.
Weber 2000 = D. Weber, *Iranian Manichaean Turfan texts in publications since 1934. Photo edition* (Corpus Inscriptionum Iranicarum, Supplementary Series 4), London.

Appendix:

Additional texts

a – f

Text a: M113

Recto

(BBB a1–a6)

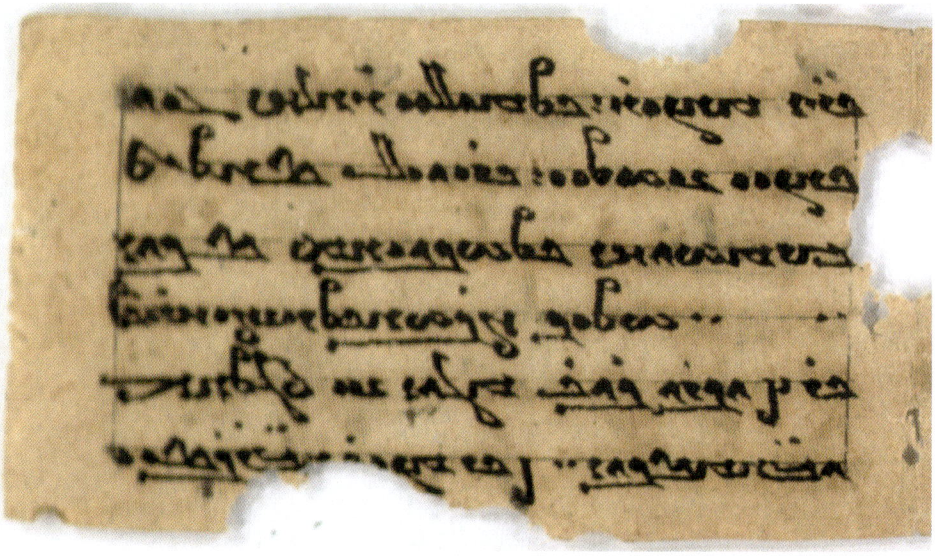

Photo: Digitales Turfan Archiv

Verso

(BBB a7–a12)

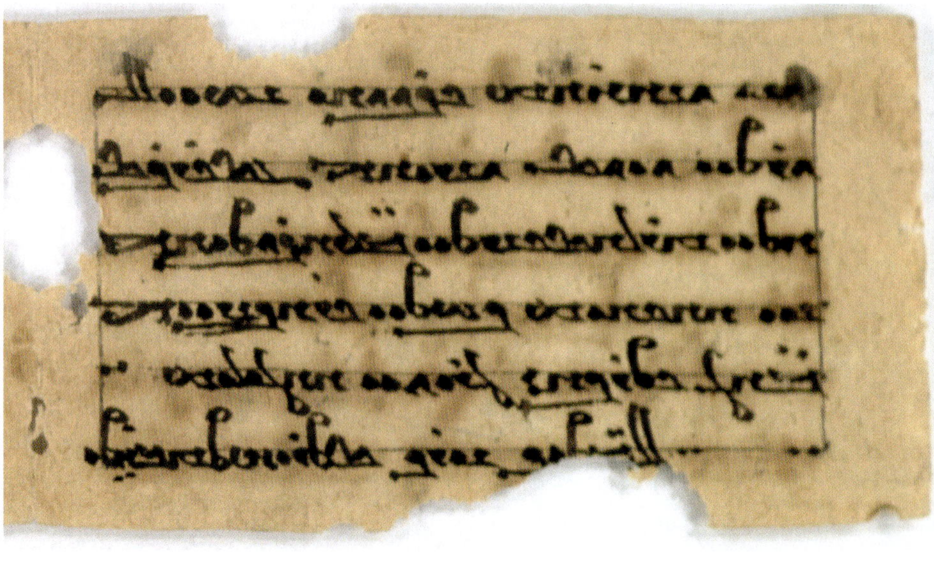

Photo: Digitales Turfan Archiv

Text a: M113

Recto

(BBB a1–a6)

a1 1/ frn mʾzyr ° pṭmyδδyy rʾδc ʿyw	... glory was damaged, each day a
a2 2/ pʾzyy nyšṭyy ° prywyδδ sʾṭṭ	'traveller', a 'guest' is destroyed;[2]
a3 3/ q(r)mšwhn pṭškwyʾm skwn	for all that I ask absolution.
a4 4/ °° °° šṭyk cxšʾpṭ dyncyhryfṭ	(As for) the third commandment,
a5 5/ pr II wkrw xwf[1] mgwn nyy jγṭʾh̲	Purity, I am not able to keep[3] (it)
a6 6/ wβʾmskwn °° I pr mz(yx ʾ)βrxsyy	properly and wholly in (its) two parts. Firstly: in great wantonness,

Verso

(BBB a7–a12)

a7 1/ (wnw) wnʾrʾm pxwwʾy nšyyδδ	lopping (or) planting a tree (or) an
a8 2/ wrṭyy wyws wndyʾh̲ ʿsprxs	orchard on a spring morning, I do
a9 3/ ʾṭyy mrδʾspndṭyy βjʾxwṭyʾh̲	not perceive[5] the misery of the
a10 4/ nyy ʾʾpʾym kšṭyy prʾkndyyh̲	buds of the trees and (the misery)
a11 5/ βʾγ pṭrkʾn γrywyy ʾʾγyδym °°	of the (light) elements; we desire
a12 6/ °° °° δδβṭ(y)k nyrk sṭryc ṭmb<ʾ>rṭy[4]	selfishly to plant (and) to sow gardens (and) smallholdings.[6] Secondly: the male (and) female bodies ...

---

[1] Mistake for *xwp*.

[2] Cf. BBB 674–5. The term *rʾδc* is probably a noun 'traveller' (= Christian Sogd. *rʾθc* 'id.', E28/11, R7, in Sims-Williams 2017, 96) rather than an adverb 'on the way' with Henning. Here it seems to be used just like *ʿyw-pʾzy* 'guest' as a 'metaphor for the light particles temporarily residing in the bodies of the Elect'; see *DMT* III/2, 166a, and above, p. 85 n. 61. The verb *nyšṭyy* can either be present 'is destroyed' (with Henning) or preterite 'was destroyed' (agreeing better with the preceding imperfect *mʾzyr* 'was damaged').

[3] The intransitive potential *nyy jγṭʾh̲ wβʾmskwn* is irregularly used here, rather than its transitive equivalent **nyy jγṭʾh̲ kwnʾm(skwn)* (as found in BBB 727–8, for example). The negated present tense could also be translated as past 'I was not able to keep'; see Sims-Williams 1996.

[4] As Henning noted, the scribe first wrote *ṭmbʾ* and then, realizing the lack of space, corrected *ʾ* to *r* and added the two subscript points to indicate the abbreviation.

[5] Or 'we do not perceive'. Again (cf. n. 3 above), a past tense translation 'I/we did not perceive' would be equally correct.

[6] For a6–a11 cf. BBB 567–82.

Text b (fragment IA): M131, i

Recto

(BBB b1–b16)

Photo: Digitales Turfan Archiv
© *Depositum der Berlin-Brandenburgischen Akademie der Wissenschaften in der Staatsbibliothek zu Berlin – Preußischer Kulturbesitz, Orientabteilung*

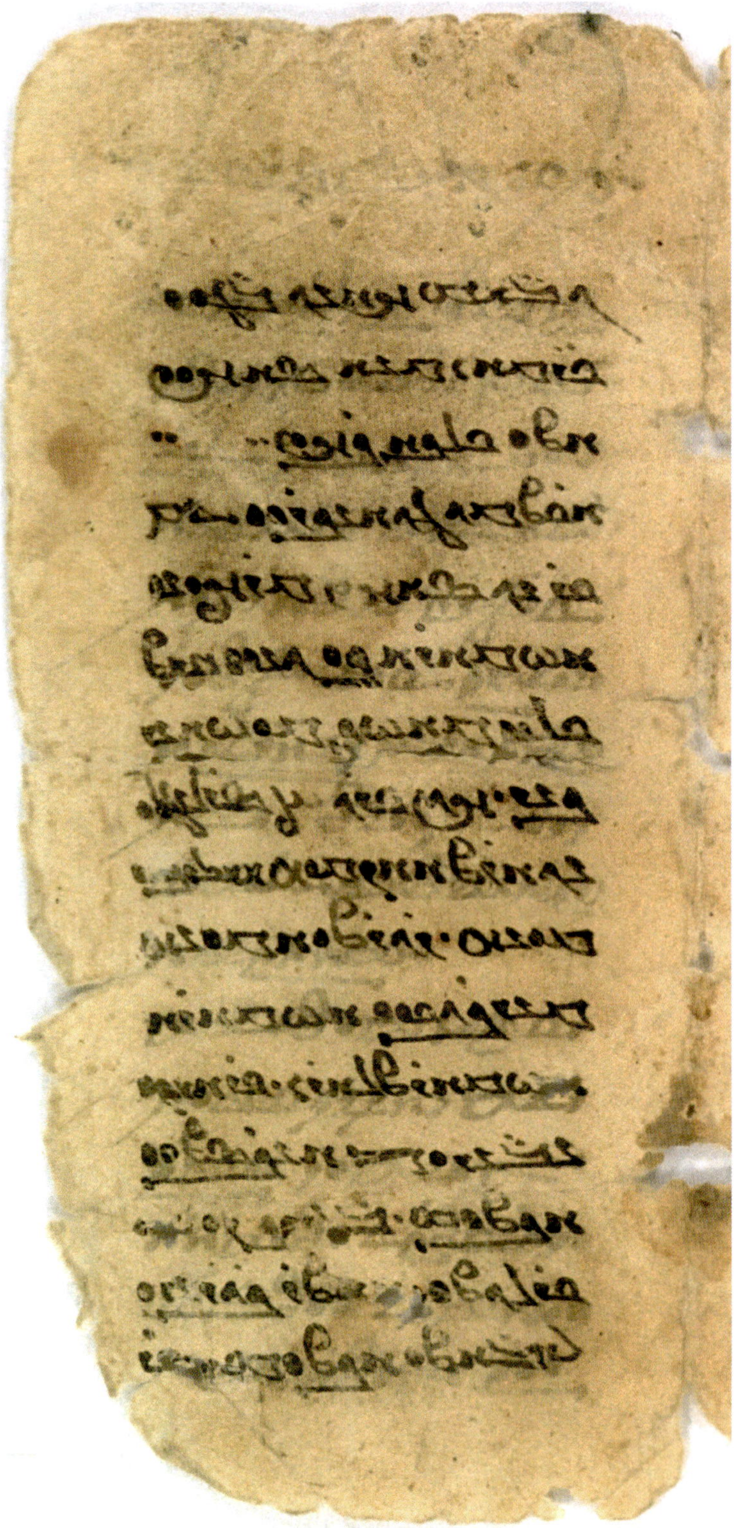

Text b (fragment IA): M131, i

Recto

(BBB b1–b16)

hdl. [?v–]IAr/ {*olive*} [...] | {*illegible*}
‘...’

hdl. IAr/ {*illegible*}[7]

b1 1/ wβ’m c’nw βγyy
b2 2/ frm’n mn’ s’cyy
b3 3/ ’ṭy pδk’ xcy ◦◦ ◦◦
b4 4/ ’fṭmw γw’nkryy ‘ym
b5 5/ pr nws’cy mrcyny
b6 6/ ’šm’r’ ky wnyy (s)’ṭ
b7 7/ pδyy m’š(k) myš’nd
b8 8/ (x)nd ◦ cw prw III srδngty[8]
b9 9/ nw’rṭ ’’zmyc ’’βrx[s]y[9]
b10 10/ mync ◦ rwrṭy’mync
b11 11/ mndxwpyy ’šm’r’
b12 12/ (’)šm’rṭδ’rn ◦ pr ’(’z)y
b13 13/ nβndyẖ ’nxsṭyy
b14 14/ ’kṭym ◦ β(jyk ryjyy)
b15 15/ prδwṭy ◦ (’’)ṭr xwr(nd)y
b16 16/ jβ’ṭy ’kṭym (◦ p)r

... I am [not ...] as God’s command is a duty and rule for me.

Firstly, I am a sinner (5) in (respect of) improper deathly thoughts—these (very thoughts) which are the foundation (and) basis[10] of all (sins); if, in accordance with the inclinations of the three ‘leaders’,[11] I should have thought unseemly thoughts of greed, of lust (or) of lewdness, (if) I have been instigated by the reins of greed (or) inflamed by evil desires, (if) I have been scorched[12] by the consuming fire; (if), through

7 Henning tentatively read a couple of letters, but these are no longer visible.

8 Written with *γ* instead of *g*.

9 The points over *βrx* are all omitted.

10 The nouns [1]*pδ*- and *m’šk* are virtual synonyms in the sense ‘basis’. Henning (hesitantly followed in *DMT* III/2, 136b) took *pδyy* as a genitive form dependent on *m’šk*: ‘the basis of all steps’.

11 On the ‘three leaders’, possibly greed, lust and lewdness as suggested by the following words, see Sims-Williams 1991, 327–8. The late Werner Sundermann (p.c.) compared MP *sn’n drwxš’n wyyb’g’n ‘ym gy’n* ‘my soul’s three deceptive she-demons’ (M174, iV9–10, in Waldschmidt–Lentz 1933, 556, 591) and Sogd. *’δry z’r* ‘three poisons’ (Benkato 2017, 86, line 197). Henning’s interpretation of the three as a group of church leaders is very unlikely.

12 Lit. ‘bitten’. See Benveniste 1938, 518.

Text b (fragment IA): M131, i

Verso

(BBB b17–b32)

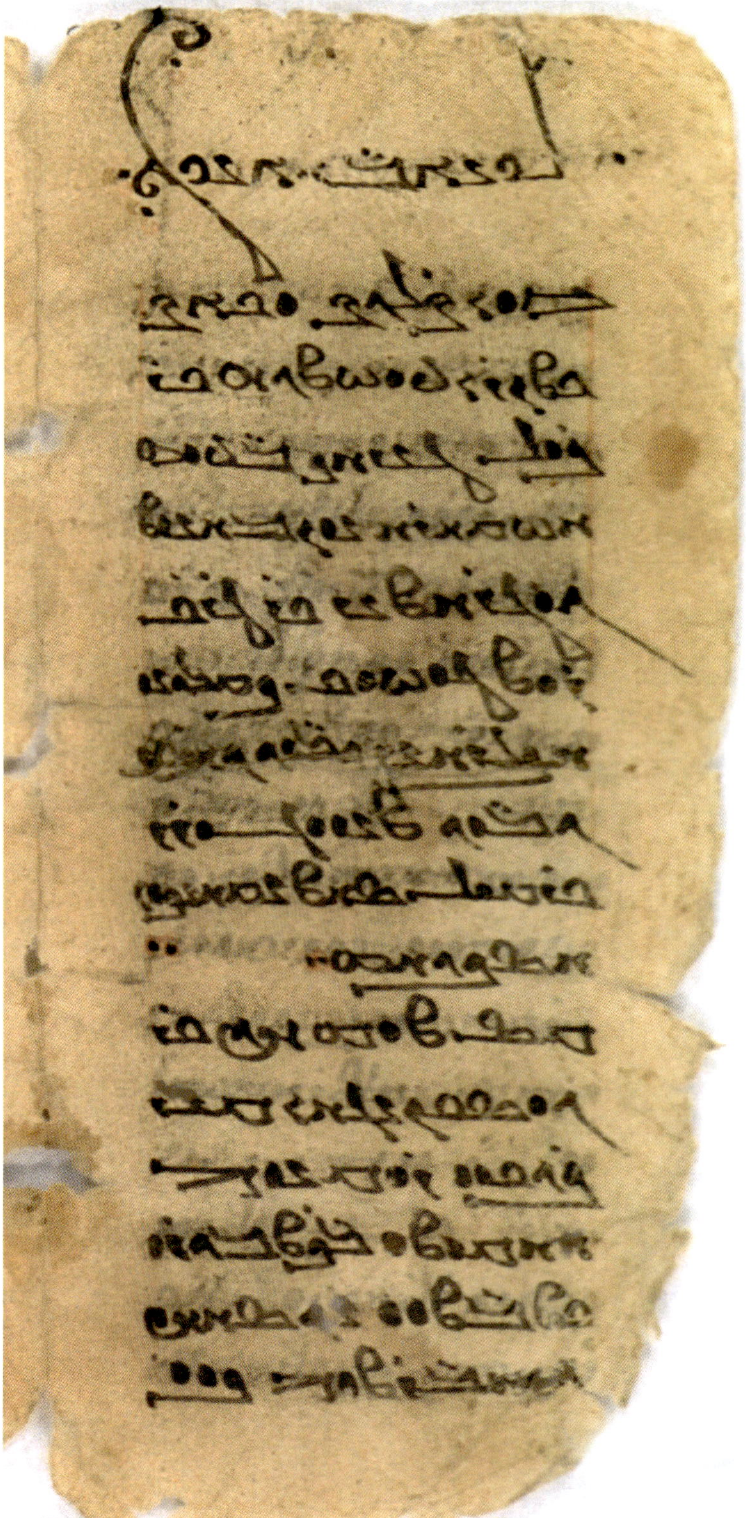

Photo: Digitales Turfan Archiv

Text b (fragment IA): M131, i

Verso

(BBB b17–b32)

hdl. IAv[–?]/ {*black*} δyn’βr’nyg | [...]
‘... (for) the elect’

hdl. IAv/ δyn’βr’nyg

b17 1/ qyn xδwk yp’k
b18 2/ pṭzrn jyšṭwc pr
b19 3/ xyδ γnd’k βjyq
b20 4/ ’šm’r’ nyz(β)’nyṭ
b21 5/ wyγr’ṭnd pr γrf
b22 6/ ryṭ γyšyp kmbwny[13]
b23 7/ ’kδr’nd[14] wβyw w(’xšk)[15]
b24 8/ wβyw ṭnyygyrd
b25 9/ prmyδ[16] s’ṭ nm’nkyn
b26 10/ ’skw’m ◦◦ ◦◦

vengeance, rage, anger, annoyance (or) hatred—through these wicked and evil (20) thoughts the passions have awoken (and) have in many ways caused damage and diminution, both spiritual and corporeal: (25) for all this I am penitent.

b27 11/ ms ṭym cw pr
b28 12/ wyspzng’n mnd
b29 13/ xwpyy rymnyẖ
b30 14/ (’)’myṭy βxṭbwry[17]
b31 15/ pṭβṭyy (nw)s’cy
b32 16/ (wy’)βrṭyẖ kyy
{*one or more folios missing?*}

Moreover, if through all kinds of unseemly, dirty, impure,[18] divisive, heated (or) improper speech, which ...
{*one or more folios missing?*}

[13] According to Henning, written *kmβwny*, but the points over *β* are no longer visible.
[14] Scribal error for **’kδ’r’nd* or **’kδ’rnd* (Henning).
[15] Abbreviated spelling for *w’xšyk* (GMS §80), squeezed in at the end of the line.
[16] Scribal error for *prymyδ*.
[17] Sic; *β* and *b* together suggest a misspelling, but the correct form of the word is unknown.
[18] For *’’myṭy* ‘tainted, impure’ (rather than ‘harmful’) see Sims-Williams 1985, 97.

Text b (fragment IIA): M5865

Recto (BBB b33–b41)

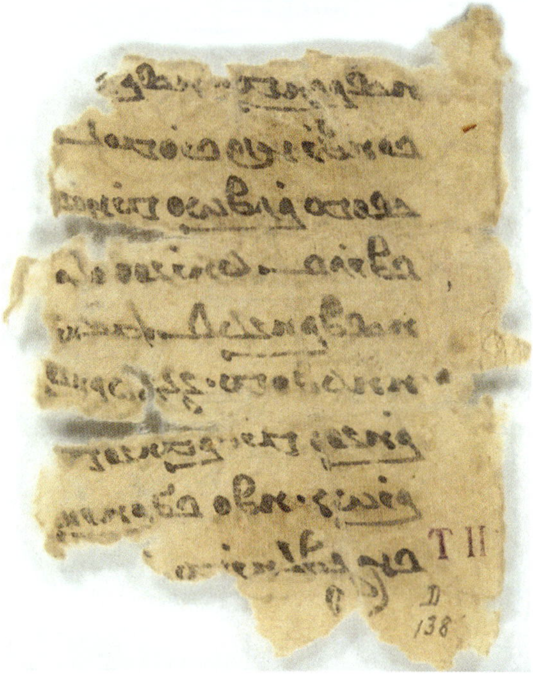

Photo: Digitales Turfan Archiv

Verso (BBB b42–b33)

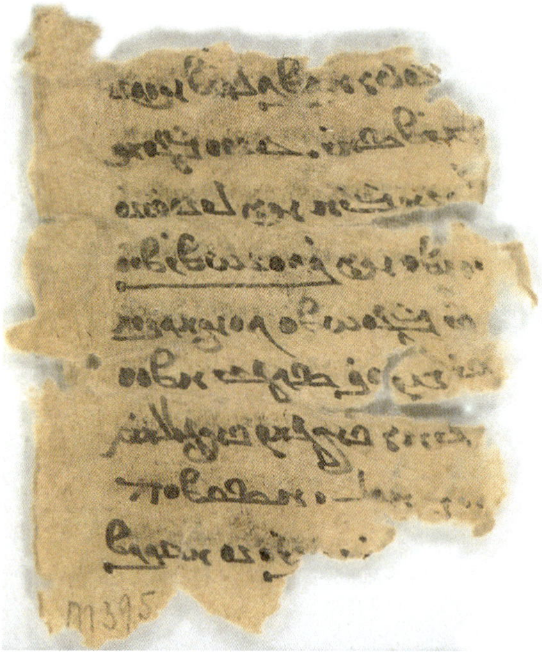

Photo: Digitales Turfan Archiv

Text b (fragment IIA): M5865

Recto (BBB b33–b41)

{*headline and seven lines torn off*}
b33 1/ ’sk(w)’m °° ’sk[’ṭr]
b34 2/ (f)y’ṭr cw prymyδ
b35 3/ sym xwṭšy mrcyn[y]
b36 4/ pṭrwp j’rnyy yδw
b37 5/ ’sṭk’njl tmb’r
b38 6/ ’’jṭym ° nγ(wš)k’(ny)
b39 7/ x’nyy m(rṭx)m’nyẖ
b40 8/ kršn ° ’ṭy pṭk’(r’)
b41 9/ pcγṭδ’rm [ ]

{*headline and seven lines torn off*}
... [for all this] I am [penitent]. Furthermore, although I have been born in this (35) ... of filth,[19] (this) fortress of death, (this) poisonous shape(?),[20] (this) skeleton[21] body, I have received human form and likeness in the house of a hearer ...

Verso (BBB b42–b33)

{*headline and seven lines torn off*}
b42 1/ (‘)yjn ’kṭwδ’rṭ cywn(d)
b43 2/ mrṭs’r ‘ynyy βγy’k
b44 3/ (δy)n’βr’ cn δynyf(r)ny
b45 4/ (° ’)ṭy cn xwynšṭrṭyy[22]
b46 5/ pr βγyšṭy wyc’wky’
b47 6/ pr mz(y)x swγnd ’ṭyy
b48 7/ (γr)’n pcγ’z pcγtδ’rm[23]
b49 8/ °° (m)’yδ ’spṭyẖ
b50 9/ [ ](r.)[ ](k)ryny ’skwṭ[24]
{*some folios missing?*}

{*headline and seven lines torn off*}
... has made me worthy. Thereafter, I received this divine status (and) elect-hood[25] from the Glory of the Religion and the elders, with the gods' witness, according to a mighty oath and solemn engagement.[26] (48) So may(?) ... be completely making ...
{*some folios missing?*}

[19] On *sym* 'filth' see Sims-Williams 2015, 149. It is also possible that *sym* is here the adjective 'confused'. The following *xwṭšy* is one of several unknown words in this passage.

[20] *yδw* is another unknown word, for which Henning suggested 'shape'.

[21] This otherwise unknown word may be a compound of *’sṭk-* 'bone' (thus Henning) + Skt. *añjali* 'the open hands placed side by side and slightly hollowed' (Monier-Williams 1899, 11a), the whole perhaps as a figurative description of the rib-cage.

[22] Sic. See *GMS* §342.

[23] Misprinted *pcγδ’rm* in *DMT* III/2, 152a.

[24] Mistake for *’skw’ṭ*, 3 sg. subjunctive (Henning)?

[25] Mistake for *δyn’βry’* (*DMT* III/2, 76b)? For a similar case see above, p. 71 n. 30. A parallel passage from the unpublished text M116, R5–7, has the abstracts *[βγ]y’k ’rṭ’wy’ δynṭ’ry’*.

[26] For *pcγ’z* 'agreement, engagement, promise' (not 'reception') see Sims-Williams 2017, 227.

Text b (fragment IIB): M395

Recto (BBB b51–b59)

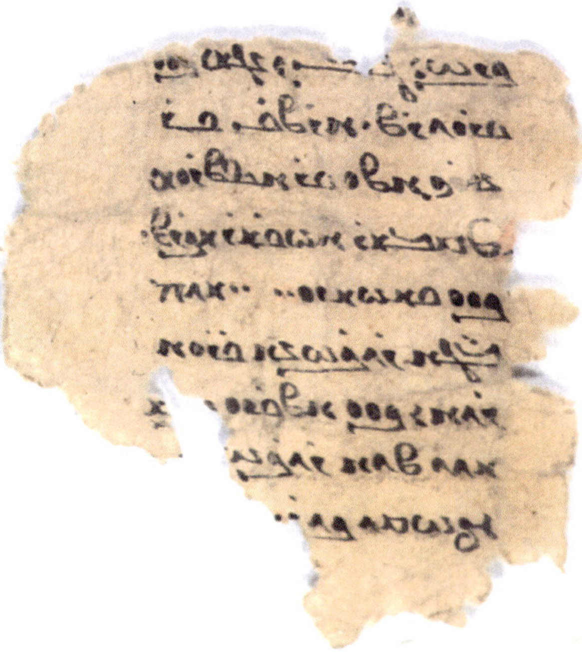

Photo: Digitales Turfan Archiv

Verso (BBB b60–b68)

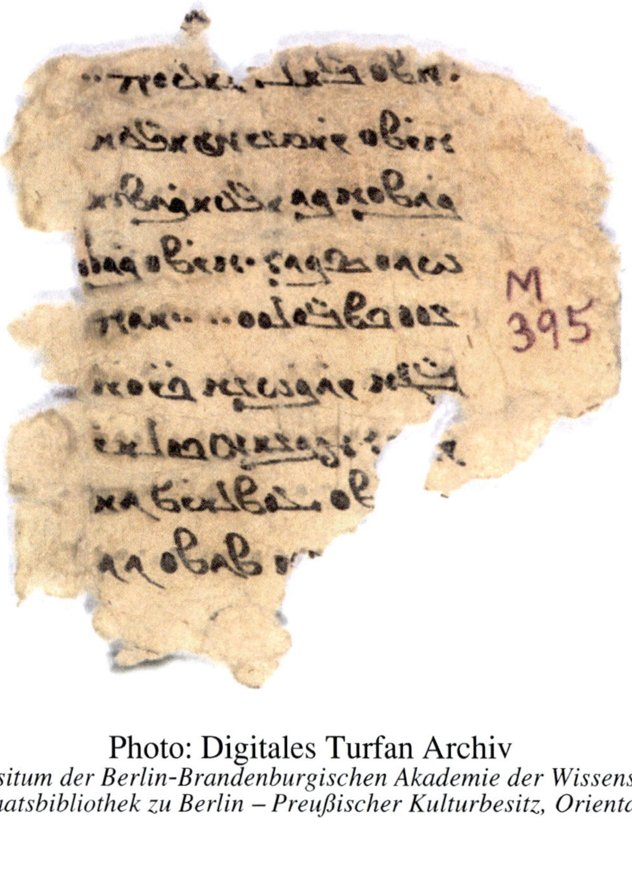

Photo: Digitales Turfan Archiv

Text b (fragment IIB): M395

Recto (BBB b51–b59)

b51 1/ k(r)šn γ[r](β) zngʾn kyy
b52 2/ prywrṭ[27] ° ʾrṭf pr
b53 3/ n(y)rk ʾṭy pr ʾsṭryc
b54 4/ ṭmbʾr ʾšfʾr ʾkrṭ(y)
b55 5/ kyy pʾšʾ(y)y °° °° ʾwẖ
b56 6/ βγʾ rwxšnʾ fryʾ
b57 7/ rwʾn kyy ʾṭfyy (k)[wn](ʾ)
b58 8/ ʾww ṭwʾ rwxš[nww]
b59 9/ cšmw kw(r °)[°]

... Who changed [you into] shapes of many kinds? And who cast you, ashamed, into male and into female bodies? O (56) light god, dear soul! Who [made] your[28] bright eye blind? ...

Verso (BBB b60–b68)

b60 1/ ° ʾṭy βʾδ (n)ʾjyẖ °°
b61 2/ ʾrṭy rʾmnd cn ʾβjʾ
b62 3/ xwṭyʾ kw ʾβjʾxwṭ(yʾ)
b63 4/ šwyskwn ° ʾrṭy xwty
b64 5/ nyy pṭβyδyy °° °° ʾwẖ
b65 6/ βγʾ rwxšnʾ fryʾ
b66 7/ (rwʾ)n cknʾc pyδʾr
b67 8/ [ ]ṭy ʿyṭδʾrṭ wʾ
b68 9/ [ ](.ʾ) ṭwṭy ww
{*one or more folios missing?*}

... [sometimes ...] and sometimes you turn, and you always go from misery to misery and you yourself do not perceive (it). O (65) light god, dear soul! Why did ... take the ... [so] that ... the ...

{*one or more folios missing?*}

---

[27] Scribal error for **prywyrṭ* (Henning).

[28] The pronoun is doubly expressed, by *-fy* and *ṭwʾ*. For similar instances see Sims-Williams 2014, 37, 72.

Text b (fragment IB): M131, ii

Recto

(BBB b69–b84)

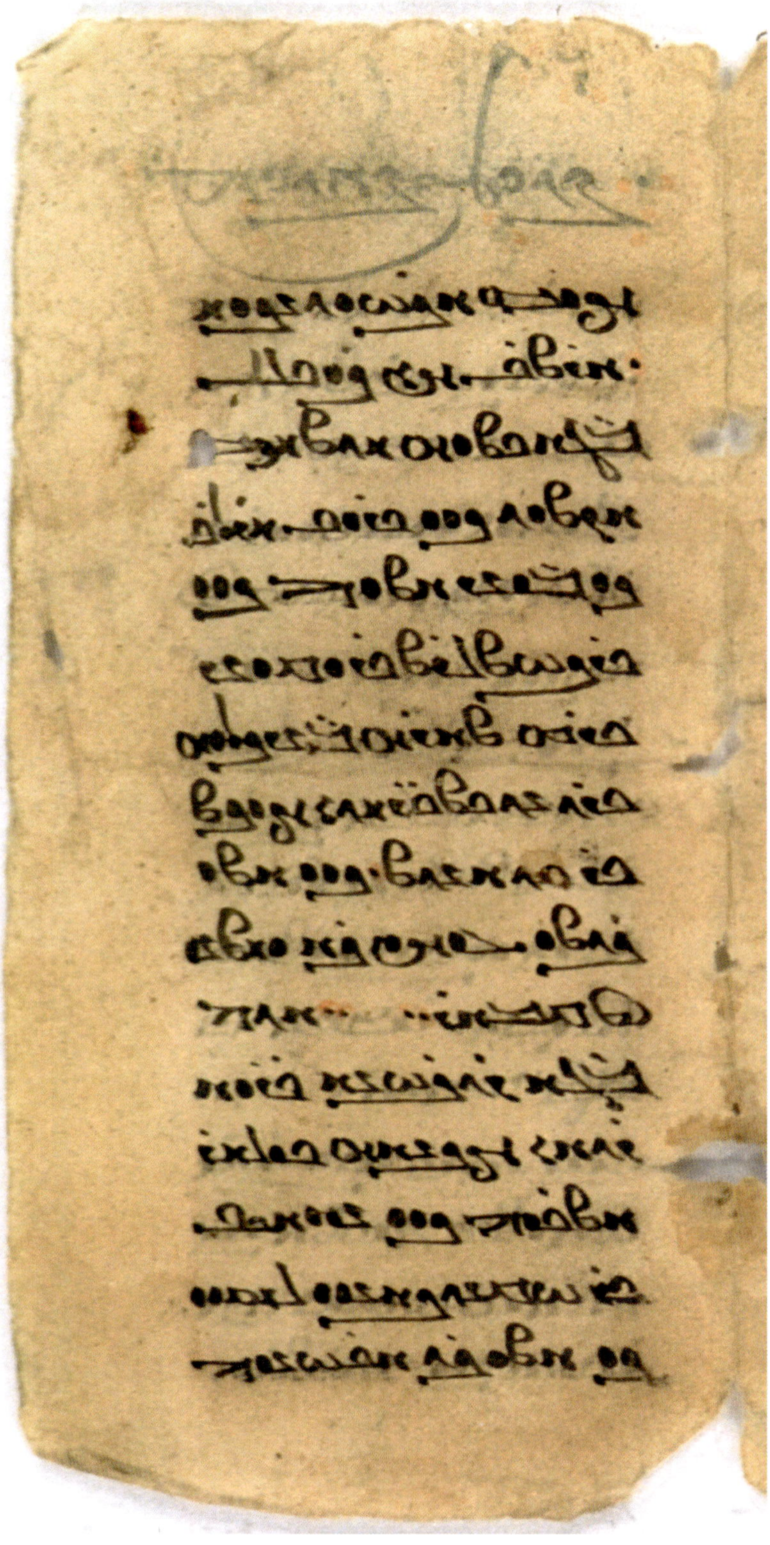

Photo: Digitales Turfan Archiv

Text b (fragment IB): M131, ii

Recto

(BBB b69–b84)

hdl. [?–]IBr/ {*blue-green*} [...] | xwyck'wyẖ
'Explanation [of ...]'

hdl. IBr/ xwyck'wyẖ

b69 1/ cyq 'xšywnky'
b70 2/ ◦ 'rṭf cn xypδδ
b71 3/ βγ'pṭyc 'wṭ'k(q)
b72 4/ 'zṭyw kyy pryp 'rtf
b73 5/ ky βynd 'ṭyẖ kyy
b74 6/ prkšṭδrṭ[29] prymynd
b75 7/ prm ṭ'rc βndktyc
b76 8/ prw nwpṭfr'wn cykṭ
b77 9/ pr pw'nwṭ ◦ kyy 'ṭy
b78 10/ xwṭy 'ycy x' y'ṭny
b79 11/ ṭmb'r ◦◦ ◦◦ 'wẖ
b80 12/ βγ' rwxšn' fry'
b81 13/ rw'n ckn'c pyδ'r
b82 14/ 'ṭfyẖ kyy nyy's
b83 15/ pr šmnwk'nyy δ'myy
b84 16/ ky 'ṭy xw 'fšnyẖ

... kingship. (70) And who led you into exile from your own place in the divine presence?[30] And who bound you, and who incarcerated (you) in this dark prison, (76) in dungeon cells, in the (place) without hope[31] which is the fleshly body? O light god, dear soul! Why? (82) And who held you in the creation of the devil which spreads(?)[32]

[29] Scribal error for *prkšṭδ'rṭ* (Henning).

[30] On *βγ'pṭyc* see *DMT* III/2, 52a.

[31] For *'nwṭ* 'hope' (not 'protection, refuge') see *DMT* III/2, 13a, and Sims-Williams 2014, 36, with references.

[32] The form and meaning of *'fšnyẖ* are uncertain.

Text b (fragment IB): M131, ii

Verso

(BBB b85–b100)

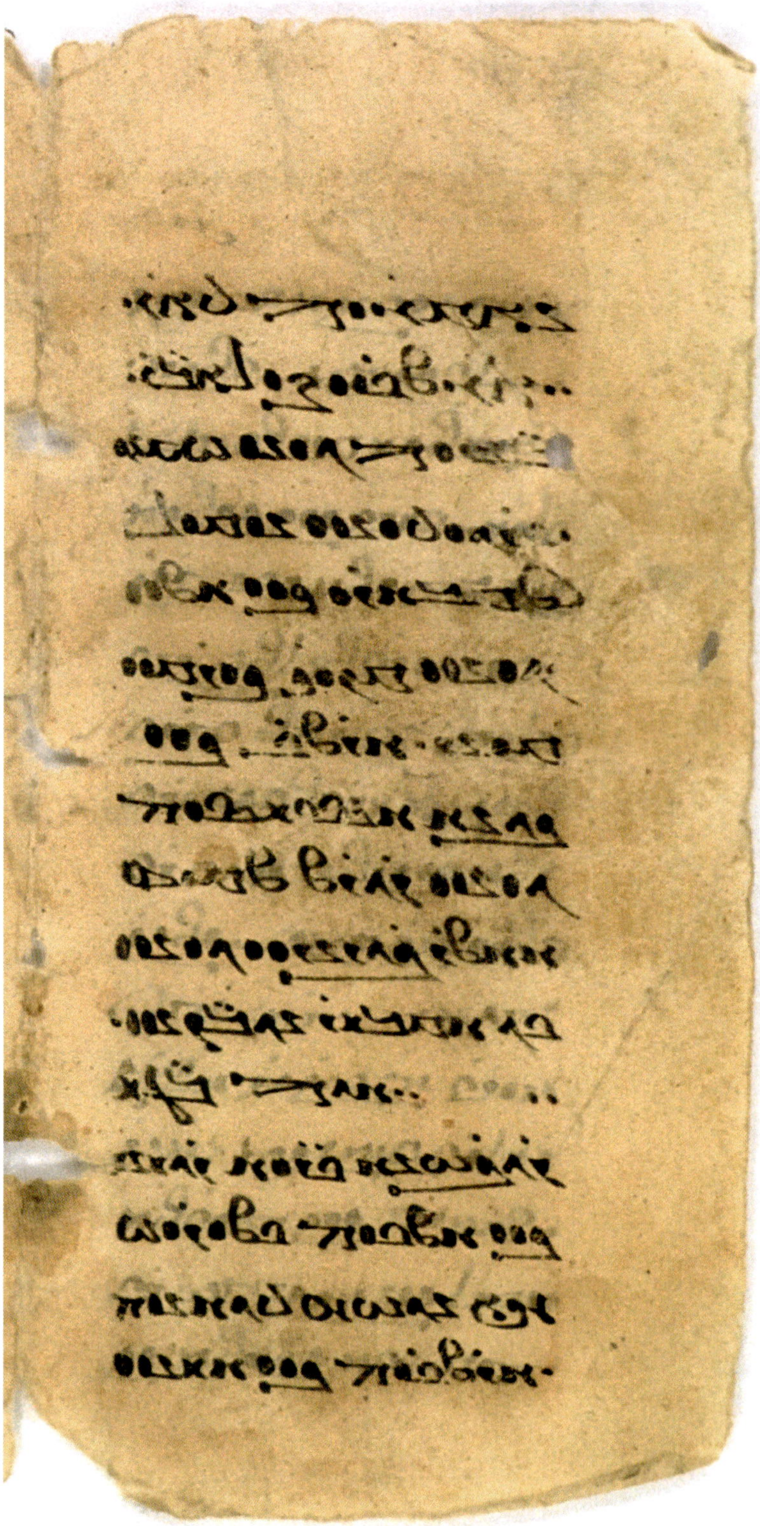

Photo: Digitales Turfan Archiv

Text b (fragment IB): M131, ii

Verso

(BBB b85–b100)

hdl. IBv[–?]/ {*illegible*} | [...]
'...'

hdl. IBv/ {*illegible*}

b85 1/ n'mryh̲ j'r
b86 2/ ◦◦ 'rṭfyy ky δ'βr
b87 3/ (βnd)yh̲[33] wyny šmnw
b88 4/ ◦ (p)rwyjynyy nymyδ
b89 5/ ṭmb'ry kyy 'ṭyy
b90 6/ (w)ynyy mzyx kyrmyy
b91 7/ myn(d) ◦ 'rṭf kyy
b92 8/ kwn' 'sp'syh̲
b93 9/ wynyy rwrṭ ṭmyq
b94 10/ "ṭr xw(r)ndyy wynyy
b95 11/ pw 'mb'r nwβznyy ◦
b96 12/ ◦◦ ◦◦ 'wh̲ βγ'
b97 13/ rwxšn' fry' rw'n(')
b98 14/ kyy 'ṭ(f)yh̲ pṭyryš
b99 15/ cn nwšc jw'nyh̲
b100 16/ ◦ 'rṭfyh̲ kyy "nyy

sweet poison? And who gave you (as) a slave to the devil, nurturing (him) in this body which (90) resembles a great serpent?[34] And who made you a servant to the lewd, hellish, devouring fire, insatiable (and) shameless? (96) O light god, dear soul! Who tore you from eternal life and who led you ...?

---

33 As there is a hole at the beginning of the line, a restoration *[n](βnd)yh̲* is theoretically possible (Henning).

34 Thus *DMT* III/2, 119a. Less likely with Henning: '(in) which his great serpent dwells'.

Text c: M5779

Recto(?) (BBB c25–c48)

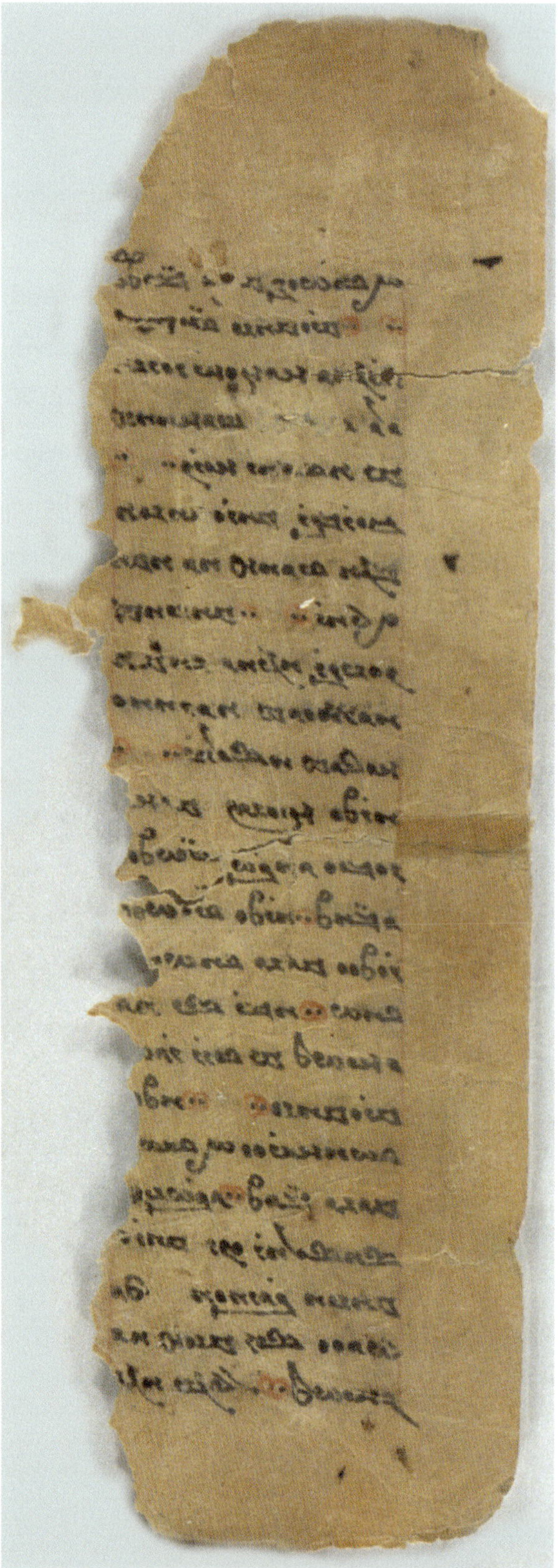

Photo: Digitales Turfan Archiv

Text c: M5779

Recto(?)[35] (BBB c25–c48)

c25 1/ III p’šyk m[wn](w) β(w)ṭṭ	... The three hymns are these:
c26 2/ °° °° {Pa.} mrym’ny frẖ	{Pa.}{Hymn 1} Mar Mani, noble maj-
c27 3/ (’)rg’w hwcyhr dydn(’)	esty, beauteous to behold; you, [father],
c28 4/ tw (p)[ydr](pd)wh(’)’m	I entreat, forgive my sins.
c29 5/ mn ’(st)’r hyrz °° °°	
c30 6/ qyrbkr m’ry(m’)ny’	(30) {Hymn 2} Beneficent Mar Mani,
c31 7/ bg’ pdw’c ’w ’m(’)	god, answer us.
c32 8/ {Sogd.} II j’r °° °° {MP} m’ny’ẖ	{Sogd.}[36] Twice. {MP}{Hymn 3} Mani,
c33 9/ zyndkr ’gr’w n’m’	life-giver, whose name is noble, help
c34 10/ ’wd’ywm ’wd’’y	me, help, forgive my sins.[37]
c35 11/ hylwm ’st’r °° °°	
c36 12/ {Sogd.} ’rṭy c(’)nw m(w)h[r]	(36) {Sogd.} And when the words of
c37 13/ dybyy w’xš (f)ršṭy[y]	the Seal Letter are concluded,[38] sing
c38 14/ wβ’ṭ °° ’rṭy fryš(ṭy)	this hymn before the apostle:
c39 15/ ryṭyy mwnw p’šy[k]	
c40 16/ p’š °° {Pa.} ’br sd ’w	{Pa.} My light father, Mar Mani, has
c41 17/ whyšṭ mn pydr rw(š)[n]	ascended to paradise.[39]
c42 18/ mrym’ny °° °° {Sogd.} ’ṭ(y)	{Sogd.} And (43) the three hymns for
c43 19/ pš’h’ryy III p’(š)[yk]	(the ceremony) after the meal are these:
c44 20/ mwnw βwṭ °° {Pa.} wxšn(’m)	{Pa.}{Hymn 1} Commander, whose
c45 21/ s’st’r yzd m’r(y)	name is fair, god, Mar Mani, lord, you
c46 22/ m’ṇy’ xwd’y’ ṭw	are going; raise me too to (48) paradise.
c47 23/ šwyy syn mnyc ’w	
c48 24/ whyšṭ °° ‘jgnd ’g(d)	{Hymn 2} A messenger has come

---

[35] Henning’s determination of Recto and Verso is reversed here on the basis of the arguments in Reck 2004, 30–31 (but his line-numbers are retained for convenience). See above, pp. xi, xvi–xvii.

[36] The occurrence of the MP word *j’r* ‘times’ in a Sogd. context in c8 below justifies interpreting the ambiguous *II j’r* here as Sogdian, like all the rubrics in this fragment.

[37] These two hymns are also attested in M782, V1 (in part) and V5–7 respectively (ed. Reck 2004, 150).

[38] On *(f)ršṭy[y]* ‘concluded’ see Sims-Williams 1985, 132.

[39] The first words of this hymn are also attested in M1, line 237 (Müller 1913, 20).

Text c: M5779

Verso(?) (BBB c1–c24)

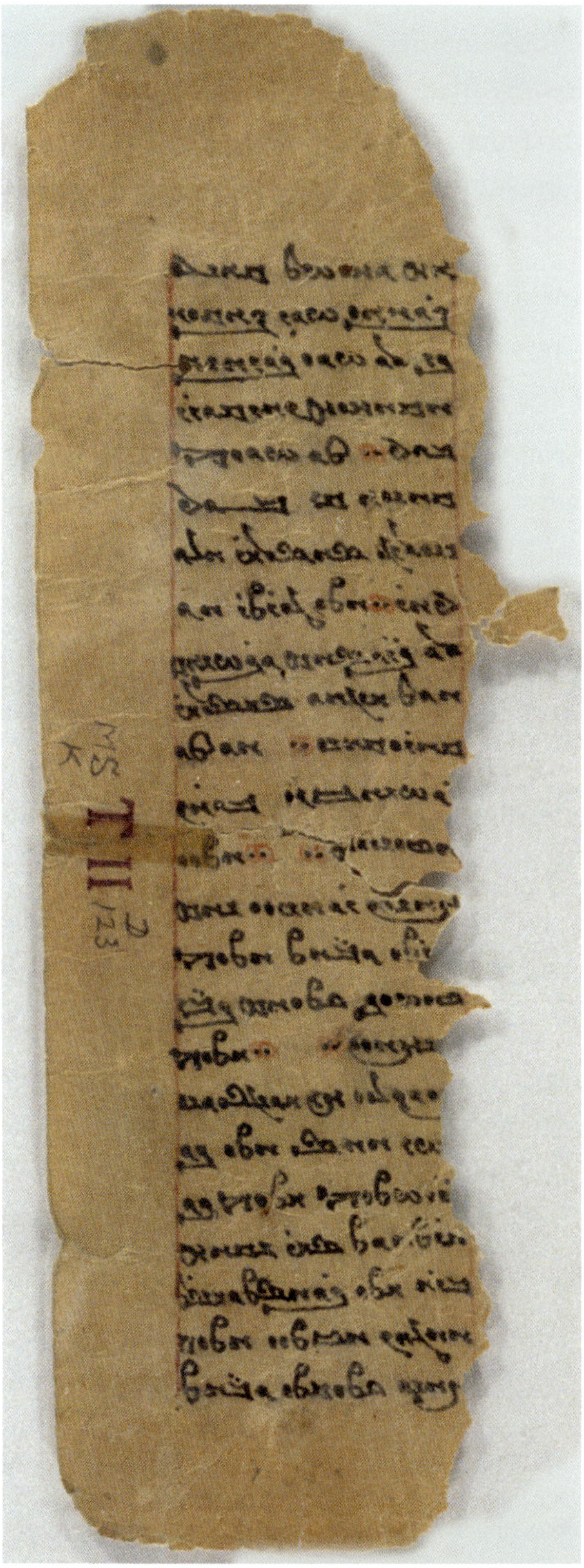

Photo: Digitales Turfan Archiv

Text c: M5779

Verso (?) (BBB c1–c24)

c1 1/ ’c wh(y)šṭ m’nʿy	from paradise;[40] lord Mani desires to
c2 2/ xwd’y šwd k’myd	go. When you go, lord, save us too
c3 3/ kd tw šwy xwd’y’	<from>[41] (the cycle of) birth (and)
c4 4/ ’m’hyc z’dmwrd	death.
c5 5/ bwj °° ṭw šwyh̠	{Hymn 3?} You are going, (6) Mani;
c6 6/ m’ny’ mn bwj	save me, commander Maitreya.
c7 7/ myt(r)g s’sṭ’r {Sogd.} ’δw	{Sogd.} Twice. And afterwards:
c8 8/ j’r °° ’ṭy γyrṭr {Pa.} ’w	{Pa.} To you will we call, fair-named
c9 9/ tw xrws’m wxšn’m	and noble commander, (11) Mar Mani;
c10 10/ ’wṭ ’(r)g’w s’sṭ’r	you, light-bringer, will we loudly bless.
c11 11/ m’rym’ny °° ’w ṭw	
c12 12/ (r)wšn’qr bwrz	
c13 13/ ’(fr)yn’m °° °° {Sogd.} ’ṭyy	{Sogd.} And when the names of the
c14 14/ c’n(w) rw’ndyy n’m	souls are brought (forth)(?),[42] finish[43]
c15 15/ [β]rṭy wβ’ṭ ’ṭyh̠	the hymn, pause briefly, and (18) there-
c16 16/ p’(š)yk pṭy’m kβn	after take ...[44] from the gospel, and pay
c17 17/ [’]nc’y °° °° ’ṭyh̠	homage to the apostle and the elect and
c18 18/ cywyδyy cn ’wnglywny	begin to make confession; and (24)
c19 19/ [ ]šn ’’s ’ṭy kw	when it is ended ...
c20 20/ (f)ryšṭyh̠ ’ṭyh̠ kw	
c21 21/ ’rṭ’wṭ s’r nm’c	
c22 22/ (β)r’ ’ṭy xw’sṭw’nfṭ	
c23 23/ ’’γ’z ’qṭyy ’ṭyh̠	
c24 24/ c’nw pṭymṭy wβ’ṭ	

[40] As Henning noted, a hymn with the opening words *ʿjgnd (’)[gd ’](c) whyšt* ‘A messenger has come from paradise’ is named as a melody in M341a, V4–5 (ed. Reck 2004, 146). However, it is not certain that c1 immediately follows c48. It is even possible that two whole columns of text (one on each side) are lost between them (see Reck 2004, 30 with n. 8).

[41] Henning suggests that *’c* ‘from’ is accidentally omitted before *z’dmwrd*.

[42] *[β]rṭy* seems to be the only known word which might fit (Henning’s *[jγy]rṭy* is too long).

[43] Thus GMS §580, but the grammatical form of *pṭy’m* is unclear (see *DMT* III/2, 159a).

[44] There is hardly enough room for *[gwy]šn* ‘chapter’, though this would make perfect sense. Henning suggests restoring *[fr]šn* ‘lection’, but no such word is attested (*DMT* III/2, 82a).

Text d: M114, i

Recto (BBB d1–d8)

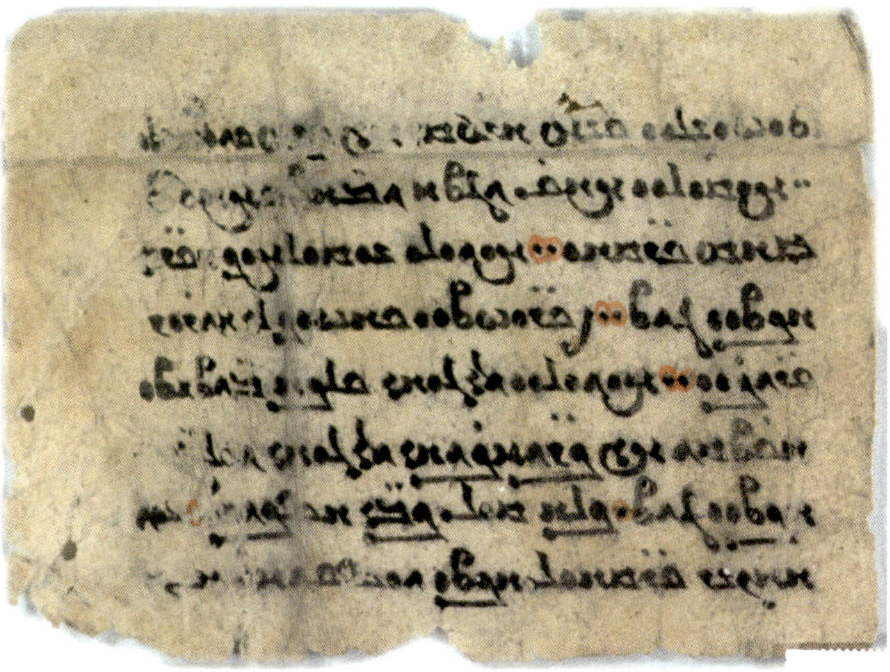

Photo: Digitales Turfan Archiv
© Depositum der Berlin-Brandenburgischen Akademie der Wissenschaften
in der Staatsbibliothek zu Berlin – Preußischer Kulturbesitz, Orientabteilung

Verso (BBB d9–d16)

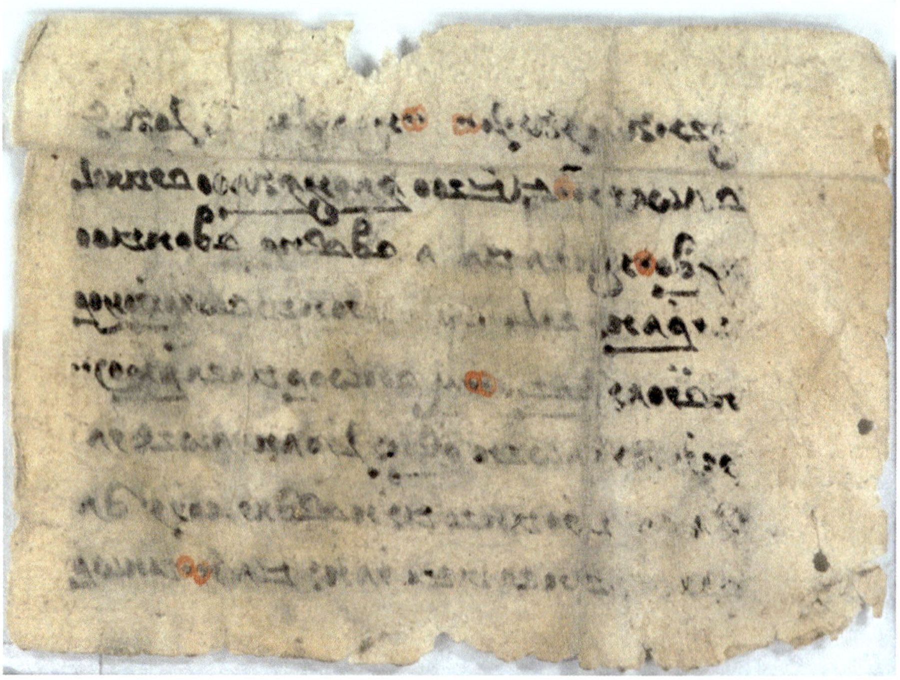

Photo: Digitales Turfan Archiv
© Depositum der Berlin-Brandenburgischen Akademie der Wissenschaften
in der Staatsbibliothek zu Berlin – Preußischer Kulturbesitz, Orientabteilung

Text d: M114, i

Recto (BBB d1–d8)

d1 1/ ṭyšyngyy pnc ʾnjm(n c)n (pn)c pwt(yš)ty
d2 2/ °° cymyδyy cʾf wγṭʾ wβʾṭ (p)cʾyṭ
d3 3/ qʾm frmʾy °° cywyδy nymyδcyk ʾfr(yn)[45]
d4 4/ ʾkṭyy γwṭ °° I fryšṭyy pʾšyk δn {MP} ʾwryd
d5 5/ frwxyy °° {Sogd.} cywyδyy tn gyʾn pδkʾ βwṭ ʾṭy
d6 6/ ʾfṭmw cn xrwhxwʾn tn gyʾn wyδ(β)[ʾγ]
d7 7/ ʾkṭyy γwṭ ° kδʾ myδ kβn ʾskwʾ(ṭ) ° (ʿ)yw
d8 8/ ʾʾznd frmʾyδ ʾkṭy {Pa.} wyspwh(r ʾd)

... ‘the five assemblies of the Mahāyāna from the five Buddhas’: it will be proper to prescribe how much of this can be said. Afterwards the noon blessing should be performed: A hymn to the Apostle, with (the opening): {MP} ‘Come hither, (5) (good) fortune’. {Sogd.} Afterwards is the Body-soul rite, and first the Body-soul sermon should be given by the preacher. When the day is ending, order a parable to be performed: {Pa.} The Prince with

Verso (BBB d9–d16)

d9 1/ cndʾ(ly)[46] zʾdg °° °° {Sogd.} c(ywyδyy ṭn) gyʾn
d10 2/ pʾš(ynd) ° qβnyy xwyckʾwyy frmʾyδ
d11 3/ (ʾ)kṭy ° cʾnw mw(n)w pṭṣʾk pṭyʾmyy
d12 4/ (pr)xwʾn nyδ (pʾš fr)yʾm pš(ʾxʾ)rycyk
d13 5/ ʾfrywn (kwnʾ) °° III p(ʾ)šyk m(w)nw xcy °°
d14 6/ {Pa.} ʾr(wʾn rw)šnʾ kl(ʾ)n grywʾ(r)wšn(ʾ {MP})dw
d15 7/ [jʾr °° {Pa.}](m)rymʾny mn ʾsṭʾ(r h)yrz ṭw
d16 8/ [mʾry](mʾny)m(nʾ) rwʾn bw(j) °° {Sogd.} mʾšk

the *caṇḍāla*ʾs(?) child. {Sogd.} Afterwards they should sing the Body-soul (hymn). Order a short explanation (11) to be made. When you finish this ceremony, sit at table, break fast,[47] perform the post-prandial blessing. The three hymns are these: {Pa.} Light soul, great[48] light self. {MP} Twice. {Pa.} Mar Mani, forgive my sins; you, (16) [Mar] Mani, save my soul. {Sogd.} The basis ...

---

[45] *ʾfr(yn)* may be a scribal error for *ʾfrywn* (Henning), an abbreviated spelling or a MP loanword.

[46] Or *cndʾ(lʾ)*? Henning hesitantly read *cndʾ(ṭy)* without excluding *cndʾ(l)*. Cf. Colditz 2018, 275.

[47] The faded words *(pʾš fr)yʾm* were not read by Henning. On this phrase, a technical term for ‘to break fast’, see now Sims-Williams 2014, 102; Yoshida 2019, 93 n. 119.

[48] On Pa. *klʾn*, apparently meaning both ‘great’ and ‘pure’, see Sims-Williams 1989, 329.

Text e (fragment I): M528a

Recto

(BBB e1–e7)

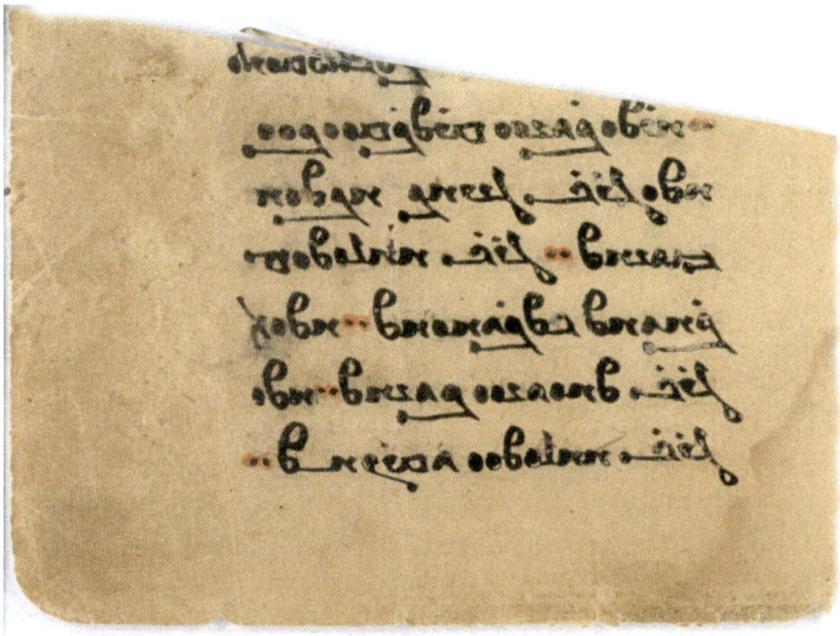

Photo: Digitales Turfan Archiv

Verso

(BBB e8–e14)

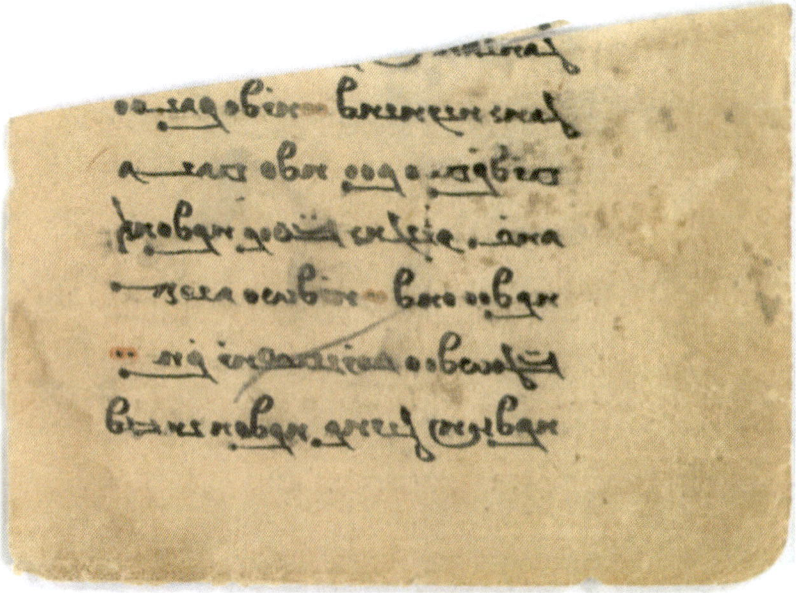

Photo: Digitales Turfan Archiv

Text e (fragment I): M528a

Recto

(BBB e1–e7)

{*some lines missing*}
e1 1/ [n’](kṭ)ptšmy(r)ty
e2 2/ ◦◦ ’rṭy xwnyy mrṭxmyy kyy
e3 3/ ’ṭy γrf γnd’k ’kṭy’
e4 4/ qwn’ṭ ◦◦ γrf ’’δyṭyh̲
e5 5/ x’w’ṭ pṭxw’y’ṭ ◦◦ ’ṭyh̲
e6 6/ γrf ṭ’ywnyy kwn’ṭ ◦◦ ’ṭy
e7 7/ γrf ’’δyṭyy wmrz’ṭ ◦◦

{*some lines missing*}
... is reckoned (as) [not] done;[49] and that man who commits many wicked deeds, (who) strikes and kills many people, and (6) commits much thievery, and ruins many people ...

Verso

(BBB e8–e14)

{*some lines missing*}
e8 1/ γw’n(w’)c[yy](x)[wj’ṭ[50] ’ṭy]
e9 2/ γw’n ’nz’n’ṭ ◦◦ ’rṭy (x)wnyy
e10 3/ mrṭxm(y)y kyy ’ṭy mwnw
e11 4/ w’f znng’n βjyk ’kṭy’h̲
e12 5/ ’kṭyy y’ṭ ◦◦ ’rṭšy wnyh̲
e13 6/ βγyšṭyy pyrnms’r x’ ◦◦
e14 7/ ’kṭc’ γnd’k ’kṭy’ n’qṭ
{*some folios missing*}

{*some lines missing*}[51]
... [he should ask] absolution [and] confess (his) sins; that (10) man (by) whom these so manifold evil deeds have been committed—before the gods the wicked deeds done by him [are reckoned] (as) not done ...

{*some folios missing*}

---

[49] For the restoration *[n’](kṭ)* ‘not done’ cf. *n’qṭ* in e14, which is not an incomplete word as Henning assumed. When a past participle in *-ty* is negated with the prefix *n’-*, the final *-y* is usually dropped as in *n’-swβṭ* ‘unbored’ and other examples referred to in Sims-Williams 2015, 36.

[50] Just a guess, but the first letter (not read by Henning) is certainly *k* or *x*.

[51] In theory one could suppose that there were never more than seven lines on each page, since the text would make excellent sense if e8 followed e7 without a gap. See however below, p. 187 n. 53.

Text e (fragment II): M528b

Recto

(BBB e15–e20)

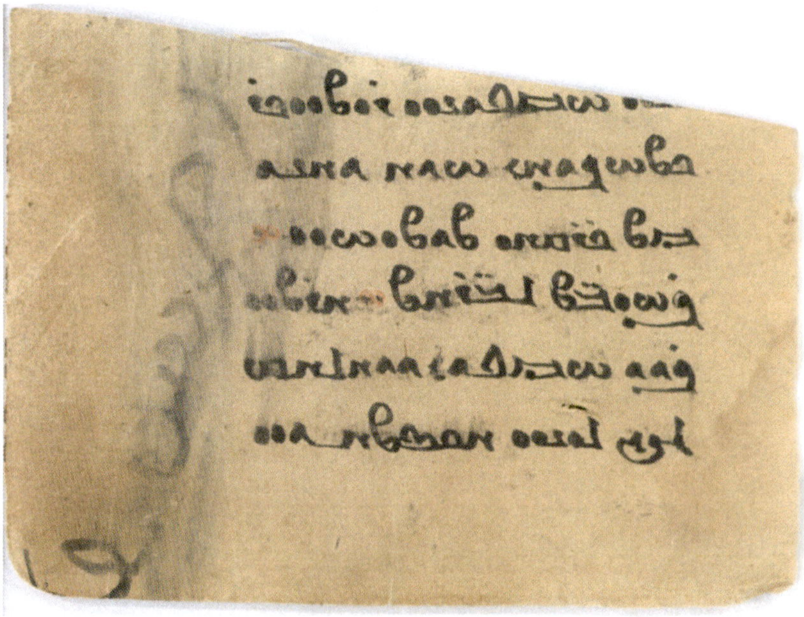

Photo: Digitales Turfan Archiv

Verso

(BBB e21–e26)

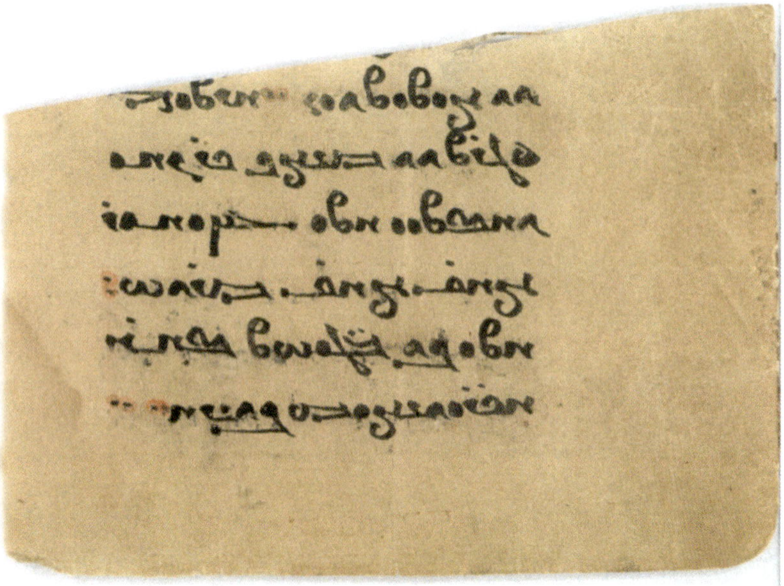

Photo: Digitales Turfan Archiv

Text e (fragment II): M528b

Recto

(BBB e15–e20)

{*some lines missing*}	{*some lines missing*}
e15 1/ [w](ny)y šqlwnyy ryṭyy pr	... [Adam] went to Šaklōn with the
e16 2/ pṭškw'n šw' w'nw	request: 'Command that she (= Eve)
e17 3/ qṭ frm'y ṭwṭyšyy ◦◦	should give him (= Seth) milk'. Then
e18 4/ xšyβṭ δβr'ṭ ◦◦ 'rṭyy	(19) Šaklōn [wanted to make] Adam an
e19 5/ xww šqlwn ww 'δ'm	apostate[52] from the (true) religion ...
e20 6/ cn δynyy 'psṭ'wyy	

Verso

(BBB e21–e26)

{*some lines missing*}	{*some lines missing*}[53]
e21 1/ ww cyṭyṭ wyn ◦◦ 'rṭyẖ	... [when Adam] saw the demons, he
e22 2/ jγrṭ ww qnck pr z'y	quickly placed the child on the ground,
e23 3/ w'sṭyy 'ṭy VII y'wr	and drew (a circle) seven times all
e24 4/ c'f c'f qrwš ◦◦	around (him),[54] (25) and made a prayer
e25 5/ 'ṭy kw βγyšṭ s'r	to the gods ...
e26 6/ 'frywncyq kwnd' ◦◦ ◦◦	

---

52 On *'psṭ'wyy* 'apostate, renegade' see *DMT* III/2, 16b.

53 While M528a (Fragment I above) has seven lines to the page and could in theory be virtually complete (see p. 185 n. 51), M528b (Fragment II) has only six surviving lines on each side, so that one could assume that just one line is missing here. However, this would imply a very abrupt transition in the narrative, so that it seems better to allow for the loss of several lines (though hardly as many as twenty as suggested by Reeves 1999, 435).

54 On *c'f c'f* 'all around' (not 'very large') see Benveniste 1940, 215; Sims-Williams 2017, 239, with references.

Text f: M139

i, Recto

(BBB f1–f25)

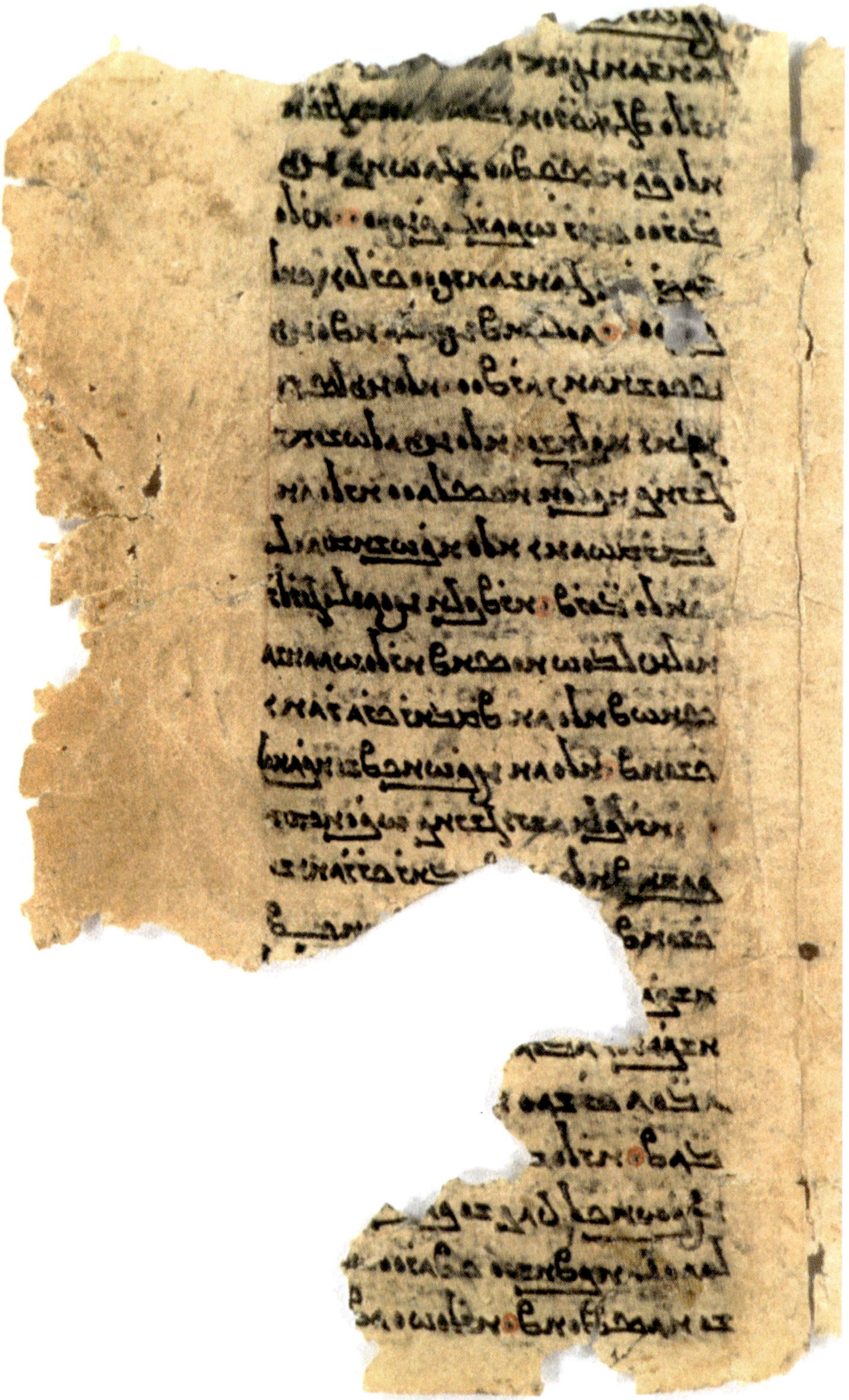

Photo: Digitales Turfan Archiv

Text f: M139

i, Recto

(BBB f1–f25)

{*some lines missing*}

f1 1/ c(x)š(’)[pṭ]
f2 2/ (γ)w’nw’cyh̲ (’.)[ ]
f3 3/ ’rty ṭγ(w)fry’ (βr’ṭ w’n)w γr(β)’
f4 4/ ’ty xw ’spṭyy nγwš’k cn
f5 5/ βyryy przr škwrδ xcyy °° ’rty
f6 6/ nwkr (xw)[55] γw’nw’cyy pr δyn I p’t
f7 7/ (x)[c](y)y °° wy(δp’)ṭ c(’nw) ’ṭy cn
f8 8/ spyn’w’ zwrṭyy ° ’ty cn δs(’)
f9 9/ z(n)g’n ’kt’ny(y) ’ty cn wtšnyh̲
f10 10/ γnd’k ’kty’ ’pstwyy ’rt(y)w’
f11 11/ qrmšwhn ’ty ’xšn’m w(y)δ
f12 12/ p’ty βyrṭ ° ’rṭkδ’ cywyδ γ(y)rtr
f13 13/ ’yδc δβyš ’ys’ṭ ’rtyšw w’nw
f14 14/ s’šṭ ’ty w’ ṭmb’r prw rw’n
f15 15/ fny’ṭ ° ’ty w’ cxš’pṭ ny ’xw’y(t)[56]
f16 16/ ° ° ’rtkδ’ wndn γnd’k šxy’q[57]
f17 17/ kw(n’)ṭ ’t(y)[w’]ṭ(m)b’r pr rw’n n(y)
f18 18/ fny’ṭ[°° ’ty w’ c](xš)’pṭ
f19 19/ ’nx(w)[’y’ṭ]
f20 20/ ’nxw(’n) w(β)yw[pr wṭšnyh̲]
f21 21/ wβyw pr nwy (’)[ ]
f22 22/ βwṭ ° ’rty (β)[ ]
f23 23/ cxš’pt jwk ny k(w)[n’ṭ]
f24 24/ δywyδ ’kṭ’(ny)y pṭwryy (šy)[’][58]
f25 25/ ny ’wsṭy’ṭ ° ’rtyšy wṭ[šnyh̲]

{*some lines missing*}

... commandment ... forgiveness of sins ... Know, dear brother, that the perfect hearer is very hard to find. (6) Now, in the religion forgiveness of sins occurs (just) once; at that time, if one turns from rebelliousness[59] and renounces the ten kinds of misdeed[60] and (one's) former wicked actions, one then obtains absolution and pardon. And if thereafter (13) some evil (temptation?) comes, one should repudiate the body for (the sake of) the soul and not break the commandment. And if one does perpetrate such great wickedness (and) trouble, and does not repudiate [the] body for (the sake of) the soul, [and] breaks [the] commandment ... (20) the breach is both [in the old] and in the new ... And [if one does] not perform the commandment wholly [and] does not bear in mind(?) the consequence of that misdeed, then one's former(?) ...

---

55 Henning preferred *(x’)* but admitted that *(xw)* is also possible. Cf. *DMT* III/2, 215a.

56 *’xw’yt* is not a mistake for *’nxw’y’t* (thus Henning) but merely a later form. Cf. *’xrwzn* (f37).

57 + line-filler?

58 Very uncertain (Henning).

59 For *spyn’wy* ‘rebelliousness’ (not ‘criminality’, *DMT* III/2, 177b) see Benveniste 1940, 202.

60 The ten sins forbidden by the ten commandments for hearers (Henning, p. 13).

Text f: M139

i, Verso

(BBB f26–f50)

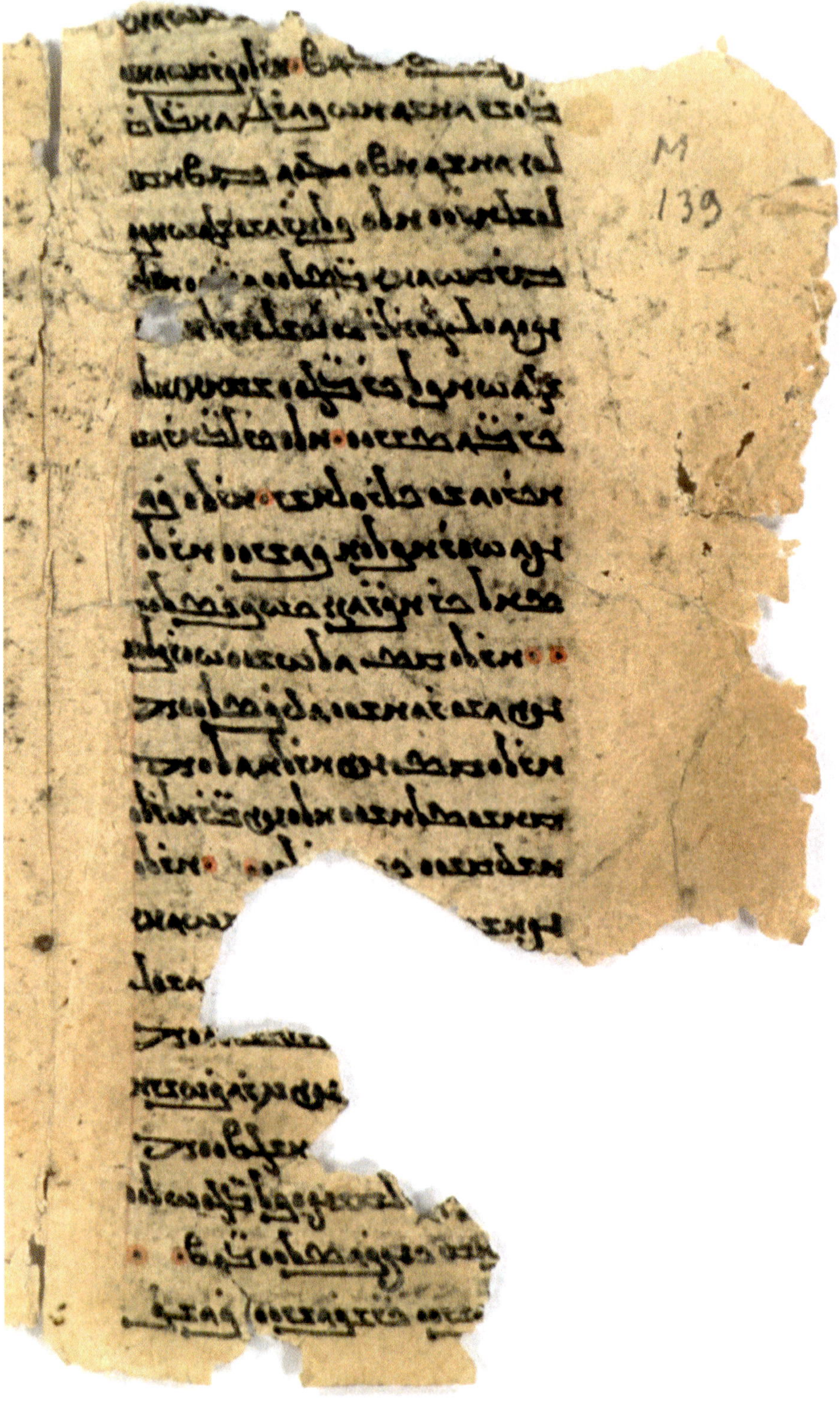

Photo: Digitales Turfan Archiv

Text f: M139

i, Verso

(BBB f26–f50)

{*some lines missing*}

f26 1/ [ ](qr)mšwhn
f27 2/ [p]c(x)[ws](ṭy[61] β)wṭ ° ’rty krmšwhny
f28 3/ βynd w’nw ’škwrd w’βt[62] pr
f29 4/ δyn w’nw ’ṭy ‘yw qṭ’m
f30 5/ δynδ’ryy ’ty kt’r wny nγwš’ky
f31 6/ qrmšwhn βstyy (wβy)y ’(rty)
f32 7/ cywyδ γyrtr (n)y δynδ’(r)t ’[ty n](y)
f33 8/ nγwš’kt pr βγyy nm’c ’ty
f34 9/ pr βwsndyy ° ’ty pr δβ’r wny
f35 10/ ’pryw ny ptryδ’nd ° ’rty xw
f36 11/ cw šyr’kty’ kwndyy ’rty
f37 12/ s’t pr ’xrwzn pškfstyy
f38 13/ ° ° ’rty ms wtšnyy šyrkt(y)’
f39 14/ cn wny rw’nyy wjxstyyẖ
f40 15/ ’rty ms cn ’rt’wtyẖ
f41 16/ m’nyst’nyy ’ty cn βr’trty
f42 17/ ’njmnyy p(š)[ky](rty)y ° ° ’rty
f43 18/ c’n(w)[qr](m)šwhn
f44 19/ [y]wnyδ
f45 20/ [mrδ’](spndt)yyẖ
f46 21/ [ ] cn II rwxšnd’
f47 22/ [wrṭnd ’ty cn]’nγṭyyẖ
f48 23/ [rw](x)[šn’](γr)δmncykt βγyštyy
f49 24/ [’](x)[šn]’m pcxwstyy βwṭ ° °
f50 25/ [frn](xwn)dyy frnxwndyy xwnx

{*some folios missing?*}

{*some lines missing*}

... absolution is witheld. And one states the ban on absolution in the church so severely that should absolution be refused to any elect or hearer, (32) thereafter neither the elect [nor] the hearers associate with him in the worship of god, and in the fast, and in the (giving and receiving of) gifts; and whatever good deed he does, (37) it is all dispersed(?)[63] in the zodiac; and also (his) former merit is removed(?) from his soul, and he is also expelled from the *mānistān* of the elect and from the community of the brethren; and (43) when ... absolution ... at once ... pardon is witheld [by] the elements, ... by the two light [chariots and by] all the gods of paradise. (50) Blessed, blessed is he [who] ...

{*some folios missing?*}

---

[61] Henning read *(cx)[š’p](ṭ)*, but it is clear that there is another letter after *ṭ*.

[62] Perhaps a scribal error for *wβ’t*, but the expression would still remain awkward.

[63] The meaning of *pškfs-* is unclear. See *DMT* III/2, 150a.

Text f: M139

ii, Recto

(BBB f51–f71)

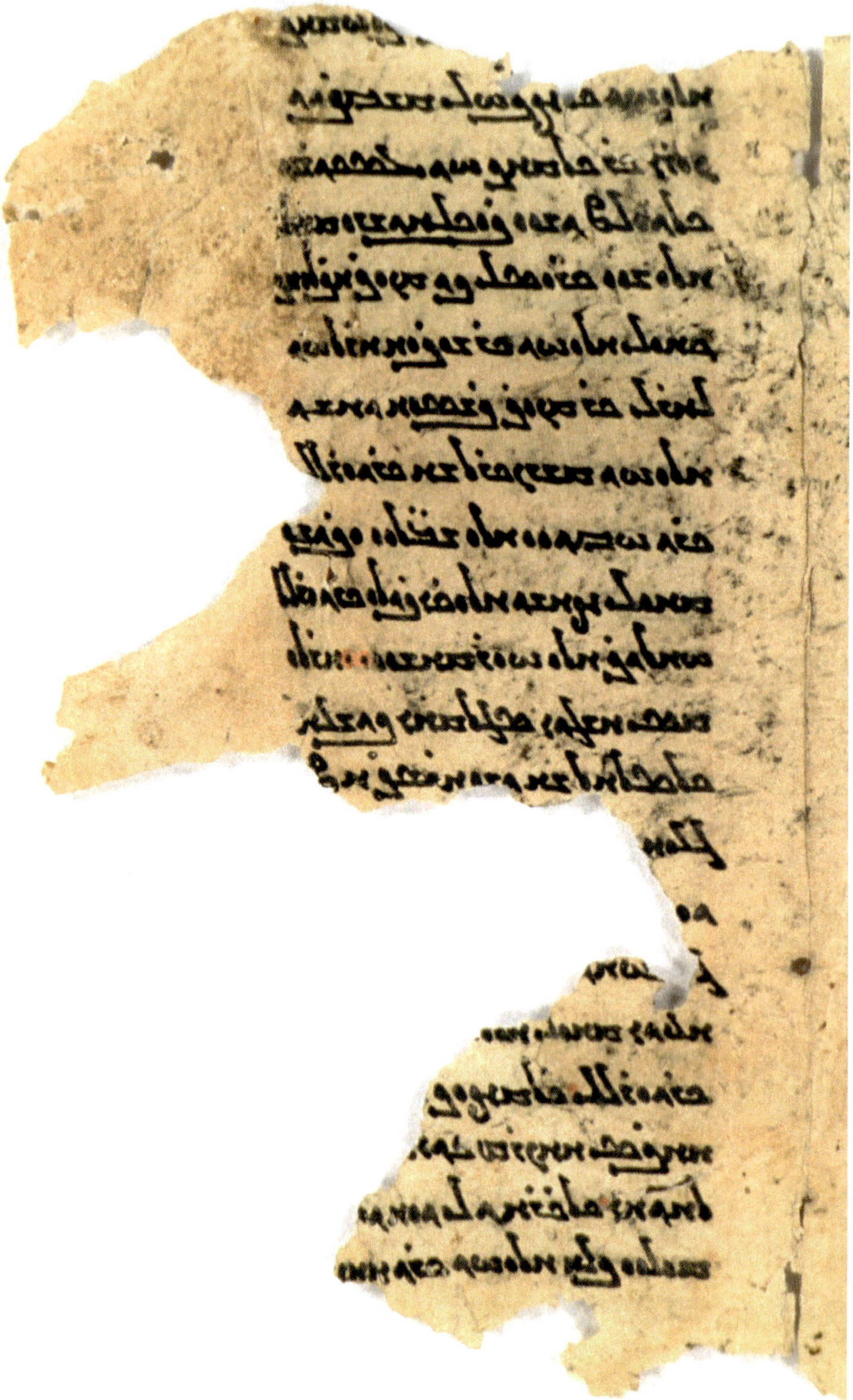

Photo: Digitales Turfan Archiv

Text f: M139

ii, Recto

(BBB f51–f71)

{*some lines missing*}

f51 1/ [k](ky) šm'(x)

f52 2/ 'tyš(w) p(t)cxšδ mnqxww

f53 3/ zyrn pr ptm'k šw 'spwrnw

f54 4/ ptwyδṭ wnyy xypδ'wndy m('yδ)

f55 5/ 'ty nyy prysδ kw mzyx 'xty'k

f56 6/ p'yδ 'tyšw pr nyxy' 'rtšw

f57 7/ δ'rδ pr mzyx xnsy' w'nw

f58 8/ 'tyšw mndzprt n' prwyrδδ

f59 9/ prw šqwyy 'ty nβtyy yxwny

f60 10/ m'yδ c'nw 'tyfn xwty prwy(r)tt

f61 11/ š'twx 'ty šyrm'nyy °° 'rty

f62 12/ ms 'nγwn sγtm'n kwnδ'

f63 13/ ptst't n' wn(y) 'rsk[64] 'ṭ[y]

f64 14/ γδy'[ ]

f65 15/ wy[ ]

f66 16/ γ[ ]š'w[ ]

f67 17/ 'jwn m'yδ '(ty)[ ]

f68 18/ prwyrδδ ftmcyk [ ]

f69 19/ ''xs ''zrm pwn.[[65]]

f70 20/ t'w'n ptfr'wδ wy' w(y)[ ]

f71 21/ myδyy kδ' 'tyšw prw ''(z)[ ]

{*some lines missing*}

... You (should) receive it like gold, offer it in full measure to its owner so (55) that you do not come to the great judgement.[66] Guard it carefully and keep it in great security, so that you do not cause it to become defiled by dry and wet blood, (60) just as it for its part causes you to become contented and happy. Likewise too (you should) all be on the defensive lest envy and wounding(?)[67] ... (67) child,[68] so that you may cause ... to become ... Remember the primeval ... conflict, the harm ... the penalty,[69] on the ... day when through Greed(?) ... it ...

---

[64] Apparently written with a point over *k* (but *'rsx* 'haemorrhoids' hardly fits the context).

[65] Or *pwr.[* (Henning); *pw'[* also seems possible.

[66] For *'xty'k* 'judgement' (not 'hostility') see Henning 1945, 468 n. 3.

[67] The meaning of *γδy'[* is unknown. Cf. perhaps *γδ-* 'wound', less likely *γδ-* 'thief' with *DMT* III/2, 86a.

[68] Or 'birth'.

[69] Cf. BBB 754–6: 'Nor was I able to remember the primeval conflict'.

Text f: M139

ii, Verso

(BBB f72–f91)

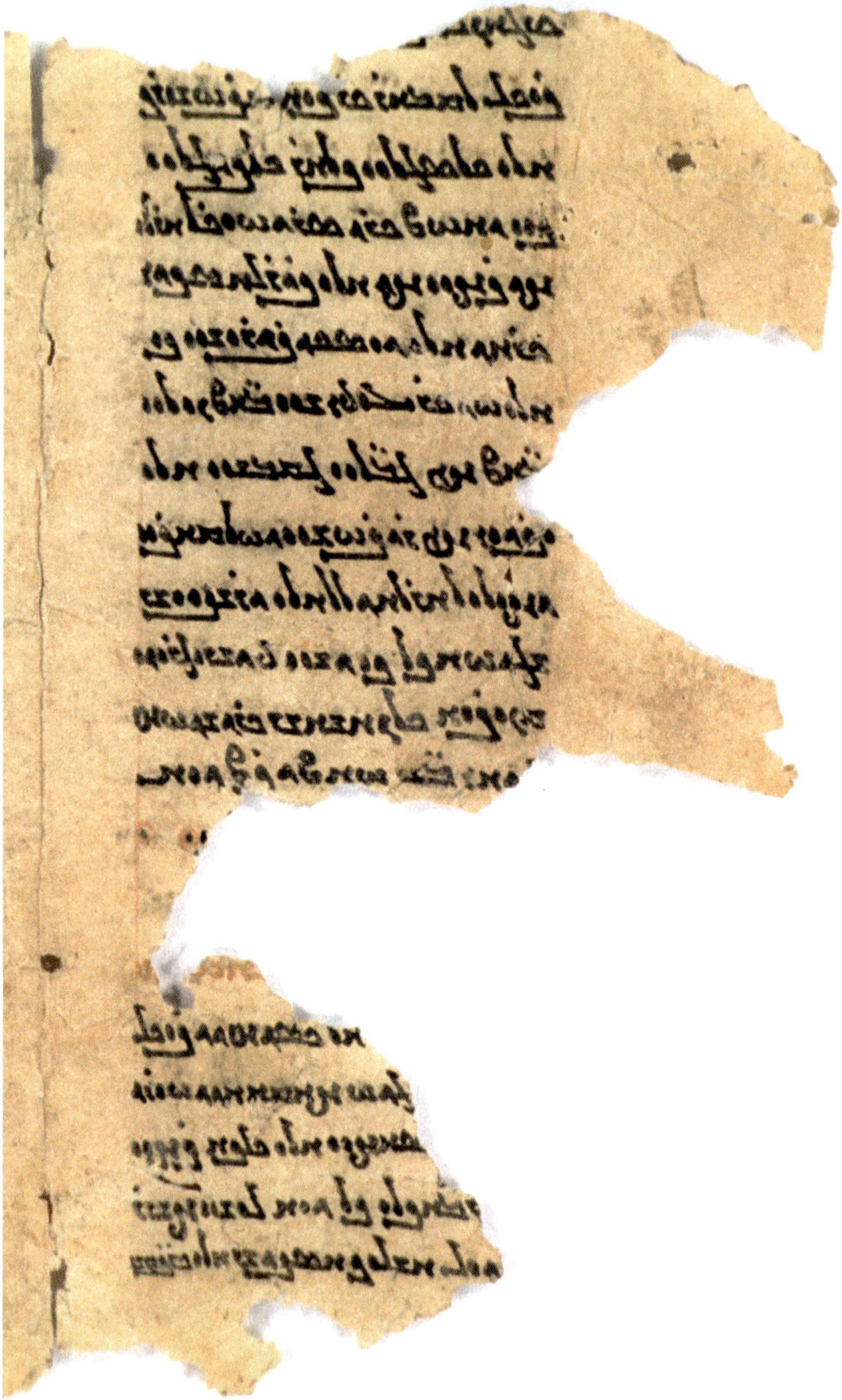

Photo: Digitales Turfan Archiv

Text f: M139

ii, Verso

(BBB f72–f91)

{*some lines missing*}	{*some lines missing*}
f72 1/ (fr)γ’z(δ k)[ ]	... Begin [to think]: (As for) your
f73 2/ xypδ tmb’r pr ky’ ’xšnyrk	body, under whose sign has it been
f74 3/ ’ty ptsγtyy kt’r ptkwγtyy	ranged or strung up?[73] (75) In
f75 4/ ky w’šṭ prw srwšyft ’rty	whose obedient service did it (take
f76 5/ cw xcyy cw ’ty xwrδ’skwn	its) stand? What is it that you are
f77 6/ pr’w ’ty wyspw xwrynyy ky	eating?[74] For every partaker who is
f78 7/ ’tyšwpr ‘yjn nyy β’ṭ zytyy	not worthy of it will be deprived of
f79 8/ β’ṭ cn γβtyy γmbnyy ’ty	(the benefit of) his laborious efforts
f80 9/ yxwyn cn rwxšnyy wštm’xyy	and (80) excluded from the light
f81 10/ wcytyt ’rt’wtt ’ty wrnkyynd	paradise. The chosen elect and the
f82 11/ nγwš’kt ky wnyy jwndy γrywy	believing hearers who recognize the
f83 12/ mzyxy’ ptz’n’nd prw nwšc	greatness of the Living Self will be
f84 13/ (jw)’n β(nd) š’ṭwxṭ wy’	happy in eternal life in the (85)
f85 14/ [rwxšn’γrδmny]ẖ[70] ◦ ◦	light paradise.[75]
{*one line left blank*}	
f86 15/ {*red*} [ ](’š)[.](q)[71]	(86) ...
f87 16/ [fry’ βr]’(t)[72] pswc ww xypδ	[... Dear bro]ther, purify your[self
f88 17/ [γryw ’ty n]γwš c’m’ ’ww šyrw	and] hear from me the good ... It is
f89 18/ [◦◦]s’cyy ’ty pδk’ xcyy	right and proper [for the] wise that
f90 19/ [wny γ](rβ)’kty kt wy’ δyn(yy) cndr	they should remain in the church
f91 20/ [pry]wyδ ’nδyk ’skwnd ’ty prxyzn(d)	[in] that manner and behave(?)[76] ...

---

[70] Thus *DMT* III/2, 171a. Henning restored *[rwxšn’γrδmny’]ẖ* as if the word were a light stem.

[71] Perhaps *m’šq* ‘basis’ (Henning)?

[72] Henning’s translation implies this restoration. Cf. f3 above.

[73] On *ptkwγtyy* and its cognates, which suggest a meaning such as ‘hanging, threaded, strung up’, see Bi–Sims-Williams 2011, 505–6, referring to earlier discussions by MacKenzie and Gershevitch.

[74] These questions are paralleled by those in BBB 757ff.

[75] Cf. 1 Corinthians 11.27–29.

[76] Or ‘serve’.